Breaking and Entering

Breaking and Entering

The Extraordinary Story of a Hacker Called "Alien"

Jeremy N. Smith

AN EAMON DOLAN BOOK
HOUGHTON MIFFLIN HARCOURT
BOSTON | NEW YORK
2019

To my guides on this journey,
who led me to new worlds

&

To Carl Smith and Crissie McMullan,
who helped me get home

For information about permission to reproduce selections from this book, write to
trade.permissions@hmhco.com or to Permissions, Houghton Mifflin Harcourt Publishing Company,
3 Park Avenue, 19th Floor, New York, New York 10016.

hmhco.com

Library of Congress Cataloging-in-Publication Data
Names: Smith, Jeremy N., author.
Title: Breaking and entering : the extraordinary story of a hacker called "Alien" / Jeremy N. Smith.
Description: Boston : Houghton Mifflin Harcourt, 2019. | "An Eamon Dolan Book."
Identifiers: LCCN 2018024873 (print) | LCCN 2018035206 (ebook) | ISBN 9780544911222 (ebook) |
ISBN 9780544903210 | ISBN 9780544903210q(hardcover)
Subjects: LCSH: Alien (Hacker) | Hackers—United States—Biography. | Computer security—United
States. | Computer crimes—United States. | LCGFT: Biographies.
Classification: LCC HV6772.A5 (ebook) | LCC HV6772.A5 S55 2019 (print) |
DDC 005.8092 [B] —dc23
LC record available at https://lccn.loc.gov/2018024873

Book design by David Futato

Printed in the United States of America
DOH 10 9 8 7 6 5 4 3 2 1

"Song to the Earl of the River" from *The Pocket Tao Reader* by Eva Wong, © 1999 by Eva Wong.
Reprinted by arrangement with The Permissions Company, Inc., on behalf of Shambhala
Publications Inc., Boulder, Colorado, www.shambhala.com.

Things are not always as they appear. This is true of locks, doors, walls, and people.

—Keshlam the Seer, "Hacking Tips"

Contents

AUTHOR'S NOTE / /

Names and other identifying characteristics have been altered to protect people's privacy. For the same reason, in a limited number of instances I have changed dates or combined individuals.

The Hacker
Next Door

*T*ALL AND TAN AND *young and lovely*...

It's Saturday night at Bally's Las Vegas and I follow a woman in black leather—jacket, skirt, boots—down the center of the casino floor. Her hair—also black—is twisted atop her head and held in place with chopsticks. She has on red lipstick and knee-high red polka-dot socks. A portable speaker clipped to her purse plays "The Girl from Ipanema."

The woman—thirty-three years old? thirty-four?—passes tables for blackjack, three-card poker, and craps. Players turn from their chips to the source of the music. Several smile, entreating her to join them, but she continues through a thicket of ringing, whirring slot machines, emerging again in front of the casino elevators.

There's a long line here, perhaps two hundred people, stretching to the end of the hallway and around a corner. Almost everyone is trying to get to the pool party a floor below or to the dozen other parties in Bally's Skyview rooms twenty-five floors above. Making sure no one cuts are two huge bouncers with crossed arms and dark red badges that say GOON.

The woman does not join the line. She smiles at the bouncers. The bouncers do not smile at her. They do recognize her, however.

The woman is a hacker. The bouncers are also hackers. And so are the two hundred people in line, and the several thousand already partying above or below.

In fact, there are close to twenty thousand hackers in Vegas this weekend.

"Access approved," the bouncers say to the woman. They part — special treatment — and the woman passes between them: first in line.

The next elevator is hers alone.

Or ours. "I'm with her," I tell the bouncers, and squeeze through before they can stop me.

A door opens and the woman and I step in together. "This is crazy," I say. "Is it always this crowded?"

The woman rolls her eyes, seemingly put off that of all the questions I could ask right now, I choose this one.

As it turns out, for the next year my life will largely become a series of such strange questions and the even stranger answers she provides.

Of all the ways I might have expected to start hanging out with a hacker, perhaps the last was an impromptu playdate for my daughter.

Alien recognized me first. We had met briefly, fifteen years earlier, when I was a senior at Harvard and she was a sophomore at MIT. By chance, we ran into each other again one fall afternoon. Each of us was out with our preschool-age daughter. Amazing — *great to see you again!* And the girls liked each other. *Can we play together?* they asked. *Please?*

We agreed. Our daughters cheered — and then ran off to a set of swings. We chatted casually for a few minutes. Then I asked Alien — not that this was the name I knew her by — what she was working on these days.

"Well . . . ," she said. "Tomorrow morning, I have to break into a bank."

My old acquaintance, I learned, was a professional hacker — or, as she put it to corporate clients, "a penetration tester and digital forensics specialist." When institutions or individuals needed to test their security, either physical or virtual, she and her team were guns for hire. And if you'd already been breached, they'd identify what had been stolen, how, and by whom — plus recover any lost information and try to ensure that the problem wouldn't happen again.

Even with frequent media coverage, hacking is actually dramatically underreported, Alien told me. Only a small fraction of discovered hacks are disclosed to the public. And most hacks are never discovered in the first place.

She knew because, time and again, she or her close associates had either done the hacking or cleaned up after someone else had.

I liked talking to Alien and she liked talking to me. Further conversations (and playdates) led to increasingly revealing accounts, including, at my request, stories about her personal and professional experiences with hospitals and law firms, airlines and art museums, police departments and the Pentagon. She also talked about finding community, fighting assholes, falling in love, and forming a mature adult life within the larger hacker world — topics completely missing in most accounts of hacker culture.

Some hackers have a well-deserved reputation for bragging, exaggeration, obfuscation, and outright lies. Alien, however, seemed modest by nature — earnest, soft-spoken, and reserved. (I had yet to encounter her as the leather-clad woman who parted the Red Sea of bouncers in Vegas.) Before becoming a writer, I'd logged time as a computer programmer, and I had enough early hacking experiences of my own to follow the outlines of her radically more sophisticated — and perilous — exploits. Every detail I could verify checked out.

One Sunday afternoon, when I was in town again where she lived, I asked Alien if I could meet her at her office. "Pretend I'm a potential client," I said. "Give me the big picture."

Alien agreed. "Here's what you probably know," she told me from across a conference table. "Hackers can break into your computer and cell phones, your company network or the network of anyone you do business with. They can read your email and texts, steal your business plans and credit card numbers, or take over your online identity in order to hack someone else."

I nodded, shifted uncomfortably in my seat, and turned off my phone.

"Here's what you probably don't know," she continued. "Only about thirty percent of hacks target a specific individual or institution. Some seventy percent are opportunistic — hackers trying to break into anything they can, and pursuing opportunities behind any open door. If your information is valuable to you, it's valuable to someone else. No one is too 'boring' to be hacked, and everything has a price on the hacker black market."

I tried to seem savvy and unfazed. In reality, I wanted to go home and turn off everything.

Not so fast. "Physical access is almost as easy," Alien said. Someone with skills like hers could enter my home or my hotel room, my office or my safe. She could copy ID cards, impersonate customers or employees, tap directly into phone lines or data centers, and uncover surprising secrets from my trash.

I'm moving to a farm, I told myself. *I'm going off grid. I'm bringing my family. And I'm buying a shredder.*

At this point the formal presentation started. For an hour, Alien walked me through examples of hack after hack. The health insurer Anthem. Retailers Target and Home Depot. Even security companies like encryption pioneer RSA and defense stalwart Lockheed Martin. The more I learned, the more I was surprised—and alarmed—by how pervasive hacking was and how diverse its forms and targets could be.

It was a story I wanted to share with others.

"Hacking today is a profession," Alien concluded. "There are well-organized cybercriminals, loose confederations of defenders, and governments and businesses often more motivated to maintain the status quo than to safeguard individuals."

"Who are you?" I asked. "A good guy or a bad guy?"

Alien shrugged. "That depends on who *you* are." At this very moment, she was willing to wager, there were hackers just like her, sitting in a room a lot like this one, only in China or Russia, Israel or Nigeria, England or elsewhere in the United States. "They're the bad guys to me. I'm the bad guy to them."

I closed my eyes and tried to remember the quiet eighteen-year-old woman I'd met half a lifetime ago. How did she become this ... *badass?* And, given that her career spans the entire twenty-first-century history of hacking, what could she teach me about the evolution of a tiny subculture to an ever more powerful industry, both illicit and legitimate, touching all of us today?

I asked Alien to turn off the PowerPoint. "I want to buy you a drink," I said. "And I want you to tell me your story. But this time, I want you to start at the beginning."

PART I

Course 19

Inside Out

Cambridge, Massachusetts. August 1998.

I T WAS A BEAUTIFUL seventy-degree night in late August. At two a.m., a young woman wearing one red sneaker, one orange sneaker, jeans, and a big, baggy button-down shirt stood in front of the public computer terminal in the empty lobby of her temporary dorm. She squinted, studying the screen. "Choose your username," it said.

Her first day at MIT — and already a test.

The default was "ETessman" — her first initial and last name. *Boring,* the woman thought. Like something her parents would have picked. Mom spent her days running the one-room restaurant supply store in Hoboken that the woman's great-grandfather, a Russian Jewish immigrant, had founded in 1915. Dad had his own small accounting firm. When she was growing up, they had been so protective that they barred her and her younger sister from crossing the street alone. Once, when she double-pierced her ears without permission, they grounded her for six months. Now, at long last, she felt free to choose her own identity.

But what?

Rock music blared in an adjacent courtyard — a party put on by one of the fraternities to recruit her fellow first-years. Finish this little login ritual and she could run out and join them. After seventeen years in stifling conformist suburbia, she could finally *play.*

With seven stabs of the Delete key, the woman erased all but the first two letters of the suggested name. "ET," it said now. Much cooler. She hit Enter.

"Too short." The grayish-blue dialogue box rejected her. "Try again."

She thought. This should be easy. Creativity was her strong suit. Harvard was just a mile and a half away, but MIT was arguably the better school—the best private research institution in the world, by many rankings. A serious place for uniquely brilliant people. Yet she had received a D in math her freshman year in high school. And because she was consistently late to school, she had a long list of unexcused absences from first-period physics. Unlike the typical MIT entrant, she wasn't an expert or genius or prodigy in anything. Especially not anything technical.

Her admissions application essay had gotten her into this place when her grades alone couldn't. In the essay—two thousand words when the limit was supposed to be five hundred—the young woman had described an abduction by well-meaning aliens. At the end, the aliens offered to make all human beings think and act exactly alike so there would be peace on Earth. To their surprise, the woman refused, preferring individual choice and variety, whatever the consequences. The essay was a thinly veiled plea: *Get me out of suburban New Jersey.* And so MIT—either by mistake or out of a wicked sense of amusement—had.

Aliens. The woman smiled. Like E.T., but even better.

Without another thought, she typed *a-l-i-e-n* and hit Enter.

The initial dialogue box disappeared, replaced by a second prompt to create a password.

Okay, Alien, she told herself. *Welcome to MIT.*

⟴

Tie-dyeing and stilt-walking, deep-frying and drilling. Balloon animals. Tire swings. Mud-wrestling matches. DIY cannons, catapults, and trebuchets. All-you-can-watch cartoons or *Star Trek* episodes. All-you-can-eat burgers, Pop Tarts, or ramen. This was Rush at MIT.

Rush was the right word for it. Ten days before classes started, one thousand freshmen arrived at randomly assigned dorms on campus. Everyone knew not to get too comfortable. In a week, all but a handful would move out again, choosing different permanent housing from among MIT's fifty-plus student-led living groups. You arrived, you chose, you moved. It was crazy, but that was MIT. Sink or swim.

Alien explored the scene all afternoon and well into the evening. The living groups competed fiercely for recruits, often via spectacular combinations of architecture, engineering, and pyrotechnics. One living group built a spinning amusement park ride from scratch in their courtyard, for example. Another made an LED dance floor. A third set off fireworks. A fourth boasted a steer roast. A fifth offered rapid passage from the top floor to the ground level of their residence via a fire pole instead of the "hassle" of an elevator or stairs.

"Want your hair dyed?" a woman at one of the student living group booths asked her.

Alien nodded emphatically.

"What color?"

"Red and blue."

Several other freshmen picked red or blue, but not both. Over the next few hours, whenever one of them passed Alien, he or she nodded approvingly, and Alien nodded back.

Soon it was midnight. This was two hours past curfew at home, but Alien, a born night owl, had finally found her natural habitat. If she could help it, she didn't intend to be asleep before four a.m. the entire semester. What to do now?

She took off her backpack in the student center and consulted the stack of handouts and fliers various living groups had pushed on her from their recruiting booths. There was another frat party, but that was too far. A water polo contest, but that was too cold. A "cruft"-smashing activity — "cruft" being an MIT term for old electronics — but she didn't quite see the point.

Finally her attention turned to a slip of bright orange paper half the size of an index card, crumpled under everything else in the bottom of her bag. When Alien smoothed out the slip to read it, she found a shorter — and surely more mysterious — invitation than that in any other handout:

"Meet in the East Campus courtyard tonight at midnight for a *real* tour of MIT."

It was already at least ten minutes after midnight. If she wanted to know who or what was behind this invitation, she'd have to hurry.

⋺⋐

Outside the student center, it was completely dark. Alien retreated briefly back indoors to find her bearings and chart a path to the East Campus courtyard on a campus map. When she pushed the door open again, gusts of wind blew up dust.

Save for a single speeding taxi, Massachusetts Avenue—the wide thoroughfare splitting the campus in half—was empty. Still, Alien looked both ways before crossing the street to the grand stairway and soaring columns of Building 7, the main entrance to MIT. Inside, she entered a lofty windowed vestibule—Lobby 7, naturally—and the start of the Infinite Corridor: a chutelike 825-foot-long hallway leading through five separate buildings.

Alien ran through it, ignoring a handful of other students she passed en route, late-night workers illuminated by weak light inside classrooms and laboratories, and the various signs and posters promoting different majors and upcoming events. Still, by the time she was outside again, it had to be closer to twelve thirty than to midnight.

Cutting hurriedly across courtyards, Alien finally found herself out of breath before the East Campus courtyard's red metal picnic tables. It was quiet here—and seemingly empty. She was alone. Alien sat down and caught her breath, unsure whether to be disappointed or relieved. She stared past tree branches rocking in the wind to the crescent moon.

On either side of the courtyard, east and west, were wide five-story brick dormitories, each fronted by three doors. A minute after sitting down, out of the corner of her eye Alien thought she saw darting movement near an open window on the top story of the east dorm. It was too dark to tell, however, and anyway, a narrow ledge running outside the fifth-floor windows blocked a clear view from below. That's why it startled her when two black-clad figures suddenly stepped out of the darkness in front of her.

They were a man and a woman. The guy was a skinny five six with Asian features and silver-dyed spiked hair. Alien saw a long radio antenna poking out of his back pocket. His companion was an African American woman at least four inches taller and one hundred pounds heavier. She had on neon-green safety goggles, presumably decorative, and wore her long hair back in thick braids. Despite their physical differences, both were dressed in dark pants and the same black T-shirt: JACK FLOREY'S OLD NO. 5, it said, in a design echoing a Jack Daniel's bottle label. QUALITY MASSACHUSETTS ROOF & TUNNEL HACKERS.

"Hi," Alien said. "Excuse me. Are you—? Do you—?"

The woman held her hand up to silence Alien, then, with a wave, bade her follow them in single file: Silver Hair, Safety Goggles, Alien.

A step behind her impromptu guides, Alien crossed the courtyard and entered the sharp-cornered triangular Building 66. They walked down stairs, turned twice in a basement, and reached a narrow passage leading several hundred feet underground out of the building and across campus. Exiting at the other end, Alien followed her hosts up a new set of stairs to the main floor of what she recognized as Building 54, MIT's tallest structure.

On the first floor, still without a word, Silver Hair opened a classroom door and Safety Goggles all but pushed Alien inside.

⟞⟐⟝

The room was your classic large lecture hall: three hundred wooden seats divided into three downward-sloping sections. Squinting a bit under the sudden illumination of fluorescent lights, Alien saw almost half the seats were already occupied by other curious, clueless freshmen. Meanwhile, twenty older students—twelve guys, eight women, all wearing the same black T-shirts—patrolled the aisles, communicating urgently about Important and Secret matters. Some even had two-way radios to talk to Silver Hair, Safety Goggles, and others outside the room. Obviously they were not to be interrupted by impertinent questions from the likes of her.

Taking a seat in the last occupied row, Alien feigned unconcern and studied a cute redheaded guy with a dimpled chin in front of her. Her very sweet high school boyfriend, Micah, was also an incoming in the Boston area, but it was time to start fresh, she felt, so she had broken things off. Convenient, because now, after what seemed an eternity, the redhead turned and noticed her smoothing her newly colored hair.

"What did I miss?" she asked him.

"I can't tell you," he said. "Punishment for being late."

"I'm not *late*," Alien said. "I was just doing something else more interesting."

"Really?" His eyebrow rose at the boast. But he smiled and said, "Invite me next time."

"What's your name?" asked Alien.

"Cal," he said. On the back of his own bright orange invitation, he scribbled his new username—CDaniels—so that she could email him.

"Mine's Alien," she told him, satisfied that he looked impressed.

The older students must have decided that Alien would be the last of their guests this evening, for they finally quieted their radios, and a big bearded guy strode to the front of the room, boosted himself atop the wide wooden lecturer's desk, and stood to speak, casting shadows behind him on sliding blackboards that held the chalky remnants of four decades of erased physics equations.

"Greetings," he boomed. "I'm Jack. By a remarkable coincidence, all my colleagues here tonight"—he gestured to the other organizers in black—"are also named Jack. We are here to help you understand your new home and experience certain sights that you might otherwise miss.

"This tour is not officially sanctioned by MIT. In fact"—he grinned—"you could say it doesn't exist. If participating in something that doesn't exist makes you uncomfortable, please feel free to leave." He paused, looking up and down the room, as did Alien. There were murmurs, and a few of the freshmen shifted uneasily in their seats, but none took him up on the offer. And how could they? Alien thought. They were special now—part of something secret. They had to see what happened next.

"All right, then." Jack cleared his throat. "Just because this tour doesn't exist doesn't mean it doesn't have rules. Like this one." He raised his hand. People murmured. Then they stared. Then, after maybe half a minute had passed, they shut up.

"Exactly," Jack said. "A hand up means total silence. We are out tonight to see—not to be seen. And not being seen begins with not being heard."

The tutorial continued for another half hour. Walk single file. Follow the footsteps of the person in front of you. If you see an obstacle en route, don't speak, but point it out clearly to the person behind you. Don't step on glass ceilings—they break. Don't touch hot steam pipes—they burn. Crouch below the walls of any roof so you stay unseen. Don't take anything. Don't drop anything. And where they were going tonight, the freshmen should never go back to alone.

"Above all, exercise common sense," Jack said. "We'd rather have you safe and sound on the ground, staring up, saying, 'Oh shit, I should have gone on the roof,' than have you up on a roof, staring down, saying, 'Oh shit, I should have stayed on the ground.'"

The room responded with nervous laughter. Good luck with that, Alien thought. No freshman would want to be the one to chicken out and miss the adventure.

"One more thing," Jack wrapped up. "We are not alone tonight. The men in blue suits are looking for us." Everyone understood that he meant the CPs, or campus police. "They do not want to arrest you. They want you not to exist. Satisfy that desire. If you hear someone coming, change floors. If you can't change floors, walk in the opposite direction. If you can't walk in the opposite direction, don't talk to them. If you have to talk to them, be friendly and polite. Have an excuse ready, like you're lost, or a question to ask, like 'Where's the bathroom?'"

Jack's eyes twinkled. "If *we* can be invisible, *you* should be able to be invisible," he concluded, acknowledging his stature and the not exactly discreet appearance of many of his colleagues. "It's amazing what you can get away with if you don't look like you're getting away with anything."

The Jacks divided the room into three groups of forty, each accompanied by seven guides. Each guide had his or her own clearly defined and obviously well-rehearsed role: Head Jack to lead the group; Scout Jack to determine their route and look out for cops; Radio Jack to communicate with other groups; Tail Jack to count freshmen and make sure no one got lost; Supply Jack to carry water, snacks, and a first aid kit; and two Utility Jacks roving the line to monitor everyone and offer help or answer questions as necessary.

Silver Hair, it turned out, was the Radio Jack in Alien's group. Safety Goggles was the Tail Jack. Alien felt lucky when it turned out that her Head Jack was the same bearded giant who had addressed the entire lecture hall. And luckier still when the freshman placed directly in front of her in the middle of the pack was Cal, her new crush.

"Stay close," he whispered, winking.

Alien put a silencing finger to her lips and winked back.

The freshmen turned over any backpacks or bags to a separate Jack, who would deliver them to their final location. Then they were off.

⊰⊱

Wide-eyed and serious, looking out for blue uniforms, Alien, Cal, and their group tiptoed out of the lecture hall and back down the stairs to the Building 54 basement, where a new, longer tunnel delivered them to the basement of another building. As they climbed stairs, Alien realized that they were back at and then above the Infinite Corridor. More halls and more stairs passed in an exciting blur. Two floors up, one floor down seemed the general pattern, with much crisscrossing along the way.

At last they reached a top floor. They turned a corner and encountered a locked door. Their Scout Jack—pale and efficient, with a long nose and wispy mustache—took a small, flexible plastic card from his pocket and slid it between the door and frame until the card was wedged securely behind the latch. He jerked quickly, the latch gave, and the lock opened. Triumphant, he led them into a narrow lounge intended for custodial employees.

At one end of the lounge Alien saw a metal staircase leading straight to the roof, which Scout Jack started climbing. Head Jack stopped short, however. He raised his hand emphatically, demanding and receiving complete quiet. Then, with his other hand, he pointed to the opposite side of the room, where a young man—janitor? student? both?—sat in a cushy chair, calculator in his lap, pencil and notebook in hand, hunched over a thousand-page biology textbook.

Was that it? Alien held her breath. Were they busted? One shout and they'd be surrounded by CPs. And it seemed unlikely that they could *all* claim to be looking for the bathroom.

But no shout came. For the biology enthusiast was so deeply immersed in his studies that he never lifted his head from the textbook even as forty-seven sets of eyes watched him scribble out cell diagrams. After a lengthy pause, and some fervent but silent hand signals between Jacks, the entire tour group marched on, up the stairs and out onto the roof.

"Duck." The whispered command went down the line, and the tour proceeded at a crouch. Ahead of her Alien saw the person in front of Cal point out a pipe sticking out of the ground, waiting to trip someone. Cal in turn pointed it out to Alien, and she pointed it out to the freshman behind her. Each stepped over it in turn.

A minute later they reached one of four squat pyramids overlooking Killian Court, the main campus's central courtyard. Here Head Jack had taken Scout Jack aside and was telling him off about not having spotted the biology student. Radio Jack, meanwhile, was warning the other tours via a central relay. While this took place, one of the Utility Jacks stepped forward to regale them. He was round-faced and genial, any pedantry undercut by a slight lisp and an overgrown bowl haircut he kept blowing up out of his eyes, as if to punctuate key statements.

"Contrary to popular conception, hacking originated at MIT in the early twentieth century, long before the advent of computers," Story Jack told them.

"The original hacks were elaborate, extremely clever student pranks — handing out colored cards at a Harvard-Yale football game to spell MIT rather than BEAT YALE when raised by eleven hundred Harvard fans, for example, or sneaking a power supply, multi-piece wooden frame, and the outer metal parts of a Chevrolet Cavalier atop the Great Dome, so it appeared that the building was mounted by a real police cruiser, complete with flashing lights and boxes of Dunkin' Donuts."

The freshmen laughed. The campus had two signature domes: the "Little" Dome, one hundred feet high and seventy-two feet across, atop Building 7, and the "Great" Dome, atop the engineering library, Building 10, 150 feet high and 108 feet across. Both were built on the model of the Roman Pantheon — and now, from this nearby rooftop, both were practically at eye level. New perspective notwithstanding, however, it was incredible to imagine having to sneak a *car* atop one of them.

"This tradition continues today," Story Jack said. In recent years, the Great Dome had had a ringing telephone booth put on it; a sixteen-foot-square, twelve-foot-high house; and a perfectly dimensioned pink nipple, transforming it into the "Great Breast of Knowledge." Most hacks lasted only twenty-four hours — if that — but the glory, Story Jack made clear, was eternal.

"At MIT, 'going hacking' still means not computer exploits but after-hours exploration — what we're doing tonight," he continued. "You 'pull a hack' when the hacking leads to something you can show off, but that's completely optional. Just by being here, you're hacking."

The tour continued with a go-ahead signal from central radio command. The group descended all the way back to one of the basements below the Infinite Corridor, and then a sub-sub-basement two levels below that.

"These are the steam tunnels — or as we call it, Hell," Head Jack told them before a squat and rusty metal door that suggested the entrance to a submarine. "You're going to have to crouch again," he warned. "And hold your hand up over your face as you walk."

"Why?" a worried freshman asked.

Head Jack shrugged. "It's a lot easier to explain a burn on your hand than a burn on your face."

The freshman gulped but asked nothing more.

Again, Scout Jack carded the door open. Even in the middle of the line, twenty students back, Alien felt the rush of hot air the moment the lock turned.

She followed Cal down a metal ladder to a dark and sweltering narrow corridor crowded on all sides with rows of burning-hot pipes. Head Jack hadn't been joking: Jacks and freshmen alike advanced slowly with their hands up, palms out, above their foreheads, crouching so low it made their knees ache, and Alien, sweating from the neck, immediately followed suit.

They emerged after what felt like hours but couldn't have been more than two or three minutes. Still in a basement machine area, the Jacks pointed out what they called "tombs": empty, unused spaces, generally created when a building was renovated or extended without updating all the floor plans.

"Knock, knock," Head Jack demonstrated, rapping his knuckles against a wall that echoed back instead of thudding, suggesting an open space behind it. Sure enough, circling the area, they found a four-by-eight-by-six-foot tomb between old staircases and a new wall. Someone had blocked the space with a thin metal grate, but Scout Jack removed this with a single pull of his pinky. Inside, the tomb even had a grounded outlet.

"How thoughtful," Tail Jack said. "Now you know where to go and study when the library closes. Just bring your own lamp."

The biggest tomb lay just beyond a ductwork labyrinth. Because Cal had to crouch again at the loudly humming machinery overhead and Alien didn't, she saw the artwork before he did. "Look!" She pointed, not bothering to whisper, given the ambient racket and the excited murmurs of others around them.

Huge logos, each ten to fifteen feet high, filled two tall walls. These were not dashed-off graffiti but carefully wrought full-color murals: a smiling yellow triangular figure holding a daisy in its left hand and the sign HACKITO ERGO SUM in its right, for example, and the now familiar JACK FLOREY'S OLD NO. 5 black label, among a half-dozen others.

"These are some of MIT's hacking communities," Story Jack explained, naming them and the general living group they were associated with: Jack Florey—Fifth East hall on East Campus; James E. Tetazoo III—Third East hall on East Campus; Order of Random Knights—Random Hall, a multi-story dormitory west on Massachusetts Avenue; TEP—the Tau Epsilon Phi fraternity house in Boston; and so on. "Each has its own culture and approach to hacks and hacking, but we all share certain ethics and aesthetics."

"What are those?" a freshman asked, pointing to what looked like tiny symbols scrawled across the high ceiling—a seemingly impossible feat without a ladder.

"Ninety-nine percent of hacking doesn't have anything to do with pulling a prank," Story Jack answered. "It's about exploration, as I said." The symbols, he went on, were "sign-ins"—the way one hacker tells all the others that he or she discovered or gained access to a particular site, complete with personal mark and date.

"Sign-ins aren't graffiti because they're small and in places so difficult to reach that ordinary people never see them," he said. "They're how hackers communicate among themselves and keep track of their history." The earliest sign-in, found on the fourth floor of Building 10, he told them, dated from *1915*.

"You should only sign in at a location that you're proud to have found," Head Jack added. "Real hackers aren't proud of 'discovering' Lobby Seven."

They walked on to a smaller tomb in which another mural, labeled HACK-ING ETHICS, listed these and other points of instruction: "Never drink and hack," Alien read. "Never hack alone.... Know your limitations and do not exceed them." The mural even said, "If you do get caught, accept gracefully and cooperate fully."

But Alien didn't want to think about getting caught. She just wanted to start exploring. Already, her mind raced with ideas for an awesome Alien-themed sign-in logo.

The group climbed stairs again, this time to the roof of Building 7. Despite hissed reminders to keep ducking single file, Alien couldn't resist staring up briefly to take in a view of the Little Dome ahead, just a stone's throw away, like a neighbor's house you could stroll up to and ask to borrow sugar. The proximity was amazing—as if they were being brought to meet the moon.

Were they going to walk right to it? she wondered. Were they going to get to *touch* it?

Halfway there, a few yards later, Tail Jack halted them. "Watch the gap," she said, gesturing to the right. What looked like the shortest path to the dome was actually a trick of perspective—ten feet of empty air between two separate buildings. Step into it and you would fall: tour—and life—over.

⊰⊱

A moment later, Alien reached the dome. "Even though this is the Little Dome, it's actually more visible than the Great Dome because it fronts Mass Ave," Story Jack told them. For one Halloween hack, he said, it had been cov-ered with six thousand square feet of painted polyethylene sheeting to resemble a Kilroy head and eyes. During a subsequent summer, it had been topped with a papier-mâché snowman. One December it was decorated with electric Christmas lights and presents; another it'd had an eight-foot-tall, ten-foot-wide Hanukkah menorah. And the domes themselves were just two of a dozen popular hacking sites.

Alien and her peers were listening so attentively to Story Jack that they didn't notice that not all the other Jacks were still behind them until the other Utility Jack, a gravel-voiced brunette, interrupted him. "Enough with the history lesson," she said. Alien looked up. This woman and Head Jack had not only *touched* the Little Dome—they had *ascended* it. The brunette was at a lower level; Head Jack was at the very top. "Care to get some fresh air?" she said. "Anyone?"

Alien hesitated only a moment, but Cal had stepped forward before her. He pulled himself up to the landing next to the brunette. Alien followed immediately. Only after she was beside Cal, panting, did she see Tail Jack bring out a hidden ladder.

"Could have told you, guys," she said.

Alien didn't care. Being one of the first freshmen on the landing was exhilarating. And the curved part of the dome, she was surprised to see, had metal rungs. Between gripping these and a little determined leg shimmying, she made it to the top even before Cal.

Looking out over Massachusetts Avenue, then across the Charles River, and then out to the bright lights of the nighttime Boston skyline and beyond, Alien felt the thrill of possession. A few hours ago, all these sights, like the dome itself, had been landmarks, beautiful but inaccessible. Now, with this climb, she had made them *hers*.

⊰⊱

The tour ended at four a.m. back in the East Campus courtyard, where the Jacks told more hacking stories and served punch and doughnuts. Afterward, Cal walked Alien back to her room. He couldn't stop talking about how cool it had all been. She agreed—and seven days later, when it was time to choose permanent housing, they both moved into Fifth East.

Alien carried her blanket, bedding, and backpack up five flights in one trip, and her suitcase and a tub of school supplies up in another. As she'd seen the night of the midnight tour, East Campus comprised two five-story buildings. Yet each of the ten halls — First East, First West, Second East, Second West, Third East, Third West, and so on — was its own independent forty-person living group with a separate, fully furnished kitchen, common area lounges, rules, and culture. Fifth East might have no more in common with Fourth East, just a floor below it, than it did with Baker House, located on the opposite side of campus.

In her immediate vicinity, the groups Alien had heard the most about during Rush were Second West, Third East, Fourth West, and Fifth East.

Second West was hands-on engineers: they built their own computers, their own stereos, and quite possibly their own desks and chairs. Third East was the home of the Tetazoo hackers, renowned for their homegrown chemistry talents, specifically with explosives. "Happy, clean-cut pyros," an upperclassman had summarized to Alien. Fourth West was said to host legendary parties with rare and unusual drugs, like opium and 2C-B, under the indulging smile of a Cheshire cat mural. And Fifth East, of course, was where the black-clad, door-busting, dome-topping roof and tunnel hackers congregated.

Black-clad, door-busting, dome-topping — and *sticky*. Everything Alien touched as she settled in — bed, desk, walls, and floor — clung to her. Obviously, the Fifth East crew's considerable powers of organization exhibited on the hacking tour did not extend to cleaning. Under her radiator was a bloodlike red stain; on the ceiling above her bed was a hardened wasp's-nest-like cluster. Cal, brave soul, tested each substance by swabbing it with his pinky and bringing the finger to his tongue.

"Kool-Aid," he diagnosed. "And shaving cream."

At midnight they walked together from her room to the lounge at the other end of the hall, traversing crumbling, paint-splattered carpeting that crunched lightly with cigarette butts, broken pens and pencils, used staples, and other discarded items underfoot.

Art partially excused the squalor. Fifth East was divided into three wings: Walcott, where her new room was, with one lounge; Goodale, on the opposite end, where Cal's room was, with the other lounge and kitchen; and Bemis in the middle.

Up and down Walcott and Goodale were beautiful murals of a forest, Pink Floyd's *The Wall*, Grateful Dead dancing bears, and other designs. Even some of the ceiling tiles had been colored, making bright overhead mosaics, while black lights in the Walcott lounge, Alien saw, made a mural of a fire-breathing dragon glow.

Bemis, the central wing, by contrast, was painted wall-to-wall black, with dimming red gels over its ceiling lights to complete the Stygian atmosphere for the hardest of the hardcore. Here, most particularly, the hall smelled of smoke, rotting potatoes, and failed experiments with uric acid.

A French flag hung across the door of the last room before Bemis turned into Goodale. Behind the door, Alien heard shouting at the loudest volume. "FUCK YOU! FUCK YOU! FUCK YOU! FUCK YOU!" a suite of strident male voices repeated.

Cal turned to Alien, eyebrows raised. She shrugged, smiling, took his hand and squeezed it.

In the Goodale lounge they found several familiar faces — Radio Jack, who introduced himself as Zhu; Tail Jack, Vanessa; Story Jack, Sam; Utility Jack, Rochelle — among a half-dozen students. Those who wanted to smoked freely. And Rochelle strolled around wearing only her underwear, which Alien noticed attracted Cal's attention. It wasn't only buildings, she realized, that hackers wanted to explore.

Head Jack himself lumbered out of the kitchen, carrying popsicles for everyone. He and Vanessa kissed.

"This is Rex, our fearless leader," Sam told Cal and Alien.

The lounge walls were painted red and black, one red side emblazoned with a scowling, geometric black-stenciled skull several feet high. The skull was Krotus, Sam said, the God of Fifth East.

"*God?*" questioned Cal.

"Well . . . malevolent deity," said Sam. He winked at Alien before grabbing and unwrapping a popsicle. "What comes up, Krotus brings down."

A little after two a.m., Alien got up to stretch her legs. Loud epithets continued in the French flag room. Now, though, the door was open. Peeking inside, she realized that the "shouting" was in fact a recording playing from tall quadrophonic speakers. A shirtless, strikingly fit older student, dressed in black combat pants with lots of pockets, stood at the rear of the bedroom, his back to Alien. He had long, smooth honey-colored hair, rippling arm and back muscles, and bare feet.

Common to all rooms on Fifth East were a bookshelf, a desk, a sink, a radiator, and a twin extra-long mattress and bed frame. To this furniture Shirtless had added a futon couch and dresser. Everything — even the radiator and ceiling — was painted the same black as the Bemis hallway. He had black blankets and black sheets, too — and piles of black clothes brightened only by white briefs. Alien watched, intrigued, as the guy cracked his window and climbed outside.

Where was he going? Alien paused only a moment before walking to the window herself and sticking her head out to see.

It was quiet — calm even — in the night air. Shirtless was sitting six or seven feet to the left of the window, on the ledge facing the East Campus courtyard. With him was another guy Alien couldn't see from her current position. Both male voices were resonant, however, discussing something to do with "the Pru" — Boston's fifty-two-story skyscraper, the Prudential Tower.

Alien crawled out to join them, the pressure of her heartbeat increasing as the clamorous "music" behind her diminished. Shuffling through the steam tunnels or climbing the Little Dome, she'd had guides near, and other students to support her. Mess up and, at worst, she burned herself or fucked up her ankle. Slip here, she realized, and she'd drop straight down five stories to pavement. And the ledge couldn't be wider than twenty inches.

As soon as she could, Alien crouched on the cool concrete. From this vantage, the courtyard's red metal picnic tables looked like tiny Legos. The surrounding shrubs and bushes seemed hardly wider — or more cushioning — than a sprig of parsley. Alien clenched her jaw and focused on a lit window across the courtyard. When she next inhaled and exhaled, the breaths came a bit easier.

Little by little, she inched left.

"Hi," Alien said when she was just a foot and a half from Shirtless.

His bicep twitched. He didn't turn.

"Nice night," Alien said, trying to be friendly.

Again, Shirtless ignored her. Alien scooted closer, legs dangling almost comfortably. The other guy on the ledge also had long hair, she saw now, chestnut brown and parted down the middle like in a portrait of Jesus. He wore an American flag as a skirt.

"So what's the power output?" Shirtless asked Jesus.

"Two hundred milliwatts," Jesus said.

"Wavelength?"

"Six hundred and fifty nanometers."

"Range?"

"Ten miles."

"Bullshit," Shirtless said. "Show me the scope."

Alien watched as Jesus lifted something that had been hidden at his side. It looked like a rifle. He passed it to Shirtless, who peered through a tiny top hole before turning and aiming the fifteen-inch-long barrel just above Alien's head.

He handed the rifle back to Jesus. "Hit it," he said.

Jesus shifted his body south, facing Boston. It was an exceptionally clear evening. All the way across the river, colored lights blinked brightly atop the Prudential Tower. Jesus slowly raised his rifle, pointed it at the postcard-perfect scene, and pulled the trigger.

Immediately, Alien saw, the skyscraper's central penthouse was illuminated by a faint but enormous green laser dot.

⊲══▶

Shirtless stood, stepped over Alien, walked back to his window as if the ledge were a normal sidewalk, and ducked inside. Alone with Alien, Jesus had a sullen, taciturn demeanor, but he answered direct questions when asked. His name was Heston, he said. Shirtless was François—hence the French flag. Both were sophomores. Yes, he had built the rifle-mounted laser himself. And he had helped run the radios during the freshman hacking orientation tour, monitoring both Jack and police channels, so the hackers were always a step ahead.

Alien suddenly remembered the initial feeling that night of being watched while she waited in the courtyard. Maybe Heston had been sitting on this very ledge a week ago, seen her, and sent Zhu and Vanessa out to get her, she thought. Before she could ask, however, François returned, carrying a gallon jug of dark liquid. He chugged for several seconds and then passed the drink to Heston.

"I thought we're not supposed to drink and hack," Alien said.

Both guys laughed at her. "It's apple cider," François said. "I don't drink, I don't smoke, I don't have sex, and I don't compromise. Ever."

Alien laughed back, happy at least that the older students hadn't told her to get lost. "Can I have a sip?" she said.

François didn't answer but passed her the jug after Heston had his fill. Alien drank. It did taste like cider. Lights turned off across the courtyard as other students went to bed.

⟨⟩

Alien didn't tell Cal about meeting François and Heston. She also didn't ask what had happened with Rochelle after she had left the lounge. When she and Cal were alone together, they were devoted to each other—that's what mattered. That's why the next night, they decided that it was time for them both to lose their virginity.

Cal had a double room to himself. Alien did too, which had seemed strange, given that they were freshmen, until they realized other prospective residents had probably visited the hall before signing up to live here and decided that the sticky walls, loud music, sketchy people, and general hacker scene was incompatible with graduating. They had chosen easily the most squalid housing at MIT. But almost certainly also the most liberated. The only way to be seen as a freak on Fifth East was to get up before noon.

Together, that evening, they visited the CVS in Kendall Square. Alien bought the condoms. Cal contributed a bag of miniature Hershey's bars and a candle. Back at the hall, they split the chocolate with others in the Goodale lounge, leaving ten minutes apart just before and after one a.m. When Alien snuck into Cal's room, he had already lit the candle and placed it on the nightstand next to the bunk bed.

They took off their clothes and sat on the top bunk together. He had cute red armpit hair. After a little kissing, it was time. Cal put on the condom and it was over so quickly Alien wasn't sure that it had even happened. But it was sweet, and they were both happy.

"Oh, that was wonderful!" Alien said, and they snuggled up together.

02

The Coffeehouse Club

C LASSES STARTED THE NEXT morning. These were essentially the same for every freshman: physics, chemistry, calculus, and something in the humanities. Spring semester would be identical, only more advanced, and with biology in place of chemistry. Then you had to choose your major.

Majors at MIT were called "courses," as in "course of study." Like the buildings on campus, they were identified not by name but by number. Computer science was Course 6, for example. Economics was Course 14. Nuclear engineering was Course 22. In the past, various majors had been designated Course 19, but it no longer had any official use. As an inside joke, those in the know appropriated the name to refer to hacking. And in this unofficial Course 19, almost all "instruction" took place between midnight and dawn.

"Follow us," Sam said. He, Zhu, Rex, Vanessa, and Rochelle wore dark tees and black combat pants and carried a slim Maglite flashlight, lock-picking tools, and a Leatherman Wave. Walking casually down the Infinite Corridor among other students there after hours, they darted off in twos and threes and wove their way up and down staircases and across corridors, trailed by Alien and Cal. Fifteen minutes later, everyone had regathered in the basement machine room with the hacking group murals.

"Are you ready for your first sign-in?" Rex asked the freshmen.

They nodded solemnly. Alien fingered a Sharpie she'd put in her pocket for this very purpose.

Rochelle and Zhu kept watch while the other upperclassmen led them around the corner. Sidling through an almost invisible opening, they entered the narrow tomb with the hacking ethics mural. The walls around the mural were covered with sign-ins dating back decades. Alien studied the names and symbols, feeling part of something bigger than herself.

Hackers and MIT administrators coexisted in an uneasy relationship, she knew. Though tombs like this one weren't exactly discreet, the Institute still allowed them — and their sign-ins — to remain. There seemed to be a kind of gentlemen's agreement: Hackers didn't get hurt or hurt others. They didn't get caught. And, except for intentionally public displays, they didn't leave any evidence behind to show non-hackers where they had been. As long as these rules were obeyed, the higher-ups let the hackers be.

Cal left his sign-in first: an *L* nested inside an *A* nested inside a *C* to form a nautilus. Alien admired the geometry but had chosen something looser and more free-spirited for herself, drawing a cute circle face topped by two bent antennae.

Underneath it she wrote "Alien" and the date.

"Congratulations," Sam told her and Cal.

"Welcome to the dysfunctional family," said Vanessa.

Rex grunted. "C'mon," he said. "Let's see how far you can go."

They returned to the main room. Alien didn't see Rochelle and Zhu, though she heard the echoes of whispered snickers.

Where were they? she wondered, searching left and right before thinking to look up.

Above them, filling three quarters of the high-ceilinged room, hung a tangle of thin red-painted water pipes and wide white-painted metal air ducts. Zhu and Rochelle stood on the duct directly over her. They waved at Alien. But how had they gotten there?

The answer came a moment later. One at a time, Rex, Vanessa, and Sam grabbed the hanging metal venting and pulled themselves up after the other veterans. In seconds, they and Zhu and Rochelle had proceeded quickly farther upward, treating the surrounding ducts like sidewalks and staircases, until they were fifteen feet above the beginners. *So that's how you do a sign-in on the ceiling,* Alien realized.

"Is that load-bearing?" Cal asked skeptically of the ductwork, at least one shaft of which wobbled noticeably when Rex stepped near it.

"The edges are safe," Sam said. "But avoid the middle."

"Tell them about the pipes," Zhu said.

Sam's face reddened. "They can hold you fine," he said, "but if they're too hot they can also melt your shoes."

"Wisdom of experience," Zhu whispered, winking.

Cal pulled himself up before Alien. He offered her a hand from the top.

"She your date?" said Rochelle.

The others chuckled.

Alien glared at Rochelle; she waved Cal off. He was taller and stronger than she was, definitely, but she weighed much less. After two failed leaps, she finally got a grip with which she could wriggle up. Inelegant, maybe, but effective, she thought proudly.

The ducts led them to a ceiling passage crowded with more sign-ins. Long ago someone had even left behind what was now a yellowed, curling copy of *Scientific American*. Tonight, though, the bulkhead-style door separating this area from an outside hall was locked in such a way even the older students couldn't open it.

Rex made a circling motion with his index finger. They turned around, Alien briefly in the lead.

At Sam's instruction, she jumped down in a different part of the room. Her ankles stung, but Alien walked it off. The others joined her, and soon, traveling up stairs and from hall to hall again, they had reached the other side of the blocked ceiling passage from the mural room. It had a padlock on this side, which explained their difficulty opening it.

"Now that's just cheating," Rex said. He stepped forward, taking a thin L-shaped turning tool and pick from a hollowed-out pen. Rex inserted the turning tool in the bottom of the keyhole, knelt for leverage, turned the lock's cylindrical casing, and then played the pick like a tiny violin bow back and forth inside the cylinder. Alien watched, impressed. In seconds, the lock popped open with a satisfying click.

"Better than sex," said Rex.

Vanessa kicked him.

"Sorry, dear," he joked.

They crossed back to the ducts crisscrossing the top of the mural room. These led over an incomplete wall and let them drop down in a new machine room. Here metal stairs led to a caged second level. Inside the cage was a huge blowing fan, helping circulate air throughout the entire building above them. The roaring blades, Alien guessed, must be at least ten feet long.

The cage was locked, but Zhu, the deftest touch among them with lock picks, got it open easily. "He's not going in there, is he?" Alien asked Cal.

Rochelle overheard her. "We don't just pick locks to pick locks," she said. "We pick locks to see what's on the other side."

Zhu entered, followed by everyone but Sam, who kept watch, just in case. Cal shrugged at Alien and then crossed the threshold.

Alien bit her lip. The hairs on her arms stood on end. She was terrified. But she hadn't come this far to be left behind. Stepping forward after Cal, she heard a final word of instruction from Sam. "Don't die!" he shouted jovially above the roar of the blades.

Because the fan blew outward, anything—and anyone—behind it was sucked directly toward it. Even before she had entered completely, Alien had to steel her heels and fight hard to resist the air current. Its force was incredible.

She looked up, curious to see how the others were handling the constant buffeting. Zhu and Cal crouched, squinting. Vanessa and Rochelle gripped the coils of the cage, as she did. Only Rex, big enough to counter the fan with gravity alone, stood free and upright. He beamed, seemingly refreshed by the hurricane. He shouted something to them. It was impossible to hear, however. Rex repeated himself, mouthing slowly. The wind rippled his beard.

Zhu understood first. He shouted too. Then Vanessa and Rochelle, then Cal, and finally Alien herself. Then all together.

"IHTFP!" Rex had been saying. MIT's mordant unofficial motto: "I Hate This Fucking Place."

Alien closed her eyes. The fan was a kind of confessional. They could say whatever they wanted here. They could tell anyone anything. No one would understand. Then the fan would suck their words away.

"Fuck, I'm tired!" Alien said. "Fuck this place!" She opened her eyes, saw everybody watching her, and unbuttoned her shirt for show. "Fuck, it's cold!"

Her baggy shirt blew open. Alien watched a button whip away, straight into the speeding blades. A second later, the fan spit back shards. Alien and the others recoiled, but the tiny bits and pieces were immediately drawn back and sucked away to some classroom upstairs.

They laughed, panting, until tears formed around their eyes—tears immediately wiped dry.

⊰∙⊱

Twenty minutes later, the roar of the fan was finally fading in Alien's ears as they had all shuffled to and halfway through the steam tunnel inferno, hands up and out over their foreheads in the now familiar protective pose.

"What's this?" Zhu said, in front again. He pointed out a side passage illuminated by what seemed like a bright but distant light. "Have you seen this?" he asked the other upperclassmen. They shook their heads.

"Well . . . ?" Zhu looked for confirmation to proceed. They were all sweating.

"Why not?" Rex said. "Can't be worse than Hell, can it?"

"Yeah," Sam said. "Let's check it out."

Alien grinned at Cal. Their first hacking expedition as official Fifth East residents and already they'd reached terra incognita for the older students. And the ceiling above the side route was bare.

"Pass those Sharpies," Rochelle said.

Alien and Cal did. Before proceeding, everyone signed in.

Zhu led them down the new passage. The light increased. At the turn, Alien saw why: above them, five feet to the left, was a metal sidewalk grate. A streetlight overhead must have been shining down through it.

This time Zhu didn't wait for anyone's go-ahead signal. Working steadily but excitedly, he opened his Leatherman and wiggled out a single screw at each end of the grate.

"And up we go," Rex said, lifting.

⊰∙⊱

They emerged to what could have been a Hollywood stage set of a city street: sidewalk, trees, parked cars, tall buildings—all, at this hour, silent and empty. The ground was wet, though; it had rained while they were down below, Alien realized. She kicked the screws, which rolled into a curbside puddle.

"This must be new construction," Vanessa whispered. She did page layout for *The Tech,* the student newspaper, which meant she knew all the MIT news. "Supposedly some old dude is about to give fifty million bucks to build a human genome something."

"Yeah," Sam joked. "They're cloning Rex."

But Rex himself had raised his hand. He gestured to Zhu, who was pointing at a driveway maybe fifteen feet in front of them. A car there had turned on its headlights. A campus police car, Alien realized.

"Do. Not. Run," Sam reminded everyone, speaking out of the side of his mouth. Still, he and they walked extremely *briskly* down the block in the opposite direction, around the corner, and back inside.

A minute later, they were back along the Infinite Corridor again, strolling innocently. When Sam started whistling, Alien had to hold back cheers.

This was magic—and they had gotten away with it! Was there anything better than entering somewhere you weren't supposed to be and then exiting somewhere you'd never been?

Hacking, the whole school—the whole city, the whole world—was your playground. You went where you wanted and did what you chose.

⟡

Alien was at the classroom by nine thirty a.m. She'd just slip in quietly, she planned. She couldn't have missed much. And if she had—well, with some subjects, less was more.

Her first class of the morning, single variable calculus, had started half an hour earlier. By coincidence, its location was the same large lecture hall in Building 54 where her hacking tour had begun. After waking little more than five hours after her emergence from the sidewalk grate, Alien had tromped outside to Building 66, where she followed the secret basement tunnel shortcut to the classroom door.

Sighing deeply, Alien stepped inside. The professor, a bald man in his mid-forties with a halo of brown curly hair and a bulbous red nose, had already filled four of the six chalkboards with equations. Some 250 students sat attentively, taking notes. Front-row center, directly in front of the professor, was a cardboard banker box for turning in completed problem sets.

There are two kinds of nightmares: the ones you wake up from and the ones you just have to live through because you're already awake. This was the latter. Cringing, Alien descended aisle after aisle, problem set in hand. "Sorry," she mouthed to the professor when she reached the front and added her work to the top of the pile.

He scowled at her and then turned to resume scribbling, raising a cloud of chalk as he went:

$$0 \leq (-x)^2 = (-x)(-x) = ((-1)x)((-1)x) = (((-1)x)(-1))x = ((-1)(x(-1)))x = (((-1)(-1))x)x = (1x)x = xx = x^2$$

"Therefore," he said, "the square of any real number is non-negative."

Alien yawned, considering whether to sit and try to copy down the entire equation in her notebook as the students to the left and right of her were doing. Why fake it, though? MIT professors were undoubtedly brilliant people. But no one had hired them because of their teaching ability. And attendance had almost no role in grading. To pass her classes, going to them any longer than it took to drop her problem sets off was a waste of time.

Alien turned around and walked out, an alternative already in mind.

⟫⟪

Strange hands grabbed Alien's shoulders. It was a crude, aggressive gesture — more pinch than rub. She knew immediately that it wasn't Cal.

Alien forced a smile and turned from preparing mac and cheese in the hall kitchen to face Alex, a pockmarked sophomore guy who'd agreed to explain her physics problem set material to her. They'd gone hacking together, but she didn't know him well. Just that he was one of the few Fifth Easters with a passing GPA and that the more she complimented him on how smart he was and how little she knew by comparison, the happier he was to help.

"Need something?" Alien asked him with strained sweetness.

Alex stared at her chest. "Just checking on you," he said.

"This will be ready in a minute," Alien told him. "Why don't you wait for me in the lounge?"

Soon afterward, she carried forks and the steaming pot out to the lounge's black-painted wooden table, where Alex waited with his roommate, a tall, pale eastern European student, Vlad. Vlad's claim to fame was single-handedly taking Romania to a top-five finish in the International Math Olympiad. Though the temptations of life on Fifth East had lured him from purely academic rigors, with a sufficiently stroked ego, he too could condescend to tutoring.

"Interesting fact," Alex was saying when Alien entered. "Forty-five percent of MIT students are women. If you look at IQ distributions, though, especially in math and science, it should be *fifteen* percent."

Vlad chuckled, already anticipating the upshot.

"So," said Alex, "every time you see three women together on campus, re-member—"

"One is here because she has brains," Vlad said. "Two are here because they have—"

"Dinner," Alien interrupted, dropping the pot on the table with a thud. While the food cooled, she pushed a problem set from her backpack on each of them. "If you could just check these for me . . . ," Alien said.

"One minute," Alex said. He surveyed her physics work: "Wrong; wrong; wrong; laughably wrong; so wrong it's almost beautiful."

Vlad laughed. He shook his head at her math equations. "I don't even know what notation this is," he said.

Alien looked back and forth between them. She laughed herself. "Can you *possibly* explain it?" she asked, taking a seat between them. "This is really hard. And"—Alien scooted in, spread her legs, and played footsie with each of them independently under the table—"I'd *really* appreciate it."

Alex gulped. Vlad's face reddened. They both nodded.

We're using each other, Alien thought as the guys competed to be the first to scribble out answers. *The only difference is that I know it and they don't.*

———◆———

Cal had his own distractions. On the black Bemis hallway, Zhu and Rex started hosting large group lock-picking sessions. Cal joined them night after night. Alien stood briefly at the periphery, gathering the general principles, but tuned out after ten minutes of pick and pin work. This was mere "practice" hacking, she felt. Persuading Alex and Vlad to finish her problem sets for her without actually giving them any play was far more interesting.

"Hey, are you ready?" she asked Cal one night the second week in a row he was spending tinkering. They had planned to grab dinner together, and she was getting hungry.

"I'm busy," he said without looking up at her.

Bored, Alien took out her backpack and idly drew a Krotus figure on the back pocket with a paint marker. To preserve the drawing, she covered it with nail polish.

"Now?" she said.

Cal shook his head. "One minute," he muttered.

Alien waited fifteen. "I haven't eaten all day," she said. "Can we go?"

Cal ignored her.

Now Alien was really annoyed. "You want to open a lock so badly? Just fucking cut it," she said.

A line of lock pickers looked up at them. They were all barefoot, following François's example, though François himself was too cool to participate in group activities.

"You're being dumb," Cal said. Playing to their audience instead of apologizing to Alien, he quoted a line from the hacking ethics mural: "'Brute force is the last resort of the incompetent.'"

"That just means it's the first resort of the competent," Alien said.

Furious, she strode down Bemis to Heston's room, where she found Heston and Rochelle playing a dice game and smoking.

Heston, the engineering wizard, had transformed spare parts into his own networked computer terminal just like the public ones at the student center.

"Let me use it," Alien demanded. "I have to dump someone."

Heston raised an eyebrow, but Rochelle was quick to second her. "Yeah," she said. "Angry lady."

Heston, amused, stood and gestured to his empty desk chair: *All yours.*

"We're done," Alien typed. She was a passionate person and had a right to her feelings, she believed. Cal had wanted to be involved. They had lost their virginity together. And now he was ignoring—or, worse, insulting— her.

"Don't just send it to him," Rochelle said. "Send it to the hall."

Alien nodded. She changed the recipient field of her email from Cal's address to that for the entire Fifth East mailing list.

At this point, François entered the room. When the others told him what was happening, he read Alien's email over her shoulder, tsking.

"You call that a breakup?" François said.

"Well, what else should I say?" Alien asked him.

"Put a picture in." François took the keyboard from her, typed rapidly, and pulled up and pasted in an ASCII text art representation of a raised middle finger:

```
......................./´¯/)
......................,/¯../
......................./..../
............./´¯/'...'/´¯¯`·,
........./'/.../..../......./¯¯\
.......('(...´...´.... ¯~/'...')
..........\.................'...../
.........."...\...........  _.·´
............\.............(
............\.............\...
```

"There," he said. "Much better."

Alien laughed. Showing off herself, she added a caption: "This is not a drawing of your four-balled dick."

Heston, Rochelle, and François all hooted. "Yes!" they said.

Alien hit Send.

———

Within ten minutes, Alien's email was part of a thirty-message thread. Within an hour, it had been forwarded across the campus. By the following afternoon, it had crossed the country and reached a colleague of Cal's mother, who happened to be a college administrator herself somewhere in Ohio.

After her colleague made the final forward, Cal's mom called him. "Are you okay?" she asked.

By nightfall, the entire story of "Four Balls Cal" was already Fifth East legend.

Although Cal quickly forgave her, laughing it off, Alien was mortified at what she had started. She spent the last of her savings—$180, accumulated in $5.15-an-hour increments at a summer office job—to buy all the flowers from the (thrilled) flower lady at the Kendall T station and arranged the seven dozen roses, lilies, snapdragons, and sunflowers as best she could outside Cal's door.

It was an apology, not an attempt to get back together. She was determinedly single now, she decided, and capped the change by dyeing her hair orange.

———

The MIT student center had opened in 1965 and looked it. Its beige concrete exterior repelled examination. Inside, scuffed linoleum floors and flickering fluorescent lights created a dingy atmosphere reminiscent of an airport security screening area. Banks, a bookstore, a post office, and other services clustered near the entrance with a small food court and convenience store, followed by computer terminals, event rooms, and group study spaces. Farther afield were student group and administrative department offices.

Alien climbed two flights of stairs to her new place of employment. Thanks to low-interest loans, her parents had said that they could cover her housing and tuition. Any money for food and clothing she'd have to earn herself.

At the third floor the stairs ended at a tight rectangular lounge decorated with stained, sunken couches and dented tables and chairs. Here, Alien had observed, there was always at least one student studying, one student sleeping, and one student planning something devious—which is not to say a single MIT student could not be doing all of those things at the same time. Sniff and the odor of burnt coffee and microwave burritos predominated. From a back room came the steady clinks and occasional whoops of people playing pool.

This was the 24-Hour Coffeehouse. Alien had a regular ten p.m. to six a.m. shift.

She was grateful for the job. Working at the Coffeehouse, she was being *paid* to stay up late. Alien had weekends off but still came here as a patron. Saturdays at midnight, Fifth Easters met others in the back poolroom to plan new hacks.

This Saturday, Sam, Zhu, Cal, and Alex showed up a little after eleven p.m., followed half an hour later by Rex and Vanessa. By midnight, ten hackers—sometimes friends, sometimes rivals—had filled the back room.

Besides her hallmates, Alien identified a hefty man in his mid-twenties, bearded and swarthy, with doughy cheeks and a neatly tied jet-black ponytail; a young buzz-cut blonde with a barbell-style lower lip piercing and a branching tree tattoo referring to a famous computer algorithm along her long neck; and a Jewfro'd figure wearing a vintage NIXON'S THE ONE! campaign button over the pocket of his bright green polyester Hawaiian shirt. These were Aziz, a Fifth East alum employed by a Defense Department contractor, who had helped lead the legendary police-car-on-the-dome hack; Rpunzel, a West Campus sophomore so named because she had entered MIT with hip-length hair, since shorn and sold to raise money for a venture that combined handicrafts and electronics; and Splotz—Seth Plotz—the Third East graduate resident tutor, expert in pyrotechnics, who set off a daily explosion, bringing a literal sonic boom every day at five p.m. to East Campus.

With them and others, in the last three weeks alone Alien had traversed the hot steam tunnels enough times that she now could do so blindfolded, built up sufficient calluses to walk back and forth over broken glass in her bare feet without injury, and been given her own hacking card, a sturdy yet flexible laminated strip little bigger than a business card, capable of being used to open many doors without lock picking.

"Well," Rex said tonight. "Where to?"

"The top of Building Thirty-seven has a nice little sign-in spot," said Aziz. "I haven't been there in years."

"What about Sloan?" asked Rpunzel, naming the MIT business school. "They just finished that new construction. We could be the first to hit it."

Splotz grinned enthusiastically. "Sounds good."

"Which one?" said Alex. He looked to Rex for the final decision, but Alien, who had largely kept quiet at previous meetings, responded first.

"Couldn't we do both?" she asked.

The others looked at her with surprise. "You plan to lead?" Alex said.

"Sure," said Alien. The goal of the Coffeehouse Club, as with any hacking, was to find unexplored locations across campus, or new ways of experiencing old locales. Style was key: you built your reputation with the most elegant, ingenious, or daring feats. "If you can keep up with me," she added.

Cal and Zhu said nothing. Vanessa, though, nodded at her in support.

"Why not?" Rex decided the matter. "Let's go."

⎯⎯◆⎯⎯

Building 37 housed the astrophysics department. The sign-in spot Aziz remembered was just beneath the roof on the fifth floor. "We can climb the elevator shaft," he said.

Alien didn't understand. "How do we stop the elevator?" she asked.

"We don't have to," said Aziz. "There's a former freight elevator. Totally dead now, but they just walled up the shaft. It's easy to get to from the basement."

"Makes sense," Alien said, feigning confidence.

Alex shrugged noncommittally. "Ladies first."

Aziz was right. Accessing the shaft was as simple as whipping out a Leatherman, removing a few flathead screws, and pushing aside a panel where the elevator had once opened in the basement. Once upon a time, the whole panel had been painted white. Now, though, the paint had peeled completely from the screws, which all turned easily—a clear sign that the panel had been opened and resealed countless times before now.

Not recently, however. When Alien entered first, she broke a cobweb and felt musty air swirl around her from the dark, dank floor.

"Cool," she murmured. And spooky.

"Here," Aziz said, passing Alien a headlamp.

Alien donned the light and looked up. Empty, the shaft appeared like a smooth square concrete tree trunk, extending to oblivion. *No place to go,* she told herself, *but up.*

Alien pressed her back against the wall adjacent to the basement opening. The chill made her spine and shoulders stiffen. She tensed to stop her whole body from shaking, hoping no one would notice in the dark.

Alien had never climbed an elevator shaft before. Yet she understood the basic mechanics from a recent sign-in trip to Walker Gym. Inside the walls of the gym was a defunct but perfectly preserved shower that had been bricked up rather than filled in, just like this elevator shaft. Visiting hackers made sure the shower always had a fresh bar of soap and rubber ducky. The only way into the shower was by climbing in from the top. The best way out was a kind of splayed crab walk.

Recalling the process now, Alien raised her right leg and then her left, catching the opposite wall with the soles of her feet. She put her palm out against the side wall. Alien grunted. She pushed back with her legs until she was inching up by her buttocks on the wall she'd started with.

Raise, catch, grunt, push: slowly but surely, she rose higher.

The first floor, marked by a doormat-sized see-through metal grate connected to the support beams, was perhaps eight feet up. Alien reached it in a couple of minutes. Her hands, thighs, butt, and abs ached, but she didn't want to rest any longer than necessary on the grate, not with everyone else waiting on her below.

"How's it going?" Rpunzel called.

"Fine," Alien called back.

"Okay to start following?" said Rpunzel.

"Yup," Alien told her.

In ten minutes, she made it to the third floor—almost twenty-five feet high. Two more stories to go. The others trailed a floor or two behind. Looking up again for guidance, however, Alien saw that the elevator shaft ended abruptly just above her. A new, even narrower passage—a chimney, it looked like, lined with red brick—replaced it.

"Aziz!" Alien called.

People shuffled below so that Aziz could face Alien and vice versa. "What is it?" he said.

"Did you know that the elevator shaft only goes to the third floor?" Alien asked.

"Really?" Aziz pondered this information a long moment. "My mistake," he admitted.

Alien swore.

"We're going to have to go around," she heard Alex say.

"No," said Alien. She studied the chimney with her Maglite. It obviously wasn't operating; they would have seen and felt smoke. And even if it was narrower than the elevator shaft, she could definitely fit inside. In fact, climbing up it might be easier, since she shouldn't have to stretch her arms or legs as far.

"Hold on," she said, rising from the third-floor grate. "I'm going to try to chimney up."

A second later, she touched brick.

———✦———

Alien was up the last two stories in less than five minutes. The excitement of leading—and showing up Alex—made her fingers tingle. Holding her Maglite in her mouth, Alien uncapped her marker triumphantly and studied the ceiling sign-ins. She was forty feet above the floor now—and inches away from adding her own name to generations of other hackers.

The Sharpie was oddly slippery, however. As Alien finally signed in, she saw something red dot her cartoon alien antennae.

Is that...?

Alien swiveled her head. Inside the chimney, she saw, the bricks glittered like diamonds. There was broken glass embedded in the walls. She pocketed her marker and looked down at her palms.

Her hands were bleeding.

———

Alien scooted down as quickly as was possible without using her hands to support her. Rpunzel and Aziz waited on another small metal grate at the third level. When she reached them, they had their own flashlights shining upward, making their faces look like disembodied heads.

"Well?" Aziz asked.

Alien hesitated. She knew everyone up and down the shaft was listening. She didn't want to *alarm* anyone. And her hands hurt only a little.

"I signed in," she said.

The chamber filled with cheers.

Aziz moved to start up the chimney himself.

"Wait," said Alien. "I wouldn't."

"Why not?" said Aziz.

Alien raised her palms.

———

Alien washed up in the basement bathroom. Back outside, Rpunzel pointed the way to the new business school building. At the site, they divided into threes and fours — Rex, Zhu, and Sam; Aziz, Splotz, Alex, and Cal; and Vanessa, Rpunzel, and Alien — each group vying to make the first and most exhaustive exploration.

After half an hour, Alien and her group were roaming the second floor.

"Look," Vanessa said. Alien and Rpunzel joined her. Vanessa's Maglite illuminated an open broom closet, the back wall of which was two feet shorter than the ceiling. Hop over that wall and one entered an interstitial space — and from there, who knew?

"Can you fit?" Vanessa asked Alien and Rpunzel. "I can't."

Alien stepped forward to the incomplete wall and pulled herself up and over it. She *could* fit, she found; she just had to wriggle sideways. She stared up, flashed her Maglite, and saw the perfect sign-in spot at the tomb's back wall.

Just to the side, though, was a carefully painted sign that that said DANGER — NOT STRUCTURAL. Big red arrows pointed at the floor.

It wasn't fair. *Too tall and you can't get in here. Too short and you can't sign in.*

If Alien really reached, though, maybe she could make it.

She stretched out in a spread-eagle position, hands and feet along each wall, until she was able to hold her body, hovering, half an inch above the floor. Pain radiated from the pressure on her bruised palms. Sweating, Alien felt her grip immediately begin to loosen.

Just a little further ..., she decided, wriggling harder.

Suddenly, her hands slipped, there was a loud cracking noise, the floor broke, and she fell.

———

Alien could hear people call down after her. First Vanessa and Rpunzel. Then the others. As yet, however, she was too dazed to respond.

Alien looked up and saw a hole in the ceiling. She peered down and saw the floor, eight feet below, covered with foam and plaster debris.

She'd landed on a huge boxy cathode-ray tube monitor on top of a rolling cart in the middle of a classroom.

"I'm okay!" she yelled. "I need help getting down, though."

The other hackers ran downstairs and into the room. They grabbed her by her legs and pulled her to the floor.

———

It was sheer luck that this setup had been here to break her fall. What if she had slipped like that in the elevator shaft, with multiple stories to drop instead of one? She might have smashed her skull or snapped her spine. Alien pushed the thought from her mind.

Cal looked worried. "Are you really all right?" he asked.

Alien nodded. "Just surprised," she said sheepishly.

Alien expected someone to make fun of her. Immediately, though, the group closed ranks. "Sam and Zhu, keep lookout," Rex said. "Alien, Cal, and

Alex—figure out a way to sweep the floor. Everyone else, help me patch the ceiling."

For the next half hour, working with silent efficiency, they cleaned up what they could. Then, from a campus phone outside, Rex placed an anonymous call to FIXIT—the physical maintenance office.

"You made it an exciting night," Alex admitted to Alien.

"We can't end that way, though," said Splotz.

"Well, what do you propose?" Vanessa said.

"We have to hang the point," Splotz said. "Am I right?"

Rpunzel rubbed her hands together in excitement. "Right!" she said.

Soon everyone was running toward Building 66.

⚞⚟

Because Building 66 was triangular, its classrooms and offices narrowed to a sharp corner known on campus as "the point." This meant wasted space inside the building, some people criticized. But if you were a hacker on the roof, the point also presented a spectacular sightseeing opportunity. *Hanging the point,* they called it, but Alien had yet to try it.

"Ladies first," Rpunzel said firmly when Alex tried to take the first spot. She gestured to Alien to begin.

Stepping past her friends, Alien lay facedown, arms extended over the edge of the roof, and felt them grasp and push her forward by her feet. She was trusting them with her life—but then, hadn't she already? Soon her hair, forehead, eyes, ears, and gaping mouth had crossed the lip of the building, and then, second by second, her neck, chest, waist, and legs, until she was dangling freely from the point, held back only by her ankles.

Alien's eyes widened. The blood in her body ran backward at the inversion; it felt like she was flipping underwater. Now, she saw, gasping happily, Ames Street and the MIT Media Lab lay before her, as on the roofs and domes—except this way, all MIT, and everyone in it, was upside down.

⚞⚟

It was eleven a.m. and already Alien had been up for three hours. First, eyes bleary, limbs aching from lack of sleep, she'd had to deep-clean her room. Then she'd had to dig out and wash enough old clothes to last three days: two button-down shirts; a pair of jeans; a pair of black leggings. Finally, she'd had to run to the secondhand boutique in Kendall Square, where she had found and bought a white wool winter cap big enough to cover her hair completely. Now, for the last half hour, she had been keeping watch out her dorm room window.

They could arrive at any moment. And when they did, they would be relentless.

Alien saw her mother first. She was pointing out fallen leaves in the East Campus courtyard to her father. Ah, yes. New England's famous fall foliage. Just in time for parents' weekend at MIT.

Alien tugged down her new cap and ran out to meet them. As she moved, the clothes she'd worn every day of high school felt funny on her body now. Loose. Impractical. Boring. Chaste.

If her parents had seen her just twelve hours earlier, one look would have been enough to tell them how dramatically the last two months had changed their daughter. With her first paycheck from the Coffeehouse, Alien had bought her own black combat pants. With her second, she'd swapped her canvas shoes for black boots. With her third and fourth, she'd added a camouflage jacket and a raft of tight T-shirts. Her favorite, in purple, said PSYCHO BITCH.

Fortunately, Alien was able to keep the T-shirt out of view in the half hour her parents spent on Fifth East itself. "I can't believe there's not an elevator!" her father said, panting hard up five flights of stairs. The muck and grime of the hall itself, meanwhile, shocked her mother. "You'll make yourself sick eating here," she told Alien in the kitchen, unloading a big canvas bag with four dozen bagels, four loaves of rye bread, four pounds of corned beef, four containers of deli mustard, two quarts of macaroni salad, and two quarts of half-sour kosher pickles.

"Elizabeth." Her mother looked her in the eye. "These are not to share. The other kids will not appreciate. You freeze whatever's left. Promise me."

"Let's go out," Alien said. There was no point explaining that she *preferred* the mess. On her suburban block at home, people scraped and paved, mowed and painted over everything that had preceded them. Choose the wrong kind of doormat and someone sent you an angry letter. On Fifth East, Alien looked the past in the eye with every mural; stolen shopping carts and other hackable objects accumulated; search under the couch for thirty seconds and she could probably pick up the perfectly preserved problem set of someone who was now or would soon be a Nobel Prize winner or millionaire entrepreneur.

People argued, sure. Sometimes they hated one another. But they could all bond over wanting to live and work with as few external rules as possible.

That's the building where my physics class is, Alien imagined narrating to her parents. *The best way to get to the roof is by jumping from the building next door.*

And that's the biomedical lab. Last year, my friends found a tomb behind a utility shaft and set up a carpet, faux fireplace, and working Atari 2600 system.

Watch your step here. I came up out of this street grate once. It may still be missing a couple of screws.

Her mother interrupted her reverie. "And who's this?" she asked.

Alien turned from the cupboard. To her horror, she saw that Cal and his mother had entered the kitchen after them.

"Cal, Mom," Alien said, blushing. "Mom, Cal."

"I'm Mrs. Tessman," her mother introduced herself.

"Elise Daniels," Cal's mother replied.

"It's so nice to meet you," Alien's mother said in perfect innocence. "I'm so glad our children have become friends."

"Indeed," Cal's mother replied drily. She knew exactly who Alien was.

The moment swelled. Then François's speakers, two doors down, interceded. "COCKSUCKER! COCKSUCKER! COCKSUCKER!" they blasted.

Alien had never been so grateful for profanity.

Her mother looked disapproving. "Well . . . ," she said. "We should probably get going. Maybe we'll see you later."

"*Yes . . . ,*" Cal's mother said. "Let's talk more."

Alien quickly steered them apart.

———✦———

Her towel was missing. Alien stepped out of the shower, reached out to the rack, and clutched empty air. "Fuck!" she said, dripping wet.

It had to be François. The last few weeks he'd made a game of stealing people's towels from the bathroom when they were showering so that he could "catch" them naked out in the hallway and take their picture.

Just to be sure, Alien tiptoed to the bathroom door, cracked it open the tiniest amount, and peeked outside.

Yup. François sat on the floor just outside the bathroom, waiting for Alien. In his lap was her towel. In his hands was his stupid camera.

François couldn't see her yet. But he was already snickering.

Alien looked down as a puddle of water formed on the floor beneath her. Already she was beginning to shiver. She considered her options: End this quickly but give François the satisfaction of seeing her naked. Try to wrap herself up in a shower curtain—or toilet paper. But others had already done that.

Or—she turned around—try to sneak back to her room another way.

It was a Tuesday evening in mid-November. Opening the window took Alien three hard pushes with her slippery fingers. Immediately, frigid air rushed in; she staggered back, rubbing down her hands and legs. It would be even colder outside, she knew. And the ledge, from this perspective, looked as narrow as a tightrope.

Alien crawled out anyway, wet and naked, her knees slipping slightly on the window frame before her feet found purchase on the ledge, five stories above the pavement below. In the bathroom, she had reflexively crossed her legs and grasped her breasts to cover up. Outside, modesty was not an option. Alien felt air strike her body in the most intimate places, but forced her gaze forward. *You can do this,* she told herself. At least it was already dark. She had five hall windows to pass, she calculated, before she reached her own.

The first window to cross was that of another female freshman, but not a hacker. The woman's room was dark, Alien realized with relief.

Alien crawled forward again, steadying herself with a hand to the exterior brick wall. She heard a car honking. *Not at me,* she prayed, already imagining the pointing onlookers.

Below, a red van had been blocked by students rushing across the street. Hence the honking.

No one had seen her—yet.

Alien looked up again, fighting vertigo. Cold bit her tits, but she ignored the pain and steadied her trembling arms.

Ahead she saw a piece of wood. Alien stood to step over it carefully. Her wet hair was stiffening, she felt. Her skin puckered; her toes froze. Alien advanced.

The next window was dark. Just one more to go before her own.

Alien's next-door neighbor Shannon was a senior in ROTC. She hated hackers and hacking. If Alien ever said hello to her, Shannon snarled. The only reason why she had chosen to live on Fifth East was because she was a smoker and cat owner and the hall allowed both. *Please don't be home,* Alien begged.

Her thigh wobbled, grazing Shannon's window frame. Afraid, Alien knelt again to a crawl—and then wanted to jump backward. Her face, she saw, was just inches from Shannon's. The senior sat by the window, smoking and stroking her orange tabby, Schwarzkopf, in her lap. Her window was open to let the smoke out; only a flimsy screen separated them. If Shannon looked up, she might throw the screen open too; in her surprise and anger, she might even push Alien from the ledge.

Alien cringed. She closed her eyes instinctively. It was ridiculous, but if she couldn't see Shannon, her thinking was, maybe Shannon wouldn't see her.

Slowly, very slowly, Alien inched forward. One frozen limb passed Shannon. Then the next. Then the next. And then the approaching window was hers.

Her own windowpane, thank God, was up. Alien popped the screen and fell inside. Her entire body was blue. Teeth chattering, she threw on clothes and then hugged the radiator.

Time to kick François's ass.

———◆———

Alien cracked the door of her room and peered down the hallway. Her towel lay crumpled on the floor outside the bathroom. François himself was gone, however. Apparently he had gotten bored with waiting for her and moved on to other mischief. This only made Alien more determined to teach him a lesson. She'd shown him up—and he wasn't even here to witness it! She had to beat him or he'd pick on her again.

Alien grabbed the towel and walked quickly to François's room on Bemis. His door was closed; she put her ear to it. Silence. She wiggled the handle. Locked.

Alien knew better than to test her lock-picking abilities. She ran downstairs to the East Campus desk, on the first floor, where a bored security guard at the beginning of the overnight shift sat listening to a radio tuned to the Celtics game. "I left my problem set in my boyfriend's room," Alien told him. "Can you let me in to get it?"

As she expected, he glanced at her ID and then simply handed a spare key to her, telling her to return it when she was finished.

———◆———

Back on Fifth East, triumphant, Alien swung François's door wide and strode inside. François could return at any moment, though. She had to work quickly.

In the total blackness of François's room, one item stood out: his underwear.

Grinning, Alien grabbed a climbing rope from a recent hall hacking outing, one end of which she strung securely from his radiator. At even intervals along the entire length of the rope, she tied all the tighty whities. Then Alien cracked François's window and peered right and left. Heston, she saw, was out on the ledge himself, taking in the evening air. And his room was six doors — or windows — down from François's.

Perfect.

Clutching the free end of the rope in her hand, Alien stepped out of François's room and crawled toward Heston.

"Evening," Heston said when she had reached him, waving with the laser rifle on his lap.

"Evening," Alien replied. She knelt over him to cinch the rope snugly around Heston's radiator. That accomplished, Alien returned the way she had come, gave back the spare key, and prepared to wait.

———⇥———

François showed up a few hours later. "Got you," he told Alien smugly when he passed her in the hallway, working through a calculus problem set with Vlad.

She shrugged, pretending to be embarrassed, but then rose and followed François on tiptoe as he entered his room and turned his music on.

A moment later, fresh shouts made Alien smile. She pushed François's door open, rustling his flag. He had discovered the rope and was already following it out his window. "You bitch!" he yelled at Alien.

They both laughed.

Alien walked to the window to watch as François crawled out on the ledge.

Given how tight she'd made the knots, Alien thought, getting his underwear untangled would take all night.

She leaned outside, eyes closed, almost enjoying the chill.

03

Earth to Alien

TWO AND A HALF months after her naked ledging adventure, Alien sat cross-legged on the floor outside her room, taking notes on taking notes. Her calculus problem set was three pages long. Her physics problem set was four pages. Her biology problem set was six pages. Each was due in a week. Even if Alex and Vlad helped her complete the assignments, she had to know enough herself to take the midterm and final.

Work, sleep, friends — choose two, people said of MIT.

A shadow crossed her papers. Alien looked up.

A tall, strong-jawed guy with dark hair and a kind smile stood over her. He had a firm, athletic build that was extremely easy to discern, since he was wearing only a towel. Alien's gaze ran quickly from three curly chest hairs to the knot of his towel. She had never met him before. She was sure of it — she'd remember.

"You're doing the right thing — trust me," the guy said, nodding to the pile of papers in front of her. "Study hard," he continued. "Don't goof off."

The stranger walked to the shower. Mystified, Alien waited to see where he went when he came out again. Was the guy Shannon's boyfriend? He seemed way too earnest to live here on Fifth East.

A little less than ten minutes later, the guy emerged from the shower. He walked whistling into an empty room. So he was her new hallmate, Alien thought — and, quite possibly, single. She studied his broad upper back admiringly. Just below his right shoulder, she saw, he had a tattoo.

Alien stared.

It can't be, she thought. *He just moved in, didn't he?*

But there was no mistaking the tattoo. A black-stenciled scowling skull.

Krotus.

⟡

That Thursday, the guy showed up as Alien and other hallmates were playing pool. It was just after midnight at the late-night lounge in the Walker Memorial building, very near East Campus. As the usual suspects opened cans of beer they'd brought or filled Styrofoam cups with drip coffee, Alien put a Hot Pocket in the microwave.

"Hey ho, neighbor!" a voice said.

Him.

Alien turned around. The guy grabbed the pool cue from Cal, who had been about to break in a new game with Rex.

"Thanks, frosh," he said.

By now, Alien had made investigations. The guy was named Mace. He had entered MIT three years earlier as "Matthew," a clean-cut professional tennis prospect with a 125-mile-per-hour serve. Then, Rush week, he separated his shoulder and found his way to Fifth East.

Mace was not a hacker in the traditional sense of the word at MIT. He didn't break into and explore buildings. Nor did he build or tinker with computer systems, the other kind of activity commonly called hacking. But he shared an obsessive, limit-pushing mindset with people who did both. Mace loved drugs, hung out with world-class chemists, and hacked his brain.

Everyone had a story. "He showed up naked on Third East, knocked on some kid's door, and started dancing," Rochelle said. "He posted telethon phone-in numbers to porn site personal ad pages, so guys calling to hook up would find themselves on a live fundraiser for charity," said Zhu. Even François was deferential. "Once at a party," Alien overheard him telling Heston, "he stuck the handle of an axe three inches up his ass and sucked a Krotus hickey into Rex's chest."

Obviously the drugs had not affected Mace's outward physical condition. But this was his third and final chance at MIT. Already he'd flunked out twice, Alien gathered. His parents were wealthy, however, and had "prevailed upon" the deans. "His dad is really sick and Mace promised him that he'd fly straight," Sam said.

The microwave dinged. Alien popped the door and carried her steaming dinner to the pool table. Everyone crowded around the game, watching Mace and Rex play. Rex never had a turn, however. Mace had flawless aim and sank all the balls in seven shots from break to victory.

"How the fuck does he do that?" Cal said.

"Me next," Vanessa said.

"No, me," said Alex.

Mace smiled. "If I win," he said, "you're carrying a manhole cover up to the fifth floor."

Hours passed this way. Mace beat everyone. Sometime before dawn, Alien wandered home alone and drew a Krotus out of shaving cream on the Bemis hallway. It took a while to perfect and looked pretty cool on the black wall under the black lights, but twenty minutes later, when Mace burst through the door, he wiped it away without a moment's thought. Alien stared sadly at the smeared remnants.

Alex, Vlad, and two other sophomore guys labored into the hall, each straining to carry a manhole cover, which they stacked outside Mace's room.

Alien coughed. If Fifth East was a cult, Mace might be its new leader.

She entered her room and eyed her alarm clock: 6:20 a.m. Technically, Sunday was already more than a quarter over. *Sleep or study?*

Alien sighed and fell back, fully dressed, on her bed.

———⊸⊷———

Ten days later, the hall threw a Mardi Gras party. By one a.m. what seemed like hundreds of students and alumni had jammed Fifth East's long black central hall, squeezing and jostling Alien before she escaped to a bathroom.

She had taken one of the red glittery streamers taped tonight to the ceiling and refashioned it as a louche top for her new black leather miniskirt, bought when her grandmother sent an eighteenth birthday check for one hundred dollars. Still, a little liquid courage was necessary to carry the outfit off with confidence. In the bathroom, a black plastic ladle and the kitchen's sixty-quart stockpot offered Florey punch—equal parts gin, tequila, vodka, white rum, and triple sec, plus lemon juice, simple syrup, Coca-Cola, and a copious amount of red food coloring.

Alien filled a cup. She had a cough, and cough medicine was basically alcohol.

Chugging, Alien emptied the drink in hand.

Zhu's room was open for bar golf. He'd simplified the rules, however: each hole made *or* missed required taking a shot. Soon this game ceded to naked Twister. Alien was topless when she toppled over into an easy chair that had lost its stuffing. Her right shoulder blade throbbed at the gash. Alien laughed. An easy chair was more dangerous than an elevator shaft!

"Rub ash on it right away," François shouted by way of assistance. "It makes a better scar."

At the time, to Alien, this advice seemed brilliant. She borrowed a lighter and a piece of paper, which she burned and applied immediately to her cut. It stung like hell, but the bleeding stopped.

Two strangers were sleeping in her room when Alien ducked in to try to find new clothing. Rather than wake them, she backed out and entered the Walcott lounge, with the glowing dragon. There she found Mace sitting on the couch, handing out bead necklaces to the nerds running naked through the corridor.

"What do you think?" Alien said, showing off the scar.

"Sweet. It looks like a Nike swoosh," Mace said. "Hey, jiggle your titties and I'll give you some beads."

Alien shrugged and shook her breasts for him. Mace grinned and handed her a necklace. Alien hopped on the couch next to him. "You look like you need help," she teased.

The only way to be accepted as Mace's equal was to match his behavior, Alien knew. She picked up a necklace. "Hey, Jen! Want a necklace?" Alien asked a nearby acquaintance. "Okay! Titties! Nice!" she said when the woman lifted her shirt.

Mace turned to her when the last necklace was given out. "Let's go to my room," he said.

Alien tried to look nonchalant. "Sure."

<hr />

They spent a long time making out, simply kissing, before either removed another article of clothing. Gradually, the clamor outside diminished. The party was winding down. Mace looked expectant, but Alien, who was starting to sober up, stopped short of taking off her panties. She didn't want to be just another girl. Soon they both fell asleep on his bunk bed.

Around three a.m., a loud snore from Mace jolted Alien out of her brief slumber. On his desk she saw crayons and paper. Quietly, she climbed down and began to draw geometric figures in overlapping black outlines.

Mace woke shortly afterward. He watched Alien for a few minutes and then picked up a crayon and moved to color on the picture. Remembering how he had ruined her shaving cream Krotus, Alien shielded the art from him.

Mace spoke softly. "I'm not going to mess it up," he reassured her. Then he very gently used the crayon to shade in a few white areas in the middle.

This was nice, and unexpected, Alien thought. She liked it.

"Up for a nightcap?" Mace asked.

Alien nodded.

Mace led Alien into the room of Don and Lauren, a senior couple. They and a group of other upperclassmen and alumni were filling a black plastic garbage bag with something from a huge steel cylinder almost five feet tall.

"Want some nitrous?" said Don, meaning nitrous oxide. Then, in response to Alien's puzzled look, he added, "Laughing gas."

Alien rubbed her shoulder blade where she had cut it, thinking. She had never done drugs. She had never even smoked a cigarette. But she was curious.

All these things you thought you believed because people you trusted told them to you . . . they weren't necessarily lies, she knew. But they weren't necessarily true. Only by experiencing as much as possible could you find out.

Someone put Pink Floyd on the stereo. They passed the bag. When it reached Alien, she inhaled for the first time.

The world spun. Alien closed her eyes and saw a narrowing darkness. The song lyrics, as they pierced her consciousness, were almost too appropriate: "You are only coming through in waves . . . Your lips move, but I can't hear what you're saying."

This was hacking too. *Don't accept—explore. Don't assume—experiment.* Breaking into buildings was one way of seeing what was on the other side of locked doors. So was sex. So was art. And so were drugs.

The bag passed to the next person. When Alien opened her eyes again, she felt like she was part of a family.

⋘⋙

Alien stood up, exhausted from studying for next week's electricity and magnetism midterm. It was two a.m. Her stomach grumbled. A second later, she started coughing in three sharp machine-gun-like bursts.

Today was the last Sunday in March. Her cough had dragged on for weeks now. Alien had gone twice to the MIT student medical center, but all they gave her was a steroid inhaler, which seemed useless. Impossibly tired, she had cut back on her Coffeehouse hours. This, though, meant less money for food, so she was stuck trying to live off canned tuna fish. It wasn't the way Alien would have picked to lose fifteen pounds.

Her parents would have gladly given her money for something more substantial, Alien knew, but she didn't want to ask them, since they were already taking out such big loans to pay for MIT itself.

And how would they feel if they knew she had basically stopped attending classes other than the thirty seconds a week it took to enter, drop off her problem set, and leave? *These are the real crazy people,* Alien thought if she strayed too far from Fifth East. Take last semester's calculus class: the professor had spent the first two weeks proving that the number 1 was positive. To care, Alien needed some connection to the real world.

Alien walked to the Goodale lounge. Inside, all the hall hackers surrounded Rex, who stood at a black wall, chalk in hand, sketching what looked like architectural blueprints.

Alien tapped Cal's shoulder. "What's going on?" she whispered.

Cal turned. "They're finally tearing down Building Twenty."

"Really?" Excited, Alien stood on tiptoe to see more of Rex's sketching. "When?"

"It's already condemned and sealed," Cal said. "Everyone's moved out."

As Rex outlined the plan, Alien forgot her cough, her hunger, and her midterm. Building 20's impending demolition had been a Coffeehouse Club obsession for months. It was an old building, and one of the most unusual at MIT, put up "temporarily" during World War II and designed to last just six months. Because it was supposed to be only temporary, everyone who used it had had free rein for over fifty years, drilling through the walls and poking wires wherever they pleased, without any administrator caring. The result was an incubator for more innovative research than anywhere else at MIT.

Scientists in Building 20 had invented the radar credited with helping win World War II. They built the world's first atomic clock and one of the earliest atomic particle accelerators. Modern linguistics and cognitive science started there. So did Bose speakers and breakthroughs in stop-action photography. Building 20 was also the longtime home of the Tech Model Railroad Club, whose members made pioneering contributions to personal computing — another kind of hacking originating at MIT.

"If you're a hacker — or even anyone who cares about science, past or present — Building Twenty is part training ground, part sacred space," Rex was saying now. "Imagine the Sistine Chapel being painted over. That's what's happening here. And I'll be honest: we can't stop it. But we have one night to get in and out before the wrecking balls come."

Alien nodded, inspired. Usually they talked about pulling a hack. This was about preserving one. Listening to Building 20 stories was like learning about a grandmother she never had known about — just as that grandmother was on her deathbed. Who knew what secrets remained untold?

They left ten minutes later, gathering Splotz and others from Third East as they filed downstairs. Aziz and Rpunzel met them on-site. Building 20 was three stories tall with a solid plywood frame and a flat tarpaper and gravel roof. A long central body fronted the street, with four shorter wings perpendicular to it and parallel to one another backing out toward East Campus. From above, Alien realized, the structure as a whole resembled nothing so much as a giant diagram of a four-pin lock.

Fittingly, a four-pin padlock protected an outside door. Working together, Zhu and Rex picked it easily. Fifteen fellow hackers poured inside, and Alien, coughing, followed.

It was dark, of course. Alien had thrown on appropriate clothing to join the others, but discovered now that in her rush she had forgotten a flashlight. For the first minute inside, she had no choice but to get her bearings from the stray beams of others' lights. These illuminated faded yellow radiation warning signs still hanging on the open doors of empty rooms.

Together the group entered a large central room dimly lit by streetlights through dirty windows. Deconstruction had already started here; rubble covered the floor where a wall had been. With the others, Alien poked through dusty boxes of resistors, vacuum tubes, and ancient electronic parts. They turned over and stockpiled biohazard signs, light-up laser warning signs, and signs about handling radioactive chemicals, to take back to the dorms. Rpunzel and Aziz climbed cabinets to walk across the exposed beams high above them.

A few feet in front of her, Alien saw a short staircase and headed toward it.

"Wait a minute." A flashlight briefly blinded her, and Cal stepped forward. "Wherever you're going, you'll need a light," he said. "I'm coming with you."

They descended the stairs together, finding a maze of empty white-walled rooms. All the doors were open. *We're too late,* Alien thought. *Everything's gone.*

Just in case, Cal searched every corner of the rooms with his flashlight. A coughing fit overcame Alien and she walked back to the staircase to recover. By the time the fit stopped, her eyes had finally adjusted to the dark. Underneath the staircase, she noticed now, were several hundred bricks, piled to waist height.

Alien made to pick up a brick—a final souvenir of Building 20. But when she grabbed the one closest to her, she found it impossible to move—as if it were glued or nailed in place in the pile.

What is *this?*

Alien knelt and dug her fingers in the narrow crevice separating this brick from the adjacent one. Working hard, Alien managed to pry them an inch apart—but then the instant she released her grasp, the first brick snapped back to the pile like a biting tooth.

"Jesus!" Alien said. She could have lost a finger.

"What is it?" Cal joined her. "What's wrong?"

"I don't know," Alien said. "I think I found some kind of super-magnets."

"*Super*-magnets?" Cal asked skeptically. "Why would they leave those behind?"

"Try to take one," Alien said. "You'll see."

Cal tried, but it took the two of them working together, one at each end, to separate a single brick.

"It's got to be neodymium"—a rare earth metal—Cal said. He gestured to the pile with amazement. "This is probably more than a million dollars in magnets. And it's lying under a staircase."

Alien grinned. "We'll each take a brick," she said. It was saving, not stealing —after all, MIT was knocking the place down the next day.

"Go tell Rex and the others," Alien told Cal.

Cal nodded and then jogged upstairs. Holding the separated brick under her arm by herself, Alien felt it tug back fiercely toward the pile. This gave her an idea.

Alien and her hallmates returned to Fifth East at sunrise, each person carrying a magnetic brick along with his or her favorite sign. They hung around the kitchen, making a huge pot of spaghetti. No one knew whether to feel exhilarated or depressed at their haul.

"It's the end of an era," Rex said. "We're the last people ever to enter Building Twenty."

Vanessa stirred the pasta. "What should we do with the magnets?" she asked.

"Don't put them near a computer — or a credit card," Cal said. "They'll erase everything."

"So where *can* we put them?" Alex demanded.

"I know," Alien said.

Everyone stared at her.

"Well, since they're *magnets* . . . ," Alien continued, "I think they belong on the refrigerator."

Her fellow hackers grinned.

"Okay," someone said.

"Yeah," said someone else.

"Try it."

Carefully, as if leading an overeager pet, Alien arranged six bricks on the refrigerator door. Then she crossed the room to the other side and opened the silverware drawer. With one hand, Alien selected a fork; with the other hand, a spoon.

"Oops!" she said, "accidentally" tossing them in the general direction of the fridge.

Rather than fall in a normal parabola, the utensils flew to the door as if sucked. They stuck like glue.

"Awesome!"

The others ran to grab their own forks and spoons — and then, inevitably, knives, and finally the kitchen's large pots and pans and baking sheets, all of which landed with a terrific *clack*. Soon the fridge was completely covered.

—✦—

Mace reappeared that Tuesday. Alien was in the student center, really, truly studying electricity and magnetism before her Wednesday morning midterm, when she took an early afternoon break to check her email. Mace had written the entire hall: "I have a 3:30 p.m. exam. Can someone PLEEEZ make sure I'm awake at 3?"

The message made Alien smile. At three on the dot, she picked up a phone in the student center and called.

"Good afternoon," she said when Mace picked up. "This is your wakeup call."

Mace grunted. "Thanks." Alien was about to hang up, but then she heard him say, "Hey, come by my room tonight. I have something for you."

—✦—

Shortly after midnight, Alien walked down the hall dressed in her PSYCHO BITCH T-shirt and black leggings. Mace opened the door and waved her in for the first time since Mardi Gras. His room was bare except for the standard issue furniture. Dense smoke filled the air.

"I made my room into a bong!" he exclaimed.

Alien laughed, and then coughed. "I've never smoked pot before."

"Sorry," Mace said. "I can open the window."

"Nah—it's been like this all semester," said Alien. "If I stopped coughing now, I'd probably miss it. Plus, it's giving me really strong ab muscles."

"Cherish that feeling," Mace said, handing her a real bong. Alien accepted it, and he helped her light it. They took turns inhaling. "Outside this hall, outside this dorm, outside this campus, people are so concerned with being safe," Mace continued. "I hate that safety net. We're so separated from the real unsafe world in America, scared to live, scared to die."

"You should meet my mother," Alien said.

Mace sat down in his desk chair. "Come sit on my lap," he said. Alien obliged, straddling him, enjoying the attention from a senior guy. "You know," he said, stroking her hair, "no one wants to admit that they're vulnerable. But if you admit you're vulnerable, if you can even get comfortable with your vulnerability, that's freedom."

Alien stared into Mace's glinting dark brown eyes. Clearly he was high as a kite. But interesting. Most MIT guys were off-the-charts smart, but way too literal-minded to understand anything that couldn't be expressed in an equation. Mace was different: smart, yes, but also philosophical. And he was so animated—so *alive*—it already seemed like they'd been talking for hours.

Alien leaned forward and kissed him.

⧫

Late morning light streaming through the window woke Alien. She turned over, stifling a cough, and then turned back, cuddling closer to Mace's warm, strong body. He responded with a loud hiccupy snore.

Alien grinned. Last night Mace had put on music and they kissed on his top bunk for more than an hour. Later—it was all coming back to her—he had reached under Alien's pants and tugged the band of her underwear. Again, though, she had gently rebuffed him. It was fun being high for the first time, moving with the deep bass of the music, feeling Mace's skin and watching him smile. For now, she had thought, fun was enough.

Alien sat up. She felt like she was forgetting something . . . but what? Gingerly, she climbed down from the bunk bed and wandered into the hallway.

"Hey!" Shannon called to her before Alien had moved five feet. "We shut off your alarm. It was blaring for an hour, dumbass."

No! Alien rushed to her door and turned the key, since whoever had broken in to shut off her alarm had been polite enough to lock up afterward.

Her clock's silent digital readout seemed to be accusing her: 11:34 a.m.

Alien's mind burned. She'd missed her physics midterm. *Stupid, stupid.*

⧫

On a cold morning two weeks later, Alien walked with Rex, Vanessa, and Sam to Joanie's, a diner in Central Square that opened at three thirty a.m. This week MIT was hosting campus visits for admitted high school students. Fifth East had held a smaller, shorter version of their fall hacking tour, and Alien had been chosen as a scout. She loved sneaking ahead of everyone, watching out for janitors and CPs. Afterward, when all the prefrosh had been returned safely to their respective campus hosts, the head "Jacks" had invited her out with them to breakfast.

Cramming into a tiny little table with the upperclassmen just before dawn, Alien ordered the $1.25 plate—two pieces of buttered toast and a fried egg.

"Nice job tonight," Rex said. He cleared his throat. "You know, Zhu's graduating. And when we become seniors, we're going to have to apply for jobs or grad school, and we won't be able to get out as much."

Alien nodded. It was strange to see her fellow hackers acting wistful—or mature, for that matter. A few days earlier they'd held a "freestyle" sprinting competition where everyone ran up and down the hall, kicking the fire doors open at each end. On Alien's final run, the heavy black door had slammed shut on her pinky finger and claimed her little baby fingernail, whole and bleeding. Alien had put it in her jewelry box. That was the hacking spirit: make every day an adventure and claim even your injuries as prizes. She knew no one made a living crawling through tunnels, climbing up elevator shafts, or dangling off rooftops for the fun of it, but look at an alum like Aziz: he was twenty-five and he still went out with them. It seemed to her that hacking wasn't something that you could just age out of.

"Anyway . . . ," Rex continued. "We're going to need new Head Jacks for the fall tour. It's a big responsibility."

"You should think about it," Sam said. "That's all we're saying."

"Don't think about it," Vanessa said. "Just do it."

Alien beamed. In one year she'd go from clueless frosh to leading some of MIT's most audacious hacking expeditions. "I'm in!" she said. "Thanks!"

Immediately, though, an unspoken caveat occurred to her: *I just have to learn electricity and magnetism first.* Somehow she was managing to scrape through most of her classes with a B or C, even the ones for which she had never bought the book and borrowed it only to read the chapter minutes before the exam. Physics, of course, was the big exception. To pass the class now after missing the midterm, Alien had calculated, she'd need a 98 on the final.

Alien thought about asking the older students for advice. But why bother? They were all, always, buried in work. MIT even had special terms to describe the perils of undergraduate existence. "Tooling" was working or studying in the extreme. You were "hosed"—as in drowning under a fire hose—when you were overwhelmed with assignments no matter how much you tooled. And "punting" was what you were doing when you should have been tooling on something but were not.

Right now, for example, sitting in Joanie's with her friends, Alien was punting.

"Hey!" Rex called her back to attention. "Earth to Alien."

Alien looked up, making sure to maintain her smile. "What?" she said.

"Are you going to eat that?" he asked her, pointing at her delivered plate. "Because if you're not—"

"I am," Alien told him. She rapped his hand with her spoon. "Back the fuck off."

Sam and Vanessa laughed.

Alien shrugged, happy, hungry, and exhausted.

<hr />

The morning of her physics final, Alien opened her eyes to white lights. Her bed felt funny—the mattress firmer, the pillows softer. She inhaled clean air instead of the usual cigarette fumes invading her room from all sides. The only sound was muted white noise.

Nirvana.

"You're up," said an unfamiliar female voice.

Alien turned her head toward the voice. Speaking to her was a reedy middle-aged woman with red hair worn back in a ponytail, dressed in nurse's scrubs.

They were in a hospital room together at MIT Medical, the university infirmary.

Alien tried to sit up, which started her coughing. "Careful," the nurse advised, moving closer. "You're still very sick."

Alien fell back. Two nights earlier, she remembered, she had been sitting in the Fifth East hallway, shooting the shit and trying to study. When she doubled over coughing and couldn't stop, the East Campus night watchman escorted her here. The first doctor Alien saw insisted that she had whooping cough, but the test results came back negative. The next gave her lots and lots of codeine. Alien broke out in a huge rash from head to toe and started throwing up. An allergic reaction, it seemed. And, in its own way, a miracle.

Now she could apply for a medical incomplete in physics.

"Do you want food?" The nurse showed her a menu.

"Thank you." Alien was amazed. *Chicken noodle soup, peanut butter and jelly sandwich, fruit cup*—the infirmary's offerings seemed like sumptuous feasts after the canned tuna she had been surviving on all semester. Even better, since IV tubes filled her arm, she wasn't even hungry. Notwithstanding everything the doctors here had put her through, she'd probably gotten more rest and nourishment in the last forty-eight hours than she had the entire semester leading up to it.

It's like a spa, Alien thought.

"Let me look and then I'll call you back," she told the nurse.

The woman left. Alien smiled and relaxed, settling into her "vacation." The *drip, drip, drip* of the IV evoked a soothing fountain.

A minute later, Alien picked up the bedside phone, eager to chat with someone now that she had free time. Her friends would all be asleep or in exams, so she called her mother.

"I'm in the hospital," she announced cheerily as soon as she could get a word in edgewise.

Silence. Then "Oh. My. God," her mother said. "I'll be right there."

⟽⟾

Alien gazed at downtown Newark through the front-seat passenger's window of her family's cranberry-colored Volvo station wagon. Five days had passed since calling Mom, who'd brought her straight home to New Jersey. Alien's childhood pediatrician had diagnosed a sinus infection and put her on antibiotics. Now her cough was finally waning. This morning she was taking Amtrak back to school.

Alien still needed a 98 to pass the class. But she wouldn't have to take the makeup final until the beginning of September. *After* the hacking tour.

She had three months to study hard, she told herself.

"Thanks," Alien told her mother as they approached the train station. "I can just hop out here, so you don't have to deal with parking."

"I can't believe you're not staying home," her mother said. "After how sick that place made you."

"It wasn't the *place* that made me sick," said Alien. That might or might not be true. But it was definitely the story she was sticking with.

No matter what, Alien was spending the summer in Cambridge. Unlike most colleges, MIT kept its dorms open. Almost everyone at Fifth East was staying. They could play all day and hack all night.

"Love you, Mom," Alien said. *But I'm not going to be you,* she added silently.

04

A Death in the Family

L *OOK GOOD, FEEL GOOD,* Alien told herself. She was late to help lead the Spelunkers' Tour—the most advanced form of the first-week hacking tour, reserved for only the most interested freshmen—but at least she looked formidable: black combat pants, black tank top, with her Leatherman on her hip and her hacking card in her pocket.

A full year had gone by since she had entered MIT. Then the Jacks had seemed like mysterious, all-knowing, all-powerful figures. Now she was a Jack herself—and a Head Jack, no less. Six days earlier, at the very beginning of Rush, Alien had paced the Fifth East ledge at midnight, watching the East Campus courtyard fill with eager, intrigued freshmen, before descending to claim her wards in the now familiar Building 54 lecture hall. Theirs had to have been the best tour. The frosh had been so excited being taken across the roofs, up onto the Little Dome, down though the steam tunnels, and finally into the sacred space of the mural room for the first time.

Grinning, Alien ran from her dorm room to tonight's tour meeting point at the MIT Chapel—the last place campus cops would think to check.

Nine p.m.—almost there. But en route her good mood shifted. Something nagged at her. Something was wrong.

"I've got to go back to the hall," Alien told Sam and Rpunzel at the chapel. "Meet you later in Sixty-six"—Building 66, where they'd hung the point and tonight planned a secret large-group ascent.

Alien walked back as fast she could. This summer, visiting alumni had given her LSD—a venerable tradition. In the 1970s, it was said, most of the LSD on the East Coast came from MIT chemists. Her jewelry box contained the last couple of strips.

Alien hadn't seen the jewelry box when she was getting ready, she realized. That must be what was bothering her. Rush was the obvious time to get busted for something stupid.

———

Alien searched her room, inch by inch. All she found that was unusual was a dried-up rose, sitting on her bureau. She moved down the hall, overturning a pile of old computers. Nothing. The LSD was gone.

Walcott was almost empty. Lauren had more classes to take before graduating, so she and Don still had their room, but the couple were at Burning Man, the tech-hippie art and culture gathering in Nevada's Black Rock Desert. Shannon was in the army, and two other hallmates had transferred to another dorm. Until any freshmen moved in, that pretty much left Alien and Mace.

Alien knocked on Mace's door. He had gone home for the summer to spend time with his father, but returned a week ago to complete his final year of classes. It had surprised Alien how happy seeing him again had made her. Mace's first night back, they had lain together on his bed, fully clothed, catching up.

"What are you going to do with your life?" Mace had asked her.

"Pass physics," Alien said.

"I'm serious," said Mace.

"Well, I don't know," Alien told him. "What are you going to do?"

"I want to be a farmer," Mace said.

"Really?" Alien studied his face.

Mace nodded. "We all have to work to benefit one another."

Alien had never seen him so earnest. They stayed up all night, absorbed in conversation, both surprised when morning light began to shine in through the windows.

Around nine a.m., they got up.

"Want to take a shower with me?" Mace asked, standing in the hallway with a towel over his shoulder.

Alien was tempted but hesitant.

"Let's wait," she said. "I kind of want to take things slow. I've moved too fast in the past."

Mace looked disappointed.

Alien smiled. "Soon, I promise," she said.

Now there was no answer from Mace's room. He must be out, Alien thought. It didn't make sense that he'd take her LSD anyway. Mace could get whatever he wanted from Don, who Alien had finally figured out was dealing what he and Lauren didn't share.

The only other place the jewelry box could possibly be was Don and Lauren's room. In fact, Alien recalled, she had last seen the box there, holding it in her hands while Don fished a beer out of their mini-fridge for her.

Don and Lauren's room would be locked while they were out of town, she thought. On a whim, Alien tried the handle anyway.

The door opened. Surprised, Alien caught her breath. Was someone in there? It was very quiet. She didn't know Don and Lauren well, and she didn't want anyone to think she was stealing something.

Alien cracked the door a little wider. The light was on. That was odd.

Alien stood outside another moment, debating what to do. She could see the white sink inside their room and was tempted to peer in a bit farther. *Should I . . . ? What if the jewelry box is in there?*

Finally, Alien looked at her watch: 9:27 p.m. No time — the tour was starting.

Shaking her head at her silliness, Alien quickly exited the hall.

<hr />

Alien chose black tea from the Coffeehouse supply cabinet and prepared to wait the fifty-five seconds the microwave was counting down to make hot water. Two a.m. had just passed. After showing off all night for the awed freshmen, she wished she'd been able to join the other Jacks in the courtyard afterward, adding her own stories to the MIT hacking legends instead of coming straight here to cover the second half of a shift.

And tool for next week's physics exam, she reminded herself. The academic axe, when it fell, fell sharply. None other than François, who projected total invulnerability, had flunked out of MIT at the end of last semester. Alien was still getting used to the relative quiet when she crossed the hallway, and the absence of his French flag.

The Coffeehouse phone rang seconds before the microwave sounded. "Alien?" a stricken voice asked when she picked up. It was Cal.

"What's wrong?" she asked.

When he told her, Alien ran back to Fifth East as fast as she could.

⸎

When Alien got there, there were deans in the Goodale lounge, talking in hushed tones with students. Everyone sat together under the drawing of Krotus. Sam gulped rapidly, as if literally having to swallow the deans' words to process them. Vanessa hugged Rochelle, who was weeping. Heston, eyes red, focused fiercely on the floor, and mechanically smoothed and re-smoothed his skirt. Even Rex seemed small and powerless. There was a nice cheese-and-fruit plate on the sticky wooden table where Alex and Vlad had helped Alien with her problem sets. It was eerily quiet.

Cal stood to greet Alien, but she turned from him and walked down the stairs. Outside again, Alien stood alone on the lawn. There was an ambulance in the middle of the grass by the picnic tables. She scanned the dorm through the full-length windows in the stairwell on every level. After a little while, she heard movement by the door she'd exited just a few hours earlier.

Alien watched as the paramedics slowly carried Mace's body on a stretcher down all five flights of stairs.

⸎

An older gentleman—either a journalist or some kind of MIT staff member, she supposed—walked up and stood next to Alien.

"Were you his girlfriend?" he asked gently.

His use of the past tense told her all she needed to know.

"No," Alien said.

The paramedics finally arrived at the ground floor. They rolled Mace's body into the ambulance and slammed the doors shut. It rolled right back out. They stopped and looked on in surprise, and then shoved the cart back and slammed the doors again. It rolled right back out a second time.

The third time, they shoved it in there really fast and slammed the rear doors quickly. Then the ambulance drove off.

The driver didn't bother to put on the lights.

⸎

Back on the hall, the police questioned Alien. She said she didn't know Mace. They were happy to leave her alone after that, already having their hands full bagging and cataloging all the drugs they'd discovered in Don and Lauren's room, beginning with the tank of nitrous.

The gas produced an intense euphoria but could deplete the brain of oxygen when over-inhaled. Mace had suffocated when the plastic garbage bag fell on his face.

Alien stepped across police tape to get to her room. She took her hacking clothes off and had a long shower, feeling the entire time like she would vomit. When she had changed, she came out again. A fresh-faced campus police officer stood outside Don and Lauren's room.

Alien nodded at him.

He nodded back kindly.

"What was the time of death?" asked Alien.

The young cop's brow wrinkled. "About nine thirty," he said.

<hr />

The next morning, a front-page story in *The Tech* suggested Mace's death might have been a suicide. "No way," his friends said. They divided up and spread across campus, stealing the issues — over four thousand copies — off the shelves as they were delivered.

Other newspaper headlines screamed, MIT STUDENT FOUND DEAD OF NITROUS OXIDE. Television crews swarmed the dorm, blocking Ames Street with their vans, harassing anyone who went into the building for an interview. When Aziz "accidentally" knocked a camera out of the hands of a particularly pushy reporter, everyone on the hall congratulated him. Once inside again, though, Alien tried to look out her window. Peering right back at her was a video camera. A news station had run it and all the necessary cables up with poles. Alien pulled down her shade. She had to get out of there.

After twenty-four hours, most of the folks from the hall had disappeared. Alien was exhausted but still too wired to sleep. Her feet grazed the clothes she'd thrown off the night before. Now they seemed like the outfit of a totally different person — as ridiculous and remote to her as a hoopskirt. No one saw you when you went hacking. No one got hurt. Those were the rules. But Mace's death had made all that a joke.

Alien grabbed her Leatherman from the crumpled clothes pile and walked back outside. She must have wandered around Cambridge for hours, because it was dawn when she reached Aziz's house. She rang the bell over and over again.

No answer.

Alien had never felt this alone in her life. She had been so sure that Mace was only interested in her for sex. But what if he hadn't been? What if he had really cared? She should never have waited to find out. If she had given him the chance, maybe she could have made Mace come out hacking with her instead of staying home alone. Maybe she could have saved him.

Before she knew it, the blade of the Leatherman was out.

Alien studied the vein in her arm, where they had fed her during her time at the inpatient ward. She lived. Mace died. It didn't make sense.

Alien sliced.

<hr />

The blade was extremely sharp, the cut thin and deep. Bright red blood ran down her arm. Alien had missed the vein by millimeters, but she still bled profusely, sitting on Aziz's doorstep. The pain was like an ice-cold bath filled with electric current.

Alien pictured knocking on a neighbor's door for help. It was a terrible idea, she decided. They might call the police, or worse, her mother.

"You know what's going to happen now?" Rex had said. "A bunch of outsiders are going to say that this means students need reining in. Someone will file a lawsuit. Then the college will hire a dozen new administrators to be babysitters. And we know—and Mace knew—that that's bullshit. MIT students have always managed themselves. That's the culture. And you can't say, 'Welcome—it's up to you to invent the future,' and then spend the rest of the year making us sign permission slips for every step we take."

Alien knew Mace would agree. *I hate that safety net.* Some people rafted whitewater rivers. Some people went skydiving. Some people hacked. You want to stay inside, playing it safe all day? Go ahead—but what was the point of living if you never took any risks? Maybe the best way to honor the dead was to push the boundaries of exploration in a new direction.

How, though? Alien wished she could ask Mace. Live—and feel this kind of pain? Or cut again—and be relieved?

Alien gagged. She tried standing. No go. Everything hurt so much.

She knocked on Aziz's door again and threw a couple of pebbles at his window. Alien felt awful, sick and woozy. He wasn't there.

She slumped over on the steps.

Aziz's door opened. A big warm body enveloped Alien in a hug. She stared up and saw wide, scared dark brown eyes staring back at her, and then a scraggly black beard and ponytail. Then Aziz carried her inside and carefully cleaned up her arm.

"What happened?" he asked.

Alien cried. "We let Mace break the rule about hacking alone."

It was a blustery Wednesday evening in mid-October. Painted pumpkins and spiderwebs, witches' hats and black cats decorated Main Street shop windows, and rain from an earlier shower still wet the pavement. Alien's last classes had ended at five p.m. and she was hurrying home for dinner before her nine p.m. Coffeehouse shift started. She stopped short, though, when she saw the sidewalk square a few steps from the entrance to the Kendall T station.

In the cement, someone had scrawled a single word: *"Mace."*

It was him, Alien thought. She knew Mace himself had written it.

Six weeks ago she had moved out of Fifth East—off campus, in fact, to the student living group with the fire pole. Alien had a tiny room, hardly bigger than a mattress. Everyone called it the Coffin.

In the aftermath of Mace's death, Alex's parents had made him transfer to Virginia Tech, closer to home. Vlad had moved back to Romania. Sam and Rochelle were both taking the semester off. Psych treatment, people said.

Zhu had turned from lock picking to launching his own software company, making a garage in Boston's Chinatown his world headquarters on the way to dot-com millions. Both Vanessa and Rex were working for him, which meant they were barely ever on campus either. Heston was never leaving MIT—he'd gotten an undergraduate research position at the Media Lab—but he had moved into the Warehouse, a communal living space for artists and engineers in South Boston, and Alien had bounced between there and a couch in Aziz's house until her new living situation started. That left Cal and a couple of juniors as the elder statesmen of Fifth East.

The entire group had gathered together one last time three days after Mace's body was found, when the charter bus to take them to the funeral arrived at East Campus at four a.m.—a fitting hour, given all their late nights, Alien had thought. The doors opened and she had stepped on wearing the same black pumps, tights, and dress in which she'd had her high school yearbook photo taken. It was the kind of outfit that everyone on Fifth East would have made fun of—except that Vanessa and Rochelle each wore something similar, and the guys all had on suits and ties. And if anyone but Aziz noticed the incongruous red bandana Alien wore over the bend in her left arm and wondered why she wore it, no one commented aloud to her.

They had ridden three hours to Mace's hometown, a few miles from the Connecticut–New York border, somewhere farmy with huge white stone houses. Mace had a beautiful blond teenage sister, Alien discovered. His father was a small thin man with graying hair—so different from the tall, strong, athletic Mace. Both shook her hand in a receiving line outside an Episcopal church in which Alien had sat in a back pew, staring up at the statue of Jesus on the cross in front, hearing the words of the service without really listening. Everyone spoke about "Matthew," not the person she'd known, however briefly—Mace.

Alien's scheduled electricity and magnetism makeup exam was the same day as the funeral. Given the circumstances, the physics department decided to let her just take the class all over again and have the new grade count for the previous term. Alien was certain that Mace would have laughed to know that he was the only reason she didn't flunk.

Don and Lauren were arraigned when they came back to Cambridge. They were charged with four counts of possession with intent to distribute hallucinogenic mushrooms, amphetamines, marijuana, and nitrous oxide, but they hired a lawyer good enough to keep them out of jail.

Alien let these and other memories wash over her as she studied the surprise sidewalk marking. She squeezed her arm where she had cut herself, an almost unconscious gesture, repeated dozens of times a day. By now the wound was almost healed. But the hacking world as she knew it—painful and cultish, addictive and intoxicating—was over.

Or so she had thought.

PART II

In Security

05

Up All Night

Boston. January 2000.

A LIEN HAD TROUBLE SLEEPING for months after Mace's death. She wanted to talk to him, and couldn't. She wanted to apologize. She wanted to say "I love you," which she never had. Mace's smile was frozen in memory, but other details—the scent of his aftershave, their last words to each other, even whether they were ever really friends—had vanished. Without her Fifth East family, Alien wondered what she was doing and why she was at MIT.

In January 2000 the Warehouse threw a party. For Alien, getting there entailed a midnight trek via T and on foot to an off-white seven-story building in South Boston. She entered, climbed black-painted, unevenly sloping concrete stairs, and banged hard—*bam! bam! bam!*—on a metal door.

The door cracked open. A trim man with a rakish beard and darting eyes shrouded monkishly by a black hoodie peered out at her.

"Hey, Frostbyte," Alien said. She knew better than to hug the reserved artist and brain hacker.

Frostbyte flashed a brief smile. "Welcome."

<hr />

Frostbyte led Alien through a maze of low-ceilinged rooms formed by makeshift walls and concrete columns at least three feet in diameter. A vast central area held bright, beautiful pulsing lights and dozens, maybe hundreds, of other partiers, dancing to computer-generated beats and some kind of amplified keyboard and string instrument combo. Their warmth — both human and electronic — was bliss-making.

Parting from her host, Alien reached a crowded camp-style kitchen offering cheese cubes, peanut butter cups, juices, sodas, beer, and liquor. The smell of pot wafted through the air. An older man dressed in a faded orange T-shirt and leather sandals stood at the counter, holding a curious-looking blue liquid in a glass pint jar.

"Have you had any alcohol?" he asked.

"No," Alien answered truthfully.

"Want some G?" he said. "You can't mix it with booze, but if you haven't had any . . ." — the guy shrugged — "good times."

"Hmm," said Alien. "How do you know how much to take?"

"A normal dose is five to ten milliliters," the guy said, picking up a clear plastic syringe. "I'll start you off at seven." He poured orange juice into the cup and squirted a dose of blue fluid into it. Then he added, "If you take too much, you just fall asleep."

"Would have come in handy last night," said Alien. "Thanks." She picked up the cup and drank, wincing at the salty taste.

<hr>

Alien wandered. The Warehouse seemed to evolve week to week. Recently she had helped to solder hundreds of LEDs on Frostbyte's giant six-by-seven-foot light wall, which she now found on display in a corner, finished. "Shadow Engine," Frostbyte called it.

Alien shifted and eleven hundred motion-sensor-paired LEDs lit up in concert with her movements.

She reentered the open area filled with dancers, minglers, DJs, and musicians. A four-foot-diameter half sphere light sculpture overhead lit everyone neon green, blue, purple, pink, red, and orange. Two guys her age approached Alien. One was white — Fred — one Hispanic — Eddie — but both were lithe and muscular, with wide smiles and short-cropped black hair. Alien danced between them, watching the shadows and colors change on their tight-fitting shirts.

Heston cut in after several minutes. As usual, he wore his American flag skirt. "You know these guys are gay," he said.

Alien laughed. "I don't think so," she shouted over the music.

"Their loss, then," said Heston. "Want to hang out some place where we can hear?"

"Sure!" They walked past a floor-to-ceiling mural of white clouds, a blue sky, and a cute frowny-faced, red-rimmed, orange-rayed cartoon sun.

"How goes it?" Heston asked her outside a relatively quiet side hall.

"Fine," said Alien, not wanting to kill the buzz by discussing her restless sleep.

"Declare a major?" asked Heston.

"Sixteen-two"—aerospace information systems—Alien said. The choice had been made without much consideration at the beginning of last semester. She'd design computers for space, Alien had thought.

Heston recoiled, which said something. The new semester started next week. All spring, he knew, Alien would be stuck in unified engineering, a two-semester, quadruple-credit forced march through eight major engineering disciplines, widely considered to be the most demanding class at MIT. "Party while you can," he told her.

They separated and Alien poked her head in other, smaller rooms until she saw another male friend talking to a twitchy, big-chinned guy dressed in a cheesy cardboard-and-aluminum-foil robot costume. Her friend himself wore a suit and tie.

"How much do you want?" he asked.

"Ten," the robot said.

Alien's friend looked up, noticed her, and smiled. "You want any?" he asked.

"Sure," she said. "I'll take ten too. Thanks."

Her friend turned, opened a freezer hidden behind a bookcase, and used tweezers to extract a page of tiny white squares—LSD—printed neatly with little pink elephants. He cut each of them a ten-strip. The robot grabbed his immediately, exchanging crumpled bills for the trouble, and ducked out. After Alien gave her friend twenty dollars, he covered her portion in flattened tinfoil he put in a Ziploc bag labeled "♥ POISON ♥" in black Sharpie.

"Remember to get that when you leave," he said, returning it to the secret freezer.

Alien nodded. She ambled through the next open doorway and found herself in an all-black hallway that curved round . . . and round . . . like a nautilus spiral. Following it felt like stepping dreamily down a rabbit hole. At the center of the maze, Alien reached a peaceful, perfectly circular room filled with couches occupied sedately by other trippers.

"Hey," she said, seeing Heston again and plopping down on the empty cushion next to him. Something bothered her. A question. "There's no *loft* here, is there?" asked Alien. She'd heard another guest mention one.

"L-0-p-h-t 'loft'?" said Heston. "The hacker group?"

Alien blinked dumbly. "Oh — *computer* hackers," she said, uninterested.

"Yeah. A couple of years ago they testified in Congress and said that they could take down the entire Internet in thirty minutes," Heston told her. "I saw one of them here tonight."

"Did they do it?" Alien wondered aloud, but Heston's response, if he had one, came too late for her to process.

⊷

Alien woke to total darkness. Her couch seat remained, but the distant music was off, along with all of Frostbyte's LED creations. And the other couches were empty.

Alien sat up. "Where is everybody?" Her heart pounded.

"You're up," a familiar voice said.

"Aziz," Alien said. Thank God. She sat up, rubbing her sore neck. "What happened?"

"You passed out," he said. "I stuck around to make sure you were okay."

"Oh. Thanks for watching out for me."

Walking together, they followed the smell of spilled beer to last night's dance floor, where wires protruded from the open back of a full-sized Moon Patrol arcade game. Surrounding walls had been disassembled as well, and a bare light bulb lit the grumpy sun mural.

Alien made her way to the freezer her friend in the suit and tie had shown her behind the bookshelf. She knelt to cache the bag of LSD he'd left her in a khaki-colored traveler's money belt she used instead of a purse, wrapped tightly around her right ankle.

Aziz waited in the kitchen, which had one of the few windows in the place. Hearing metal grates roll up in the building across the street, Alien looked out. It was still dark, but people in a bakery were loading fresh bread onto trucks.

"What time is it?" she asked.

"Five thirty a.m.," Aziz answered.

Alien raised her eyebrows. Maybe fifty minutes had passed between taking the G and passing out, she estimated. *So I slept only four hours.*

Still, she felt totally refreshed.

⟨⟩

A week later, Sunday, two p.m., Alien sat behind the student center Coffeehouse counter, shunted to a day shift, and staring at the first page of chapter two of one of her textbooks, *Engineering Materials,* as she had for hours. Beside her was a day planner in which she'd segmented her to-do list in fifteen-minute increments — "9:30 a.m. Wake/9:45 a.m. Shower and dress/10 a.m. Bike to Radio Shack/10:15 a.m. Get alarm clock battery ..." — but the crossed-out accomplishments ended at noon: "Study!" Instead, Alien had filled the edge of the present planner page with a pencil sketch of a male profile.

Alien looked up, exasperated at herself and her predicament. Her aerospace information systems professors wanted rule followers — not artistic types. They created for an intended purpose or specification, whether physical or digital. No one told a space shuttle or airplane designer to "improvise."

Thud. Something heavy hit the counter, toppling her textbook to the floor. Two fellow sophomores, Brett and Ben, waved from the opposite corner of the Coffeehouse, from where they had sent the object — a bright purple bowling ball — tumbling.

"Sorry!" the guys called.

Alien stood. She returned her textbook to the counter, retrieved the bowling ball, and gently rolled it back.

Halfway across the room, the ball jogged left. Brett, though, hit a button on a black handheld remote control and the ball corrected course, traveling neatly through his legs to Ben.

"You're getting there," said Alien. The guys had told her that they were entering bowling's U.S. Open. Making it to the championship with raw skill would be impossible, so they'd hollowed out the middle of a ball, replaced the core with a remote-controlled gyroscope, and then filled it back in to restore the ball to legal weight and remove any sign of tampering. Now they were debugging.

To have that much free time, Alien thought enviously as Brett and Ben gave her the thumbs-up.

⟨⟩

Alien trudged from the Coffeehouse to the library at ten p.m., and from the library to Cal's room on Fifth East at one a.m. Neither helped the textbook pages turn. Packing it in around five a.m., she walked back to her cramped room off campus. Then, starting at six thirty a.m., just after she'd nodded off, alarms sounded on all sides. Floors creaked, doors slammed, and sinks and showers ran. Her housemates talked, played music, and ran up and down the stairs. Alien tossed and turned.

She got up, eyelids heavy, at two p.m. Still, she *had* to start studying. Her first big quiz was midday Tuesday. But how to stay awake as long as necessary? How to learn?

Alien walked downstairs to the empty kitchen.

<hr>

She opened the freezer and rummaged for private Tupperware. Checking to make sure no one else was watching, Alien pulled out the pink elephant LSD from the plastic bag her friend at the Warehouse party had given her. Then she used a pair of nail scissors to snip off a teeny, tiny piece of a square—maybe one eighth of a tab—and swallowed.

Acid, previously, was a very emotional and intense experience for Alien. Take almost a whole tab and she could listen to music or draw for hours. On a bad day the drug could turn on her, propelling her into nightmarish paranoia.

The meager quantity of an eighth of a tab would be different, she reasoned. Her brain was a machine—a kind of computer. With a tool like LSD, she could manipulate it for maximum performance.

Spreading out her unified engineering materials across the floor of her room, Alien sat, double-clicked her mechanical pencil, and turned her notebook to a fresh page.

<hr>

Within twenty minutes, Alien's mind cleared and she enjoyed a creative, caffeine-like buzz.

"The change in the rate of consumption = the fractional rate of growth × the current rate of consumption," Alien wrote as she read:

$$dc/dt = r/100$$
$$C = C_0 e^{r(t-t_0)/100}$$

Hours passed. Housemates returned. The sun set. "Dinner! Dinner!" came shouts below, but Alien remained engrossed in *Engineering Materials*. Close to seven p.m., feeling like she was coming down, she took another eighth of a tab, and then, at midnight, when her roommate went to bed, pushing her to the first-floor living room, another eighth.

Block letters became cursive in her notebook. Cursive letters became tighter, neater, almost calligraphic. Equations flowed:

$$N/m^2 = Pa$$
$$Mw/m^2 = MPa$$
$$\theta = F/A$$

"Tensile stress is caused by a force pulling at right angles to the face," wrote Alien. "Shear stress is caused by a force pulling parallel to the face. Stresses are positive when they PULL." She sketched shimmering three-dimensional drawings to illustrate each lesson.

Alien filled nine pages with notes, switched textbooks to *An Introduction to the Mechanics of Solids,* and filled seven more.

When she looked up again, it was four a.m.

———◆———

Drugs solved two problems. Hacking her brain for productivity with microdoses of acid, Alien could focus as long as necessary to study or complete her class assignments. Afterward, measuring out and taking exactly seven and a half milliliters of G, she could fall asleep within minutes and wake refreshed four hours later. Working and sleeping were still not *fun,* however. For that, Alien had to find her friends.

One base was a 150-person dorm called Senior House (though freshmen, sophomores, juniors, and seniors all lived there), kitty-corner from East Campus, where Alien moved the fall of her junior year. Another was TEP, MIT's Tau Epsilon Phi house, in Boston. Others were Frostbyte's lair, the Warehouse, and the Cambridge-area apartments of other recent alums like Aziz, many in well-paid jobs, but still choosing to live communally if they could, with the continued counterculture ideals of artists, misfits, and explorers.

Linking these and hundreds of other locations on and off campus was the college's computer network and Athena, its operating platform.

Athena had been designed in the 1980s, before most students had their own computers, and its core functions operated via text-based UNIX operating system commands—green type against a black background—not the usual point-and-click icons and menus of Macintosh or Windows. Even now, though, the system, which combined remote storage and distributed applications, was far more powerful—and more popular—than any other form of personal computing at MIT. The idea was, you could connect from anywhere and access central servers hosting your individual files, like papers, problem sets, email, or instant messages, and hundreds of programs for work or play.

Rush week freshman year, for example, it was a public Athena terminal at which Alien chose her username. Later that fall, from another Athena terminal Heston had set up on Fifth East, she sent her viral email dumping Cal. In addition to class work, Alien stored personal photos and digitized music files on her Athena account instead of her own PC, so she could see, play, or share them wherever she went. And, using a standard UNIX command, "finger," which reported if a user was logged into the computer system, at what Internet address, and how long it had been since his or her last activity, Alien used Athena to locate and keep tabs on friends.

One Tuesday evening in late October she raced through the Infinite Corridor on Rollerblades, narrowly dodging fellow students, carrying a bright yellow sunflower to surprise a new guy she liked, Patrick. Alien knew he was home at Senior House as of seven fifty p.m.—fifteen minutes ago—because she'd just checked from an Athena terminal in the student center.

Alien dashed across sidewalks, streets, and jarring cobblestones, pulled open the heavy wooden door to Senior House, and then continued inside, following carpeting to the elevator, where she hit the button for the fifth floor. Patrick's door was closed when she got there, however. Alien knocked and opened it. No one was there. At the public Athena terminal in Senior House, she logged in and typed "finger pmurphy" again.

As of 8:07 p.m., the system responded, he was in the basement cluster in Building 66, from whose roof Alien had hung the point.

Alien sighed and rode the elevator back downstairs. Outside again, she shot over slick concrete to the bowels of 66.

One lone screen-lit figure sat in the cluster. Not Patrick. Alien frowned. She skated in and plonked down at a workstation. Fingering Patrick once more, she found he'd just logged in from the office of MIT's student computer club, SIPB — three floors up from where she'd started.

Dammit.

One more stop, Alien told herself.

SIPB, pronounced in two syllables — "sip-b" — stood for the "student information processing board," a sign of the club's origins in the late 1960s, when the entire Internet, then called ARPANET, consisted of a single buggy link between UCLA and Stanford. Inside the office, MIT alumni, dropouts, and random Cambridge-area computer nerds mixed freely with current undergraduates. They shared an almost comically worn tan couch, two shelves of technical books and papers, scattered tools — a drill, an ohm reader, an industrial stapler — and geek art like a Froot Loops cereal box hacked to say "ROOT OOPS" (*root* being the special username of someone with full and unrestricted access to a computer system) amidst twenty or so high-speed networked terminals.

Alien swept wet hair out of her eyes and searched the room for Patrick, tallying a half-dozen occupants but not him. She logged in herself and saw he'd logged out four minutes earlier — eight forty p.m.

Seriously?

She could find another guy to give the flower to, Alien figured. She had no shortage of worthy crushes on campus. But her new night-shift job at the campus Center for Space Research started at nine p.m. There wasn't time — there was never enough time — to finger everybody she knew, one by one, just to see who was near enough now to hang out with.

"Hey!" Alien addressed the other people with her in the office. "Is there a command like 'finger' that could tell me who's logged on at a specific machine?"

The first response, from the middle of the room, was a snort. This was Gabe, a junior with silver earrings and close-cropped blue hair, who was sitting next to a squeaky-voiced freshman called Crunch who had graduated from high school the year before at the age of twelve and then entered MIT, no puberty necessary.

"What?" asked Alien. "Is there?" she repeated.

"Yes," said Gabe.

"Man finger," Crunch said.

They both laughed.

"Thanks," she said. *Jerks.*

"Man," in this case, meant the UNIX command to search the system's on-line manual pages.

"man finger," Alien typed.

Finger a username and you got the Internet address of the machine he or she was on, she read. Finger *at* a machine address, though, and it told you who was logged in there.

Got it, Alien thought.

She entered another command, "ifconfig." Her terminal window filled with numbers. For human use, different locations on the Internet were generally communicated with names: mit.edu, for example, or whitehouse.gov, or yahoo.com. But behind each name was a unique numerical value, its exact position online: x.x.x.x, where each x was a number between 0 and 255. Her computer's Internet address, it said, was 18.181.0.2.

"finger @18.181.0.2," Alien typed.

"alien," the screen returned.

"Cool!" Alien logged out. She leaped up and rolled past the SIPB microwave, soda fridge, and electric tea kettle to a filing cabinet full of Oreos, Chips Ahoy, Pop Tarts, and ramen packs. Alien deposited two quarters for a pack of Oreos she brought over to a rear-corner terminal at which a tall, thin man in his early forties was typing furiously.

"Hey, Plitman," Alien said, calling the man, as everyone did, by his username.

Plitman typed on, ignoring her. He had thick glasses and unkempt curly hair, wore a dark blue button-down shirt tucked into beltless khakis, and occupied both his seat and the one next to it, where he had placed a bulging black backpack. "Can I move this for a minute?" Alien asked him, trying to sidle in beside him.

"No, you can*not*." Plitman enunciated oddly and avoided eye contact, but his verbal manner, when he spoke, was as direct as a mugger's knife. "That backpack is holding radio equipment worth two hundred and *fifty* dollars."

"Sorry," Alien said. She straightened her body and stepped back without stepping away. Though neither a current student nor an alum, Plitman basically lived in the SIPB office—he was almost never not here—and he knew as much as or more about Athena and the UNIX operating system than their inventors.

"I'm trying to save time with something," Alien told him. "Can you help me?" She placed the Oreos on Plitman's keyboard, along with the drooping flower.

Plitman double-blinked. He nudged the flower aside but took the cookie pack, opened it, ate one Oreo, and then cut a tiny piece of Scotch tape from a roll next to him and carefully resealed the pack.

"I have time to answer one question," the expert said.

"How can I find out all the machine addresses?" Alien asked him.

Plitman wrinkled his brow in confusion. "At SIPB?" he said.

"No," said Alien. She raised her arms in an all-encompassing gesture. "At MIT."

Two a.m., Alien blasted the *Rocky Horror Picture Show* soundtrack at her post at the Center for Space Research. Earlier this month, a new satellite had launched. In their job manning the lab, the chief responsibility of Alien and other interns was to print out charts and hit the letter "s" once an hour, every hour, day or night, a sort of virtual shoulder tap, it seemed, to make sure the satellite stayed awake.

Alien sang along with the music—"Don't dream it . . . be it!"—as she rolled back from printer tray to computer terminal. Her to-do list had had her chained all night to her problem sets, but Alien had yet to begin them, and, for the moment, she did not care. If she could pull off the idea she'd had at SIPB, her social problems would be solved for the year.

The concept was straightforward even if it had taken her hours to get the exact details right. First, pressing Plitman into duty beside her, Alien had searched SIPB's online file system until they found a one-page document labeled "Topology Overview," mapping physical locations to Internet addresses across the MIT campus network. The public cluster in Building 10 —halfway through the Infinite Corridor from either end—had addresses 18.90.0.1 through 18.90.0.21, for instance. The cluster in Building 14—Hayden Memorial Library—had an equal number of addresses starting with 18.51. A few blocks away, the cluster in Building E55—Eastgate Residence Hall—had addresses starting with 18.97. Close to two thousand addresses were included in all.

The analogy to physical buildings was obvious. If someone who had never been to MIT needed directions to Senior House, you couldn't just tell him or her the name. You had to say the full address: 70 Amherst Street, Cambridge, Massachusetts 02142. The finger command worked the same way, but better. Given a full machine address, it turned into a virtual census taker. *Knock, knock,* finger said. And then the networked computer on the other end said who was there.

As midnight had come and gone, Alien had written her first computer script, or automated series of commands. She called it f.

Alien told f to finger each machine address, one by one. That accomplished, the script checked to see if any of her friends were logged in. Finally, it formatted and presented the findings in a simple list:

```
Splotz is @ 64.
Vanessa is @ 14.
Heston is @ E15.
```

And so on, through any contacts Alien chose, connecting virtual address to physical location (Building 64, the east side of East Campus; Building 14, Hayden Memorial Library; Building E15, the Media Lab) for everyone logged in anywhere at MIT.

Or so she hoped.

Alien considered how to proceed. Her f script was starting strong, but slowing pace as it tried to cover the entire campus, like Alien herself trying to chase down Patrick.

The lab door opened. Alien shot up, startled, and killed the music. A guy in his late thirties entered, six feet tall with shaggy hair and a scraggly beard, dressed in a knitted red-, white-, black-, and gray-patterned woolen poncho and a floppy brown canvas hat, as if he had just been herding sheep.

"Jake," Alien said, excited. Her friend looked like a hippie but split his time between Los Alamos National Laboratory, where he had some kind of staff position, and MIT, where he was a visiting scientist. Jake was a brilliant computer programmer and an ardent believer in free software, meaning any program people could use, improve, or alter to their own ends, without cost or restriction. Computing, to him, had taken a wrong path with the development and popularization of commercial operating systems, particularly Apple and Microsoft products, which locked you in to a limited way of doing things and hid a computer's underlying power and flexibility from its users.

His idealism extended to other areas. Her second night in the lab, Alien had found him sleeping here on a wooden table. "I hate hotels," Jake had said, and Alien had shown him to a basement bathroom below the Infinite Corridor where he could shower.

"Hey, kid," he said warmly now. "How's it going?"

Alien cleared her terminal window before waving Jake over. "I'm trying to write this script," she said, as if the idea had just occurred to her. "Say I have a really long nested number series. How would I iterate through it quickly?"

"You can condense this into a single 'for' loop," Jake said. "May I?" he asked, leaning over to type three lines of sample code when Alien nodded.

"There," he said smiling. "Quite efficient."

Alien took his word for it, unwilling to try the code while Jake might see her purpose. He lingered beside her, though, seemingly bubbly with energy himself, though Alien knew he took no drugs — not even pot — appearances notwithstanding.

She checked the time: 2:04 a.m. Tonight the lab had her sharing the night shift with another undergraduate intern, who took over at two thirty.

Alien stood. "Want to see something cool?" she offered.

"Sure." Jake straightened. "Hat or no hat?" he asked.

"Gloves," said Alien. The Center for Space Research lab was located in Building 37, in whose old walled-up freight elevator shaft she had cut her hands. Alien turned off her computer screen. "I'm going to take you on a *real* tour of MIT," she said.

⟺

Five hours later, Alien stepped outside Building 37, grimacing in the sudden sunlight. Jake, at last, was curled up on a couch. Time to test her f script. Unsurprisingly, almost everyone Alien knew was fast asleep too. The only person she knew who was awake and online at seven a.m., f reported, was Fred, one of the guys she'd danced with at the Warehouse party.

Given that Fred lived on Fifth West, Alien would have expected him to log in from there, if anywhere, this morning. Moments earlier, however, f had knocked at the student center, on the opposite side of campus, and gotten back his name.

Was that right? Alien wondered. Or had her program failed?

Blading hard now across MIT, she'd see if her discoveries had taken her as far as she thought.

Alien's charge ended at the student center lobby. Using the only occupied public terminal, she saw, was a short, squat woman wearing jeans and a red flannel shirt, the top of her shoulder-length straight black hair encircled by a rainbow bandana. Definitely not Fred.

Alien looked left and right. Shit.

"Hey!" Someone tapped her shoulder. "Alien?"

She turned. A familiar smile greeted her.

"Fred!" Alien embraced him in a hug that felt like fate. Her script had criss-crossed campus to connect them! "What are you doing here?" she asked.

Fred, dressed in a maroon mesh shirt and cute white athletic shorts and sneakers, pointed outside, toward the athletic center. "I finished a run by the river and I'm headed to the weight room," he said. "Just checking my email in between. What about you?" he asked.

Alien smiled. "I'm Rollerblading," she said, pulling down her T-shirt where it had ridden up in her sprint.

Fred followed the brief glimpse of bare skin appreciatively. "Want to get breakfast or something after I work out?" he asked.

"Sure," said Alien.

They made plans, and then Fred jogged out, waving. Alien waved back.

⎯⎯◆⎯⎯

The f script was a little bit addictive. Where were Alien's friends? Her boy-friends? Her dorm mates? Who was hanging out together? Who was hooking up?

You could tell a *lot* by watching who was logged in from where.

The power to see through walls let Alien maximize her social life. But if she could peer out at everyone, she realized, everyone—at least in theory—could peer right back.

Take the week before Halloween. Tuesday, just after her unified engineering lab let out at five p.m., Alien found Patrick, her Senior House crush, in the Athena cluster in Building 56. Wednesday evening, she Rollerbladed over to TEP when she saw Eddie, the second of her chiseled Warehouse party dance partners, was logged in there. Thursday, Alien realized that Fred had come to see her when he connected from the public terminal in Senior House. Friday, Patrick, Eddie, and Fred were all MIA, but Cal, she saw, was up late at a student center ground-floor Athena terminal, so Alien walked down from the SIPB office, surprised him, and they took a "for old times' sake" hike up to the Little Dome.

Saturday afternoon, a friend on Fourth West, the floor below Fred's, emailed Alien to say he had "new CDs" to share if she wanted some. That night she Rollerbladed to East Campus and into the dorm room of a tan, greasy-haired guy dressed in corduroys and a baggy black T-shirt, carefully stocking a white mini-fridge. "Hey!" she called.

The guy turned. "Good timing," he said, offering Alien a fresh foil-covered five-strip of LSD, or forty microdoses — more than enough to keep her focused through finals.

"Thanks!" said Alien, handing him a folded wad of bills. Then she passed the five-strip back. "Can you keep it cold for me? I'll grab it later."

Next door, another friend, Walter, had drawn a half-dozen people around his computer. Taking advantage of the height boost her Rollerblades gave her, Alien angled to see what he was showing them.

Onscreen was Walter's personal Web page on the MIT servers. "WELCOME TO THE MOOD RING," it said. "I made it for my art class elective," he explained.

Below the title was what seemed like a simple smiley face. The face was animated, however. Alien watched for close to a minute as the line of the mouth moved from grin to flat expression to outright grimace, then back up a bit to frown, and then another brief smile, and back to flat solemnity before briefly changing up again.

"What is it?" she asked as the other onlookers wandered back to the party.

Walter, a skinny kid with puckish blue eyes, chuckled. "It's the mood of the dorm," he told her. "Here." He opened a new terminal window underneath the Web page and typed rapidly for a few seconds. "See for yourself."

His screen filled with seemingly meaningless characters. In the middle, though, Alien recognized two words as they scrolled by: "need sex."

Walter hit the space bar. New text replaced the old. This time Alien made out the phrase "depressed a lot lately."

"This is everyone's traffic, unfiltered," Walter said. "Their email, their Web browsing. And their Zephyr" — instant message — "sessions. You name it."

Alien studied the streams of raw text. "You're sniffing packets," she said.

The dorms at MIT delivered Internet traffic—packets—back and forth via basic routing devices called hubs. When you plugged your computer into a port on the wall, everything you did online traveled down the hall to that hub before being directed to the broader network. And everything everyone *else* on the hall did traveled the same way.

By default, each computer listened only to traffic about itself. But changing that was as simple as flipping a single setting on your dorm room machine. *Promiscuous mode,* manufacturers actually called it. MIT banned the practice, but technically it was easy. Plenty of times on Fifth East, Alien had heard François and Heston shouting across Bemis, loudly announcing each other's most prurient Web surfing stops. "If it's not encrypted, it's public," François had said.

"Sniffing, aggregating, and averaging," Walter said now. He explained: "Using smiley face emoticons, the Mood Ring counts as happy points. Using sad faces, it counts as unhappy points."

"So if happy points are greater than the unhappy points, the face smiles?" Alien guessed. "And if the points are about equal, it's neutral?"

"Right," Walter said. "Of course, this is MIT . . ." He gestured back at the Web page. By the face's current expression, you'd guess someone was feeding its fingers to piranhas. "Happiness never wins for long."

———◆———

When she got home that night, Alien logged into Athena via her personal computer. Using f script to track everyone had been a touch too stalker-ish for her to tell anyone about it. But Walter's Mood Ring, cute and clever as it was, was a million times more intrusive.

Imagine Fred reading the instant messages she'd sent to Patrick, Alien thought. Imagine her mother reading her emails from either guy. Imagine MIT administrators or her boss at the Center for Space Research hearing every song she listened to or viewing every image she loaded online.

Using a free program called GPG—GNU Privacy Guard—Alien already encrypted any confidential emails. But not other private digital information, like photos, diary entries, and the rest of her online communications. Not until now.

"gpg -e -r," Alien typed, followed by the names of her most sensitive files.

06

I Spy

W HEN ALIEN WROTE HER f program to find friends, she never thought what she was doing was hacking. She just wanted to be efficient and approach life creatively. Look at Frostbyte and Walter. One made art out of programmable light bulbs, the other out of packet sniffing. Or Brett and Ben, the bowling ball boys, putting engineering work worthy of a Ph.D. into a ridiculous prank. These were the examples that surrounded Alien at MIT. Fitting in, paradoxically, meant emulating no one else. If Alien *was* a hacker, it was in large part because she rejected the label. "Objective: To learn interesting things, do interesting things, and be happy," her résumé declared throughout the remainder of her college years.

But the longer she stayed at MIT, the further away happiness seemed.

Mid-fall 2000, new construction started across the street from Senior House. Monday through Friday, jackhammers jolted Alien awake at seven thirty a.m., only a few hours after she had gone to bed. As far as her formal schooling went, aerospace information systems was nothing like the imaginative adventure she had thought it would be. The rewards for having survived the unified engineering prerequisites were more courses she didn't care about, with a smaller, even more intense student cohort, and regular recruitment "opportunities" with Boeing and other straitlaced companies that supplied the airlines and armed forces.

Does this excite me? Alien asked herself. The answer was no. Moving fast got her adrenaline going again. She joined the women's ice hockey team.

Zap! Pow! Alien loved the rush of speed and physical contact. Yet hockey, too, proved to be a terrible reminder of the MIT grind. The Sunday before Thanksgiving, a friend and teammate committed suicide.

In early December came what MIT students called "hell week," the last days of classes, when any uncompleted assignments were due. After "hell week" came "dead week," when you were supposed to be studying for finals. Instead, Alien walked to the office of the dean of undergraduate education. On one wall inside the office were boxes containing forms for a range of academic options.

Alien had come to complete the paperwork necessary to withdraw from MIT. She knew how fortunate she was to have gotten in, and how much her parents had invested in enabling her to pursue her education. She didn't want to waste this chance or let them down. At the same time, she couldn't stand life at the Institute anymore.

Alien looked at the box with the withdrawal forms, but couldn't bring herself to actually reach up and take one. She couldn't disappoint her parents.

Then another form caught her eye: "Application for Study Abroad."

In January 2001, Alien entered the drama program at Trinity College, Dublin—a situation as close to the opposite of MIT as she could picture. Alien had told her parents the time abroad would be just one semester and a summer. Secretly, though, she imagined leaving Cambridge behind forever.

Going from the United States to Ireland, and from the tech nerds to the drama kids, represented two simultaneous culture shifts. Her first week in the new program, the entire class turned and stared at her whenever they heard her accent. "America? That's really dangerous, isn't it?" a girl with gorgeous bright red hair asked. (Alien's mother had asked the same question about Ireland.) Another demanded, "Are you Catholic or Protestant?" When Alien said "Jewish," the class gawked at her.

At MIT Alien had felt out of place for being more artistic than technically minded. At Trinity the reverse was true. Naturally enough, her drama classmates all wanted to be actors. When Alien mentioned her past space research lab job, or casual interests in virtual reality and robotics, they looked at her like she was, well, an alien.

In June, Alien traveled to the tiny, isolated Aran Islands, population twelve hundred, off Ireland's western coast. Walking along the islands' ancient stone walls, visiting homes without electricity or running water, listening to the Irish language spoken and sung, taking in the gray-blue sky, she thought: *I could live here for years*. Immediately, though, came the next thought: *No, I couldn't. I would get bored*.

When she returned to Dublin, Alien saw an email from the Senior House mailing list, soliciting ideas for Rush recruitment. She replied immediately. Two months later, back in Cambridge after all, Alien dangled her legs from a fourth-story roof overlooking the Senior House courtyard. Simultaneously with other upperclassmen, she turned over one of six suitcase-sized cardboard boxes ordered from the Rhode Island Novelty Company.

Thousands of tiny multicolored bouncy balls poured down on the gathered freshmen.

Either MIT had changed her or Alien had belonged here all along.

———

Alien was back, but on what she hoped were more tolerable terms, though the time away from technical classes meant she had three more semesters until graduation. In August 2001, she switched majors to Course 6-2 — electrical engineering and computer science. Now she just needed a new job.

Alien wanted to work in the MIT Media Lab — a world-renowned research hub for everything from holography to digital music, electronic ink to emotionally responsive robots — where she thought she could build things and be creative. Before she could apply, though, another, perhaps even more attractive position presented itself. "Do you like eating pizza and staying up late?" the posting said. "Come work at I/S."

I/S stood for MIT Information Systems, an administrative rather than academic department. They ran Athena and other IT services and infrastructure at MIT. The document Alien had found at SIPB, matching campus physical locations to Internet addresses, mapped their territory. And by the first night of the fall semester, it was hers to help protect as a newly hired member of I/S's network security team.

Alien flew. The ends of her naturally dark hair were freshly dyed a color called Nuclear Red that glowed under black light. She caught air as she skipped down the Building 7 steps in Rollerblades. Alien zoomed across Mass Ave, wove through a group of freshmen bunched outside the student center, and zipped down Vassar Street, where she took a left at MIT Police headquarters, and then braked at the I/S offices, a new two-story redbrick building on the far west side of campus. Alien tromped up a front flight of stairs and inside at ten p.m.

I/S employed several hundred people, divided into more than a dozen teams. Many were fellow students, night owls, or both. As Alien rolled forward under fluorescent lighting, over thin carpeting, and through a small foyer leading to a warren of indistinguishable cubicles, she saw that at least ten out of fifty desks on this side of the first floor still had someone working at them at this hour. Yet Alien was the sole network security team member present. Like physical security guards, they worked in shifts, responding 24/7 to viruses, outages, targeted attacks, and other threats.

MIT helped invent the Internet. As a consequence, it controlled vast swaths of cyberspace—far more than any other university, as much as AT&T, IBM, or major portions of the U.S. military. Unlike these other mammoth organizations, however, the Institute had long prided itself on its powerful computers and high-speed network being independent and open, absent any overriding central authority or firewalls beyond a NetID and password to block unauthorized access.

The virtue of the decentralized, open network was that it facilitated the free flow of information vital to a great research university. As a member of the MIT community, you could set up virtually whatever systems you wanted, however you wanted them, which encouraged experimentation. And you could use the network without restrictions on speed or bandwidth, which encouraged collaboration. Together, these principles inspired innovation, invention, and discovery, the goals to which the Institute was most devoted.

Freedom, however, had its liabilities, especially as the network grew. First, it was hard to manage the monumental traffic, particularly when system updates were needed or problems arose. Second, MIT's high profile made it a major target for attackers. Thirty years earlier, a few thousand people had used the Internet. Fifteen years earlier, it was a few hundred thousand. Now it was more than 500 million. Anyone, anywhere could be a kind of hacker, doing the online equivalent of testing doors, picking locks, sneaking in, and trying to leave his or her mark.

Alien logged in at an Athena workstation when she reached her desk. CaseTracker, a Web-based program, loaded: forty-five new messages. These might come from her boss, Marie—an Indian American woman in her thirties — other network security team members, anyone else at MIT, off-campus sources, or any of a host of automated scans, internal or external.

In 2000, the so-called Love Bug virus, a malicious Windows script masquerading as a love letter, for example, had circulated via people's email contacts, hiding or deleting certain types of files as soon as it was opened. Countless copycat viruses followed, along with "worms," or self-propagating programs, that spread back and forth between Athena and other university networks and commercial Internet service providers, hogging bandwidth and overloading the routers that let computers communicate online. Local to MIT, there was a student-run UNIX server hijacked by someone selling email accounts to white supremacists. Actual foreign agents on the prowl for classified information from the Institute's many defense department contractors. The random high school kid (and likely prospective applicant) in Iowa City — or Istanbul or Irkutsk — who wanted to brag that he'd hacked MIT.

"Trouble runs both ways," Marie reminded everyone. One issue was packet sniffing, as Alien had already witnessed. Another, even more common, was copyright infringement. Students who would have howled if they'd known someone was reading their email had no qualms about storing and trading vast amounts of intellectual property online. Free-software evangelists like Jake believed computer programs should be written to be shared. Others extended the idea, claiming that if "information wants to be free," any copyrights should be ignored.

In 1994, a Fifth East resident named David LaMacchia had been caught, arrested, and indicted by a federal grand jury for running his own secret file-sharing site to store and trade copyrighted software and games, using MIT servers. The case was ultimately dismissed, however, because LaMacchia charged nothing for his services.

Congress subsequently moved to close the "LaMacchia loophole," as it was called, passing the No Electronic Theft Act in 1997, followed by the Digital Millennium Copyright Act in 1998. Still, Napster, the first popular music file-sharing service, had thrived at MIT before record industry lawsuits shut it down. And now many students, Alien among them, had moved to so-called peer-to-peer file-sharing services like LimeWire, through which individual users connected directly with one another, no central server necessary, essentially letting everyone online access anything online anyone had stored.

It was with a healthy sense of irony, then, that Alien started work tonight processing a half-dozen takedown notices from aggrieved music and video and computer software copyright holders, angry at MIT students for downloading and distributing their content without payment or permission.

The next two messages Alien saw were easy: new virus reports. The network security equivalent of police APBs, these described viruses by name, appearance, and behavior, including the specific systems they targeted and what countermeasures could stop them.

"Thank you for bringing this to our attention," Alien replied in both cases. "We will investigate this notice and take appropriate action." After moving the reports to active, open status in CaseTracker, Alien signed off: "Elizabeth, for the Network Security Team."

The following incident was trickier. A tenured physics professor, the head of a large research group, had yet to respond to repeated warnings to update vulnerable system software. Now his desktop machine was infected, and actively attacking several multimillion-dollar supercomputers.

Alien wrote to the professor again, sharing the relevant virus report and pasting a link to a Web page where anti-virus software could be downloaded.

"Please either use this software now to remove the virus from the computer, or else disconnect the computer from the network until you have time to use the anti-virus software," she concluded. If he did not follow her instructions, she made clear, "the network connection may be shut off at any time."

When she finished typing, Alien checked the time—11:18 p.m.—and then her personal email.

"Are you going to poker night?" Heston wrote her via Zephyr, referring to a weekly Thursday night game a group of recent Senior House graduates hosted at their Somerville apartment.

"Yes!!" Alien replied.

They chatted briefly, and then Alien toggled back to CaseTracker.

It was now 11:23 p.m., she saw. The network security team had nine new messages. The price of a five-minute break was that she had as many cases as she had started with.

I'm playing whack-a-mole, Alien thought.

———◆———

Alien liked the network security job despite—or, really, because of—its challenges. Even to sophisticated users, MIT's network was largely out of sight and therefore out of mind. They didn't have Alien's level of access and inside knowledge. There was so much more risk than people realized.

More than mere workplace, the I/S office became a hangout. Marie treated Alien and the other student staffers like adults, and welcomed their help brainstorming how to do an almost impossible job better. To that end, Alien wrote new computer scripts to automate her most common CaseTracker activities, crafted Web pages and other outreach materials explaining security fundamentals to ordinary users, and learned how to log into routing equipment called switches and remotely disable someone's port, or point of access to the Internet, if his or her machine was causing problems.

Soon, scanning the network, she had the same sensation as reaching a rooftop and feeling like everything in sight belonged to her. *Except now,* she thought, *it's my job to protect it.*

"I want you to join us tomorrow night," Marie messaged Alien one evening in early December. "To observe and learn."

The next day was Tuesday, December 11, 2001, exactly three months since the airplane hijackings that had attacked the Pentagon and destroyed the World Trade Center. In Afghanistan, the United States and its allies were now at war with international terrorism in a campaign called "Operation Enduring Freedom." Like so many others, Alien had been stunned by the 9/11 attacks. They had a special personal dimension for her, since she had worked in the Wall Street area one summer only a few years back, when she was in high school, and was haunted by the virtual certainty that she had known some of the three thousand victims. The terrorists hadn't used computers, but they had certainly taken advantage of other vulnerabilities. They had made the entire world feel less secure, making any kind of breach a source of anxiety.

Alien arrived in the office at eight p.m., performing CaseTracker triage while she waited for Marie. The same physics professor Alien had emailed in early September had a new computer virus. The man was a Nobel laureate, she'd discovered. Rather than change his habits after I/S pulled his port the first time, he'd called Chuck Vest, the president of MIT, personally to complain. As a result, I/S had been forced to reactivate his connection.

Maybe forty minutes in, Marie arrived at Alien's cubicle. "Glad you could make it," she said. "Sorry I couldn't give you more background. Ready?"

"Sure," said Alien without any idea for what.

She hadn't been summoned because of anything to do with the physics professor. They crossed the campus and, at nine p.m. sharp, entered the MIT economics department lobby.

"They'll be doing forensic acquisition," Marie said quietly. "Watch carefully and don't say anything."

⇜✦⇝

Four people awaited them. Clearly in charge was a handsome man in his late thirties, with sandy blond hair and a goatee, dressed in a dark suit. He conferred with a junior colleague in his late twenties. From their clothing and manner, neither looked as if he worked at MIT.

Off to the side, watching a little nervously, Alien thought, was the economics department's IT guy, who couldn't have been older than twenty-five. Beside him was a red-haired sixtyish employee of the physical maintenance office.

"Okay?" the older of the men in suits asked everyone. His tone was crisp and curt, his posture straight-backed in a way suggestive of military training. They had spent only a few seconds together, but his eyes were sharp and observant. Alien felt certain that the man had already committed her height, weight, age, and other identifying characteristics to memory, just in case.

Fascinated, she nodded with the others.

"Okay, then," the man said. "Let's go."

⇜✦⇝

The physical maintenance guy unlocked the department office door and then left. The econ IT guy entered first. Next came the younger of the men in suits, tugging a black roller suitcase behind him, and then the older, who beckoned Marie and Alien to trail him closely.

The group stopped opposite a department lounge at what looked like a closet door. Marie and the men in suits looked to the IT guy, who seemed jittery as he stepped forward. After stumbling on the first try, he unlocked the door with an electronic keycard.

Following him, the others squeezed inside one by one.

⇜✦⇝

The space was approximately five by eight feet, with a white linoleum floor. As Alien crossed the threshold, her first sensation was of noise from several large fans going full blast. Since the room was already air-conditioned, her second sensation was of feeling cold. Goose bumps formed on her exposed arms. Adjusting to the new environment, Alien saw the younger of the men in suits opening his roller case in front of black metal racks along the wall.

The racks were stacked with hard drives connected by labeled cabling to MIT network ports.

This was a server room, Alien recognized. These machines were loaded with data generated by the department's faculty and students. Typical of where she had gone hacking freshman year, it was the kind of place hundreds of people passed every day but almost everyone ignored. In Course 19, however, Alien had focused almost entirely on empty or abandoned spaces, which this most certainly was not.

On the hard drives in front of her were gigabytes of economics information and equations, the product of decades of research and analysis, humming toward thousands of results — some dead ends, some future Nobel Prizes, and all of supreme interest to those who'd put them there. And on them too, apparently, was something of interest to the men in black.

Alien watched and listened closely as the older man shouted out specific Internet addresses. The IT guy darted back and forth, seeking the cables with those labels. Meanwhile, the younger man removed external hard drives from the suitcase and mounted them on the designated machines. He controlled all he was doing from a monitor and keyboard he had also brought with him. With assistance from Marie and the IT guy, he ran the UNIX program dd, a disk duplicator that copied or "imaged" what was on the servers.

"Okay, we're starting the imaging process," the younger man said, looking up long enough to make brief eye contact with Alien. He made a note in a little book next to him.

Alien kept a discreet distance. Another person would have wanted to know why they were here, but she was completely focused on the technical processes. The difference between using CaseTracker and tagging along tonight was that between reading an anatomy textbook and watching a live medical procedure in an operating theater. It wasn't the patient that interested Alien but the surgery.

"Good?" the older man in the suit mouthed silently when everything was up and running.

His associate at the keyboard signaled a thumbs-up.

⟦✦⟧

They let the imaging run for a few minutes and then calculated the pace of their progress. In the meantime, the younger man snapped photos of the server room and filled out what appeared to be a detailed inventory.

"Okay—it looks like we're good for now," the older man shouted over the fan noise when his colleague had finished writing. "We'll follow up at four a.m."

They left. Outside, back in front of the department building, without any explanation, Marie told Alien to go home. "Good job. See you tomorrow" were her parting words.

Alien walked slowly to Senior House. For once, winter weather cleared rather than clouded her head. Because I/S had extraordinary access privileges, the first rule of the network security team was to respect user privacy. That they had come to the economics department at night, led by these two men, in order to copy hard drives in secret suggested something very serious. *Forensic,* Marie had said. It hadn't registered until now.

Alien realized that she had just seen a computer network treated as the scene of a crime.

⟦✦⟧

INTERNET PIRACY IS SUSPECTED AS U.S. AGENTS RAID CAMPUSES, read a headline in the following morning's *New York Times.* "Federal law enforcement agents seized computers and raided computer networks at M.I.T., the University of California at Los Angeles and other large universities today in shutting down what they described as one of the Internet's largest and most sophisticated software piracy networks," the paper reported.

The pirates, collectively called DrinkOrDie, used the university servers as "drop sites," storing and distributing huge portions of their haul via campus servers. Like David LaMacchia before them, individual participants seemed to have no personal profit motive, working instead for bragging rights, the technical challenge of being the first to crack copy protections, and access to the free software, games, music, and movies provided by fellow members. Once a file was up, though, outsiders, including organized criminal groups, could download and package it for resale.

DrinkOrDie had posted Windows 95 two weeks before Microsoft released it, the *Times* said. Now they had up *Harry Potter and the Sorcerer's Stone* and *Monsters, Inc.* — films that were still in theaters. According to federal investigators, the financial loss to the producers of all this content ran into the hundreds of millions of dollars.

Before the new year, a twenty-three-year-old computer sysadmin — systems administrator — for the MIT economics department was identified as a ringleader. In August 2002, he was sentenced to thirty-three months in prison.

⟨⟩

Alien didn't follow the DrinkOrDie case closely. Others could debate whether the rogue sysadmin's punishment was merited by his actions. What intrigued her was how he had gone undetected for so long — and then how he had been discovered and tracked.

The fall semester of 2002 was Alien's final one at MIT. Through hard work, helpful TAs, and her own talent for the types of hands-on projects required in labs, she'd escaped aerospace information systems and actually boosted her GPA in electrical engineering and computer science. She'd also sweet-talked her new adviser into letting her replace several Course 6-2 classes with credits from unified engineering, even though the topics covered were completely different. The only significant requirement standing between her and graduation was her AUP, or Advanced Undergraduate Project.

"I want to do something with security for my AUP," Alien told Marie.

"Want to take a look at network flows?" said Marie. "Flick" — a fellow SIPB member — "wrote a script to gather the records from all our routers. We're not really doing anything with the information, though."

Alien nodded. "Cool!" All of MIT's internal traffic flow records . . . now that would be an interesting extension of her desire to see inside the Institute and understand what was going on. Flow records stored the source, destination, time, and amount of information involved in any data transfer. Because the records captured traffic flow by size, not content, personal information was still protected, but a digital piracy drop site, virus-spewing supercomputer, or other significant security issue would be obvious by its imprint.

"I could create a new tool to analyze the traffic and display stats," she said. She just needed a little help.

First, there was Flick with the flow records. He was happy to share, he said, but he suggested he and Alien meet for drinks to discuss the matter first.

"Night is highly preferable," Flick wrote. "I only get smashed early on weekends and national holidays."

They met at John Harvard's Brewery in Harvard Square. In exchange for an hour of smiles on top of explaining what she wanted to do, Alien had her data.

Now to interpret it. Next poker night, while her friends bet and bantered, Alien searched the wood-and-cement-block bookshelves in the Somerville apartment living room, flipping past *The Feynman Lectures on Physics*, *The Procedure Handbook of Arc Welding*, and *The Collected Poems of Langston Hughes* to grab *TCP/IP Illustrated*, volume one, the standard reference on Internet communications protocol, in front of a tank of gaping clownfish.

She started coding on what she was calling NetVision. Senior House was too distracting. SIPB was too bright. The Building 66 basement Athena cluster was just right, but there was no one there to hit up for help if she had questions. One midnight in mid-October, the last warm week of fall, Alien swallowed a micro-dose of LSD emblazoned with the Senior House logo—a grinning red, white, and blue skull—and Rollerbladed across the river to a century-old five-story brownstone on Commonwealth Avenue, Tau Epsilon Phi.

"François?" she yelled, left and right. Her old Fifth East hallmate had recently reenrolled at MIT and Alien had used her f script to locate him here.

A voice came from the first-floor lounge. "He's in twenty-two," a slouched figure on a beat-up couch answered.

Alien climbed a flight and entered 22. It was a four-person room that was pure MIT. In order to use space efficiently, the TEP brothers had used metal rods to bolt the room's beds, feet detached, to the ceiling. Also hanging from the ceiling—in this case from metal chains rather than rods, so that it could swing—was a legless leather couch that looked like it had been rescued from the curb on the night before garbage pickup.

One reached the beds and couch via narrow wooden stepladders. This left most of the floor available for four large metal desks, two more battered couches, a black refrigerator, and a mirrored cabinet topped by empty Jack Daniel's bottles. The bottles themselves were illuminated in ever-changing colors by computer-controlled LED lights running behind them, a legacy of Frostbyte, who had lived at TEP as an undergraduate. Mounted on the walls were a blackboard, pirate flag, and various band posters and purloined street signs. The final touch was a functioning four-signal traffic light.

"Hey," Alien said, waving to the room's residents — all sophomores — one in bed, reading, one at a desk, tooling, and two on the floor-level couches, talking about tooling — i.e., punting. François, she saw, had dropped his straight-edge stance on never smoking. He was on the hanging couch, passing a bong to Eddie, from the Warehouse party.

Alien unstrapped her Rollerblades, took her laptop from her backpack, and climbed the ladder to join them.

"Hit?" Eddie asked, giggling.

"No thanks," Alien said. Pot made her inefficient. "Do you have a minute?" she asked François.

"Sure," he said.

Alien grabbed a long purple Ethernet cable dangling helpfully from the ceiling, logged into Athena, and loaded NetVision.

Nothing happened.

"See?" Alien asked. "It's taking so long to get through all the data, I have to kill the process" — force quit the program — "before I get results."

"Show me your code," said François.

Alien did. The screen filled with Perl programming language algorithms and instructions.

"There's your problem," François said. "Why did you use Perl?"

"Pattern matching," said Alien. Perl was designed to make extracting individual elements from long files — like every Internet address, and only Internet addresses — easy.

"Database and query in Python" — another programming language — "will be much faster," François told her.

Alien nodded, tight-lipped. Computer science classes at MIT emphasized conceptual principles over practicality. They didn't teach programming languages people actually used.

"Do you *know* Python?" François asked after several seconds of silence.

Alien shrugged. "Not yet," she said.

⎯⟨⟩⎯

Two a.m., three weeks later, music played in the Senior House courtyard, and parties beckoned from all directions, but Alien had barricaded herself in her room to debug her program—finding and fixing the tiny flaws that could open it up to unexpected failure. Getting up to stretch her legs, she found Jake, the visiting scientist at the Center for Space Research, taking up her open invitation to bed down on a common area lounge couch.

"I'm graduating," Alien told him. "Remind me to introduce you around so you'll be able to crash here next semester."

Jake sat up on his elbows, curious. "What are you going to do, kid?" he asked.

"Escape MIT," Alien said. "Maybe move west." Her parents were pushing grad school, of course, but she wanted to travel, not tool, stare at canyon walls, not computer screens. It had been right to return and finish her degree, Alien believed, but now she was eager again for something completely different. All she had to do was get NetVision working first.

"Hey," Jake said. "You should move to Santa Fe."

"Yeah?" Alien smiled. "Sunny Santa Fe!" they sang in the musical *Rent*, she remembered. "*Yeah*," she repeated.

Jake continued. "You could work for me at Los Alamos," he said.

"Sure," said Alien, less deliberation than impulse, like all her best ideas. She had no idea what Jake really did. As far she was concerned, if he ran a pizza place, that would be fine. As long as it was a change.

New home, new job, new life.

Alien clapped to herself when she got back to her computer screen. And then she began to type again.

⟞⟝

NetVision went live in December. It was Monday of finals week, and a rare hush covered Senior House when Alien lowered her laptop screen shortly after eight a.m., surprised when invading daylight broke her concentration. Her room was stripped and empty, her belongings packed beneath a mural she'd painted of a lush wildflower garden. Now, with snoring classmates surrounding her, her code worked, and she couldn't wait to show it off.

Alien walked out to a balcony overlooking the Senior House courtyard to get dressed. The air was freezing, but she stripped first, enjoying the sun on her bare skin and the panoramic view of the Charles River and Boston.

Totally naked, she saw sudden movement in a window of the only building between her perch and the water, a three-story white stone villa, the house of the MIT president.

Two wide eyes stared at her. The window shade slowly lowered.

Alien laughed. *I just flashed Chuck Vest,* she thought, putting on her pants.

Thirty minutes later she was outside again, grateful at least that the strong wind was at her back as she skated to work.

Only a handful of other I/S cubicles were occupied at this hour. Alien logged on at her desktop machine, and then rolled into Marie's office and asked through chattering teeth if she would join her.

"You remember how long NetVision was taking?" Alien said, warming herself by talking. "Then how it was fast enough but kept crashing?"

Marie nodded.

"Well, I rewrote it all — twice," Alien said. "See . . ." She typed a moment and then pointed excitedly at the monitor. "Now it responds in real time."

The screen filled. In a neat all-text grid, it listed the top ten Internet addresses on the MIT network, ranked in order of the amount of data transferred to and from them. Its latest update was 9:07 a.m. — just four minutes earlier — the program said.

"Not bad," said Marie. She reached around Alien, took the keyboard, and hit the up arrow and Return key to repeat the command. A moment later, a new list appeared. Six of the top ten "talkers" had fluctuated, NetVision showed, while the others — including three of the top four — held steady.

"Can you make it visual?" said a male voice.

Alien and Marie turned to see the I/S network manager, Jeff, standing six inches away, smiling behind a bushy brown mustache. Jeff was only in his mid-forties but already a legend to Internet geeks on campus, who spoke of his contributions to Athena and the MIT computer network the same way, and for similar reasons, architecture buffs did Louis Sullivan ("form follows function") and Ludwig Mies van der Rohe ("less is more"). He had honored Alien and appeased the computer science department by agreeing to serve as her AUP adviser, though actual oversight, up to this moment, had been Marie's.

"One minute," Alien responded, loading her source code in the same terminal window as Jeff and Marie caught up on other matters.

NetVision worked by inputting Flick's flow records to a database. Sorting

Internet addresses by the size of their uploads and downloads was one function. With a few more lines of code in two spots, Alien quickly added other functions to calculate each listed address's percentage of the total network load and create a Web page displaying the results.

"How does this look?" she asked when she had finished.

Jeff turned. "You did it already?" he asked.

Alien pointed proudly onscreen at a blue horizontal bar chart. The top address was responsible for just under 15 percent of total traffic at MIT, the Web page showed. The next address was responsible for just over 10 percent. Every other address on the list had a much smaller fraction of the total—1 percent or less.

"Are you kidding?" Marie asked, scrutinizing the findings. "That's got to be a mistake." The MIT network had 25,000 active Internet addresses. But if what they were seeing was accurate, a full quarter of the total traffic came from just two computers.

Jeff moved closer. "Whose addresses are they?"

Whenever someone at MIT brought a new machine online, he or she was supposed to register it with the name, phone number, and email address of a human contact. No one verified the accuracy of this information, and once established, a machine's records were rarely updated, but the registry was the first thing Information Systems checked when investigating a potential problem. Alien had configured NetVision to pull the registered hostname and details when displaying results.

Alien glanced at the readout and laughed. "It's *us*," she said. "The top talker on the MIT network is a server here at I/S."

"Mail?" Marie asked.

"Web." Jeff scooted around Marie's desk to see his own name listed under the point-of-contact field. He nodded. It made sense that MIT's public website would top NetVision's list.

"What about number two?" he asked.

Alien frowned. "Funny, it didn't resolve." She manually typed the second address into MIT's system registry.

"No machine(s) found matching query in the database," the program returned.

Marie frowned. "Try again," she said.

Just in case, Alien retyped the numbers, double-checking for any typos.

The directory results were identical, however. No computer with that address had been registered at MIT.

Alien turned. "It's an unregistered system."

Silence.

"Are you sure this is right?" Jeff said. "There's an unregistered computer responsible for ten percent of all of MIT's network traffic?"

"It's right," said Alien.

No one spoke for a long moment. The computer in question could be a virus launch point, a new software piracy server, a secret military installation, or something else altogether, good or bad.

Alien refreshed NetVision. A new blue bar chart appeared. In the last couple of minutes, it showed, the percentage of traffic from the mysterious site had actually *increased,* going from 10.1 to 10.7 percent.

Marie looked at Jeff. He picked up a piece of paper and handed it to Alien. "Write down that address for me, okay?"

"Sure," she said, scribbling it down.

As she did, Marie and Jeff consulted about the phantom user, but Alien barely listened. Inventing the tool to facilitate network inspections and investigations had been what excited her. Anything that came out of it—even another federal raid—was ultimately just another step on the CaseTracker treadmill. And that wasn't her problem anymore.

"Oh, hey," Alien asked. "Can you sign off on my project? I need it to graduate."

⋙━⋘

The getaway car was her mother's old cranberry-colored Volvo, its rear bumper still proudly festooned with stickers advertising her and her sister's high school honor roll student status. Alien's accomplice was a fellow off-semester graduate, a guy with thick ringlets of long blond hair, one of her boyfriends of the last year, none serious. They were driving together to Santa Fe. In January, Alien started work for Jake at Los Alamos. Her friend would keep traveling. Who knew what would happen after that?

Stepping into the car, Alien brushed snow flurries from her eyes and frozen dress, changed out of Rollerblades, and leaned over to embrace him.

"We're free!" she exclaimed as they pulled out. Alien rolled down the sunroof, in spite of the winter weather.

They sped down Memorial Drive as the student center and Killian Court, the Great and Little Domes, Building 54 and Building 66, Fifth East and Senior House all receded in the rearview mirror.

"Good-bye!" yelled Alien — to MIT and, she thought, to anything to do with security.

Sixty seconds later, her mind was already shifting to the next adventure. The yellow line of the highway pointed the path ahead.

07

Wild Wild Web

ALIEN WAS TWENTY-TWO YEARS old when she arrived in Santa Fe in January 2003. After her childhood in suburban New Jersey and college years in urban Cambridge, and even after the rugged green splendor of Ireland, New Mexico's natural wonders — pink and purple mesas, an infinite landscape washed by golden sunlight as far as the eye could see — astonished her. Just as dramatic were the cultural differences, with café bulletin board notices advertising flute meditation and acroyoga, ecstatic dance and belly dance classes, mindfulness workshops and hydrotherapy. She found a room in a communal living environment residents called "The Island," a long brown adobe ranch house almost alone on seven acres in southwest Santa Fe, shared with a carpenter, a masseuse, a student of Chinese medicine, an experimental rock duo consisting of a singer and a drummer, and a "fire artist" who juggled blazing clubs and extinguished a torch by putting it in his mouth.

This was just the kind of setting she'd been looking for, she thought. Artistic. In harmony with nature. Relaxed rather than high-strung. Outside the mainstream. Both destination and escape.

Then came her first day of work.

The Island was separated from Los Alamos National Laboratory by about forty miles of highway that wound past a series of small Native American reservations, over the Rio Grande River, and up to a succession of mesas. At the perimeter of the lab, before Alien could glimpse anything inside, she was halted by a tollbooth-like row of seven guard stations, white with blue aluminum roofs.

"ID?" a man in a brown collared shirt that said SECURITY OFFICER asked her.

Alien produced her driver's license for examination and he pointed her up a rise, set against ponderosa pines and the Jemez Mountains, 11,500 feet at their peak.

Moments later, Alien reached a sign with the words LOS ALAMOS NATIONAL LABORATORY and a logo that was a simple drawing of an atom, with electrons looping around a nucleus. To her left were several blocks of drab, boxy concrete buildings. First was the badge office. Here, Alien presented her passport, which Jake's office administrator had told her to bring as proof of her identity, and recited her Social Security number.

"Okay." The clerk directed her to a side table where a colleague waited with a green-lit glass-topped electronic fingerprint capture device, like a tiny photocopier, and a separate electronic signature pad, both linked by thin cables to a black laptop.

"Sign here," he said, pointing to the signature pad and handing her a stylus.

Alien signed. With practiced ease, the second clerk grasped Alien's hand, rolling her right thumb firmly over the fingerprint capture device's glass. The machine beeped loudly and her thumbprint appeared on the screen of the laptop. He repeated the process with the other nine fingers, and then took separate impressions of the left four fingers together, the right four fingers together, and, again, the left and right thumbs, so that his laptop screen showed twenty black whorled forms—two impressions each of every finger.

Last, a third clerk took a head shot. "The badge will print in five minutes," the woman said.

While Alien waited, she studied a large map of the lab mounted on the wall. It was remarkably vague in detail except for the obvious fact that the place was enormous. In all, there were more than one thousand buildings in forty-seven distinct "technical areas" ("TA-1," "TA-2," and so on) dispersed across its remote forty-square-mile plateau.

When her badge was ready, Alien was handed an eight-paragraph information sheet. "Protect badge against loss, theft, or misuse," it instructed. "Report a lost, stolen, or misused badge within 24 hours of discovery. . . . Surrender/return the badge when requested. Wear the badge conspicuously, photo side out, in a location above the waist, and on the front of your body." Whenever she left the lab, it concluded, "protect your badge from view."

Where am *I?* Alien wondered. *What the hell does this place* do?

———

The heart of the orientation session that followed was a video history of Los Alamos. Native farmers. A boys' outdoor school. Then army barracks built sixty years earlier for the ultimate security—or insecurity—project: the creation of the atomic bomb.

Alien had known—vaguely, intellectually—that her new workplace was associated in some way with nuclear weapons. But it had never registered that they were actually conceived, built, and tested *right here.* Seeing grainy footage of an early mushroom cloud, Alien sat back, staggered, and said, out loud, "*Wow.*"

"The Los Alamos National Laboratory plays a key role in our nation's defense and security, and because you are now an employee of this laboratory, you can become a target of a hostile foreign intelligence service or terrorist group," she read in her training packet materials. "Regardless of your clearance status, your access to sensitive and classified information at the Laboratory makes you a potential target of nations and individuals who want and need our information."

Alien was still processing the warning when Jake came by a little while later to greet her and take her to lunch in the cafeteria. "That's the building I work in," he pointed out as they walked the sprawling campus after the meal. "It's behind the fence."

Alien craned her neck to see where he was pointing, but couldn't tell which of the distant buildings he meant—or, for that matter, which of the many fences. Half a mile later, they reached a low-slung pale brown complex. NOTICE, said a sign outside in red letters. "Each person that has access authorization into this area/facility must: Individually run his or her badge and be authorized by the badge reader/hand geometry unit. Those who do not have access authorization must be escorted."

Following Jake's lead, Alien slid her new badge across a scanner. With two beeps, the door clicked open. He led her down a long linoleum hallway dotted at short intervals with gray civil defense sirens but otherwise identical to countless passages just like it at MIT, including the low hum of heating and cooling pipes and the aroma of burnt coffee. They stopped at a door marked "NIS"—"Nonproliferation and International Security," Jake translated.

Inside the NIS administrative offices, Jake introduced Alien to five men and one woman. They were all dressed pretty much the same, in khakis or jeans and a button-down shirt (and, for Jake, his usual multicolored woolen poncho). But their badge colors were different: gray (Alien and one of the men), red (a single person), yellow (three people), and blue (two people, including Jake). Four workers also wore a CRYPTOCard, which looked like a solar calculator and generated a time-synched seven-digit passcode necessary for certain computer logins. Hanging from a separate lanyard for two of them was a thin garage-door-opener-sized black plastic rectangle with two thumbnail-sized slots for metal film.

"Dosimetry device," Jake explained. "It measures radiation exposure."

Jake walked Alien back outside the office. In the hallway just beyond it was a steel-barred floor-to-ceiling revolving turnstile, like those in a subway station. LIMITED AREA, said a sign colored blue and yellow, indicating the badge colors required for entry. Alien watched as one of the men she'd just met swiped his yellow badge at one scanner, placed his palm on another, and then pushed on through the turnstile before disappearing from sight. She and Jake turned left instead, around a tight corner, and up metal stairs to a dingy, low-ceilinged niche where four black computer stations faced a white concrete wall.

"This is Sanjay and Toyo," Jake said, introducing her to two more of her new co-workers at NIS. Both men were grad students—Sanjay from India, Toyo from Japan—and both wore red badges. "You'll be working next to them."

Alien nodded. She realized that "next to them" also meant "on this side of the turnstile," excluded from areas—like Jake's office, or anywhere "behind the fence"—where only those with yellow and blue badges could go.

<hr>

Even if Los Alamos was a huge, high-security research lab, the "mezzanine of doom," as Jake called it, where Alien worked alongside Sanjay and Toyo, was, like the hallway leading to it, straight out of MIT. Unpretentious. Utilitarian. A place to log in and work.

"Okay, kid, let's get you started," Jake said. "Go ahead and type in your username."

Stiffly, she typed "etessman." It felt strange. Her fingers wavered. The computer system was different from the Athena boxes she was used to, but still controlled primarily via a UNIX-based command line.

"Good," Jake said. "Now we're going to set up your environment right."

From her time at MIT, particularly her early experience writing f script and, later, her work coding NetVision, Alien already knew the essentials of computer programming, including what command line tools she liked to use and how to automate and combine them. But Jake expected efficiency as well as proficiency from his staffers. "The biggest part is key bindings"—keyboard command shortcuts—he told her. "You work most effectively when your fingers never leave the keyboard. Learn the quickest ways to accomplish your most routine tasks, and you will find that you are enormously more productive."

What followed was the beginning of Alien's transformation as a programmer. "These skills will serve you for a lifetime," Jake continued. Instead of a series of almost haphazard, improvised steps, Alien would need to break all of her tasks down into a careful sequence. Internalize this process and it would become automatic and nearly effortless, like a race car driver shifting gears, or a soldier assembling a rifle.

Jake spent a full hour with Alien, side by side. They began with her core programming tools, customizing Emacs and GDB, her editor and debugger, and then moved on to the operating system environment itself.

Along the way, he kept stopping and correcting her, half driving instructor, half drill sergeant.

"Do it right," Jake ordered when Alien used the left arrow key to move to the beginning of a line of text. "Is that the most efficient way to do it?"

"No . . . ," she said, without yet knowing how to improve. "Is there a better way?"

"Control-A goes to the beginning of the line," Jake said. "You don't have to hold down the arrow key."

"Okay." Alien tried the command, and her cursor shot over. "Got it," she said. And then they continued.

"Back a line," Jake tested her afterward.

"Forward to line one hundred and twenty-nine.

"Switch windows.

"Save buffers.

"Merge files.

"Compile.

"Good."

"You're a slave driver in a poncho," Alien joked. But she appreciated that Jake's instructions, especially when taken together, changed the relationship between herself and what was happening on the screen. The more he pushed her, the faster and more elegantly she moved, until the commands at hand felt *hers*—extensions of Alien's body—to be used intuitively, as the challenge at hand demanded.

This was hacking of a kind, not in the sense of breaking into something, but of moving from outsider to insider, user to ace. She was surprised to feel a similar thrill, in its own way as energizing as scaling an elevator shaft or the Great Dome.

Finally, Alien had the keyboard shortcuts down well enough to dance across anything onscreen in seconds.

Jake looked on approvingly.

"*Now* you're ready to work," he said.

———◆———

Alien circled twice, but every single parking spot by her building was taken when she arrived at work at ten a.m. one day in early March.

"Shit," she muttered to herself. "*Morning* people."

If this were Cambridge, Alien might have circled again, waiting for someone to clear out. At Los Alamos, though, everyone holed up all day once they'd gotten here.

She could park in the overflow lot, a mile away. Or—Alien smiled—she could "invent" her own spot right here.

She eased the Volvo forward, past the first parking space closest to the building, and drew to a halt atop a striped yellow "no parking" area. *There*—she backed up, straightening the rear of the station wagon to align precisely with the car beside her, so the imaginary space looked official. With the car parked over the yellow stripes, you couldn't even tell.

Alien stepped out of the Volvo, walked to her building, swiped her badge, and strolled inside.

———◆———

While Jake's research group worked in nondescript buildings, there was nothing mundane about what they did. They helped manage a unique combination of satellites and multimillion-dollar telescopes and supercomputers. The system operated automatically. When the satellites spotted gamma ray bursts — sudden, seemingly random flashes of high-energy light — across the sky, the telescopes shifted to focus on the action. Then the supercomputers correlated millions of points of observation data to identify patterns or track the presence of new objects, passing word to involved scientists in real time.

It was an outer space surveillance system, of vital interest to the U.S. military because it could detect clandestine nuclear weapons tests. To a scientist like Jake, what was far more exciting were the breakthrough discoveries in astrophysics it might produce.

Alien's job was to improve the underlying code.

"It's a rat's nest of nested 'If' statements," Jake had warned her. "Figure out what everyone before you did and clean it up. If you do a good job, we can release it as free software."

Free software. To an outsider, the proposal might have sounded disparaging: free as in *worth nothing.* But Alien understood it in the sense intended by Jake and the programmers she most admired: free as in *contribution.* The chance to enrich both the lab and the community of computer scientists and astrophysicists around the world. Proof, with Jake's guidance and encouragement, that she was participating in a larger aesthetics and ethos of coding.

At work today in the mezzanine, Alien spent hours, eyes narrowed, analyzing a particularly convoluted section of the software, like a police accident investigator at the scene of a ten-car pileup. Except that, as Alien typed rapidly, using a keyboard shortcut every few seconds, she could reverse time, start over, and replay the pileup again and again, until she realized what each line of code *meant* to do. Then, rewriting, Alien could take the entire program apart and fix it so that, in effect, the accident never happened.

"Modularity. Flexibility. Abstraction," she remembered one of her computer science professors preaching. *Modularity* meant separating a program's functions into clear-cut, independent building blocks. *Flexibility* meant programming in such a way that those functions could be easily modified in the future. *Abstraction* meant emphasizing the big picture over nuts-and-bolts details — in this case, creating a general tool to identify objects in a collection of astronomical data, not just the data generated by the system specific to the lab.

Alien's room was a mess. Her closet. Her car. Her *programming*, however, was crisp, clean, concise, and clearly commented — meaning she documented everything she did so that any coders who used the software after her could easily understand it.

"Got you," she said, rerunning the once problematic section shortly before four p.m., bugs squashed and needless inefficiencies eliminated.

Alien wished she could show Jake. But the only way to talk in person was for him to come to her. Try entering the high-security areas and guards would stop her in seconds. Her gray badge screamed: *I can only be trusted up to a point — literally.*

⎯⎯◆⎯⎯

Alien started dating an officemate, David, who took the seat next to her in the mezzanine after Sanjay's and Toyo's stints there ended. He was three or four years older, with a great jawline, wheat-blond hair, striking blue eyes, and a ripped runner's build. Come spring, he introduced her to a social group of fifteen or so fellow lab employees, ages twenty-five to fifty, who organized off-beat collective Wednesday evening running events at local trailheads, more in the spirit of nerd fun than Los Alamos's high seriousness.

"Better drink this quick." The eldest guy passed Alien and David each a cold Coors. "Hares leave in five minutes," he said.

Everyone swigged for the duration. Then a guy and a girl, both redheads in their late twenties — dashed off into knee-high dry yellow grass, trailing flour behind them. Another ten minutes passed and someone yelled, "On, on!" The activity was a hunt of sorts, as elaborate as it was benign.

Alien, David, and everyone else gave chase.

The pack spread out, laughing as they followed false and real trails set up in advance by the hares. False trails were marked with three lines: *wrong path, backtrack.* Real trails led to new beer stops. Here, again, everyone drank, which inspired loud group chants, the more obscene the better.

It was now almost dark. Alien stumbled, ducking tree branches, tripping on buried rocks. Looping two to three miles — and one or two more beers — she and the others reached the trailhead again, where the hares by now had built a campfire.

Everyone but designated drivers drank more. They all sang more, too, and then piled back into cars.

The Los Alamos Hash House Harriers, the group called itself. *A drinking club with a running problem.*

——⟫⟫——

Alien wasn't a big beer drinker. But it was good to hang out and have fun without the usual security measures separating everyone, and to know she wasn't the only lab employee looking to blow off steam. Afterward, she and David drove to his rental place, a wide-windowed house in rural El Rancho, halfway between Los Alamos and Santa Fe. They stepped out of their sweaty clothes, showered, and then slipped into his outdoor hot tub.

Alien lay back, communing with the bubbling hot water and sweet sage-ash-scented breeze, taking in the blue-black sky and dense silvery constellations. Perhaps thirty seconds passed, and then—goose bumps—she saw a shooting star.

"We're watching space," she reflected. "But do you ever feel like it's watching us back?"

"Isn't it?" said David. "Satellites and such?"

"Right." Alien grimaced. "One, two, three, four," she counted separate sets of blinking lights among the natural celestial objects.

They lingered in the tub for another hour, but Alien's cheery sense of total freedom, she found, had vanished.

"If the government put telescopes in space instead of on the ground, they could track us or anyone else on Earth," she said. "They could use *my* software."

David's wrinkled hand found hers underwater. He squeezed.

"Probably," Alien said, "they already do."

——⟫⟫——

As summer approached, Alien explored more outside the lab. She visited Ghost Ranch, where Georgia O'Keeffe had lived and kept her studio, and the hand-carved cave dwellings of Bandelier National Monument, rich with intact petroglyphs. She liked to walk barefoot and sometimes topless, better to feel the earth and sun on her skin. The sand burned her feet. She winced and walked on, knowing calluses would make her stronger.

The first weekend in June, five months after Alien arrived, The Island threw a party. One of the guests, a trim, thinly mustachioed thirtysomething, was the ringmaster of a small traveling circus to which her fire artist house-mate belonged. The show needed one more member, he said.

Alien immediately volunteered, not even asking what she was volunteering for.

Her debut was the afterparty for a vintage car show in Tucumcari, about 175 miles southeast of Santa Fe along the old Route 66. The stage was the large open lot next to a local biker bar.

First to perform were silk aerialists — acrobats swinging and spiraling into different positions while hanging from strips of long, stretchy fabric tied to anchors on the roof of the bar. Then the ringmaster strode onstage in a cherry red Sergeant Pepper uniform. Cheered on by the car collectors and bikers, he bound up his girlfriend/"lovely assistant" in an apparently inescapable strait-jacket and watched in histrionic astonishment as she twisted and turned herself free. They bantered a bit, and then she somehow passed her whole body though the triangular opening in a wire coat hanger before slipping away to assist the fire artist in setting up for the grand finale. A white-haired guitarist strummed and sang the old Tex Williams song "Smoke! Smoke! Smoke! (That Cigarette)."

"And now," the ringmaster announced, "the Amazing Alien."

She stepped forward, fetchingly attired in a miniskirt, billowing white blouse tied high above her midriff, and oversized red heart-shaped sun-glasses.

The ringmaster winked as he made certain the audience got a good look at a half-inch-thick plywood board, two feet wide and five and a half feet long.

Protruding from the board, an inch apart from one another, were approximately fifteen hundred eight-inch nails, pointy ends gleaming.

"Sleeping Beauty," he declared, gesturing toward Alien, "and," drawing attention back to the prop before him, "the Bed of Nails." He laid it on the ground, nails up.

From a dainty crouch, "Sleeping Beauty" prepared to settle down on her back for her rest. The engineer in her knew the secret to the stunt: since only one fifteen hundredth or so of her weight rested on any single nail, she'd be fine. The sensation, Alien had found, practicing by The Island's garden, was like floating on a sea of toothpicks. But she made a big deal out of holding her breath along with the audience, and then grimaced before breaking out into a huge smile.

"*Amazing* indeed!" The ringmaster egged on the clapping crowd.

The act wasn't finished. Grinning devilishly, he presented another board, half the length of the first, filled with another thousand nails. This the ringmaster placed on Alien's stomach and chest, sandwiching her between the spikes.

Keep smiling, Alien told herself. The top plank rose and fell as she breathed in and out.

The ringmaster covered Alien's face with a pillow. On the top plank of nails, mid-chest height, he placed with exaggerated effort a thirty-pound cinder block. And then, Alien knew but could not see, he lifted a sledgehammer by the handle.

The ringmaster swung, smashing the cinder block to bits — and dissipating the force of the hammer's blow. He lifted the top board with a flourish, and Alien gracefully leaped up to wild applause.

—◆—

Alien was the youngest resident of The Island and — with a salary of $3,200 a month — made more than twice as much as anyone else. The housemate she became closest to was the oldest, the carpenter, Piñon. Part Hispanic, part Native American, he was somewhere in his early fifties, about the same height as Alien, with nut-brown skin, wiry white hair, a bushy salt-and-pepper mustache, and round frameless glasses.

Following Piñon's example, Alien started smoking Eagle 20's Menthol Gold cigarettes. They grabbed green chili burritos together and spent free weekends hanging out, him taking her fishing, her taking him to cruise for fashion finds at Goodwill. Twice married and divorced, with two adult sons and a Zen demeanor, Piñon was very different from anyone Alien had encountered before. A typical tech guy, if he socialized at all, might loudly explain to you what he knew and you didn't. Piñon spoke seldom, and quietly. When he did, he was insightful and funny.

One day, a friend of Piñon's offered to hook him up with an old black Yamaha motorcycle. Alien clambered onto the back of the black leather dual seat for the test ride. Piñon donned the same safety goggles he used when machining wood. Neither of them wore a helmet, but Alien took comfort in Piñon's casualness and a half-inch-wide strip of pale pink skin, visibly distinct from the darker hue of the rest of his body, running from neck to waist below his T-shirt. Scar tissue, she felt in this case, meant wisdom of experience. The dividing line between recklessness and the rewards of taking risks.

The engine started. Vibrations shook her from the rear foot pegs: ankle to calf, calf to thigh, thigh to ass. "Hang on tight," Piñon said. They shot off loudly. Alien looked down and saw black asphalt spinning wildly beneath her like the end of an old movie reel. By the time she looked up again, trees blurred beside them. Street signs. Rooftops. It felt as if they'd been shot out of a cannon, hurtling through the air entirely exposed. She loved it.

Wind whipped her hair, fresh purple-painted highlights stabbing backward ten inches behind her.

"That was so *awesome*," Alien exclaimed at the end of the ride.

Piñon's reply, when it came, was so soft she had to ask him twice to repeat it.

"You should get a motorcycle too, sweetie," he said.

Alien's bike, bought used for eighteen hundred dollars — a steal — was a red Honda Nighthawk 750. Alien nicknamed it Pepper. By mid-July, after taking a fifteen-hour motorcycle safety course, she had her license. To celebrate, Alien and Piñon rode to a bike shop, where she purchased a pretty silver Arai helmet, and the local Harley-Davidson dealer for black leather boots, riding pants, and two jackets — one regular, which she lent Piñon, and one with zip-off sleeves, for herself.

"Want to ride up to Taos?" Piñon asked. Their route would be a fifty-six-mile scenic byway.

"Sure!" Alien grinned, arms bared, as she shifted into first gear. She closed the throttle with her right hand and then, with her left, pulled in the clutch while toeing downward on the shifter. Slowly trading clutch for throttle, she felt the 470-pound machine beneath her lurch forward with a sudden upsurge in its throaty baseline hum.

Leaving parking lot for street, Alien upshifted, and then again when she reached the U.S. 285 on-ramp, and again a third time hitting the highway itself. Still, cars and trucks whooshed by on all sides. Each time, Alien's bike wobbled and shook, which, in spite of all the physical risks she had taken at MIT, she found terrifying. The New Mexico highway seemed far more hazardous than the rooftops and hidden recesses of the Institute. As a novice, she had uncertain control of the motorcycle. And she had no control at all over the other vehicles. "If they accidentally try to move into your lane," Piñon had said, "kick their door."

Alien forced herself to accelerate into fifth gear, as Piñon, visible just behind her in her mirror, nodded encouragingly. Wind whistled. The engine whined. Right and left of the road, grassy dirt gave way to low green brush and cloud-topped mesas.

Twenty miles in, U.S. 285 met New Mexico 503 in Pojoaque, followed by New Mexico 76 near Chimayó, elevation 6,050 feet. Into the Sangre de Cristo Mountains they climbed, past Córdova (6,950 feet) and Truchas (8,050 feet), among a half-dozen other tiny villages, each with its own artistic specialty — painting, pottery, jewelry, rugs, woodcarving, basket weaving — and centuries-old hand-hewn church. Ponderosa pines and other evergreens hugged the highway now. Far-off mountain peaks appeared to be at eye level. Clouds overhead, cool and smooth as scoops of vanilla ice cream, seemed close enough to touch. The exhaust from hundreds of woodstove heaters filled the air with a roasted-marshmallow aroma.

Dogs barked. Ravens honked. Pickup trucks whizzed past. The road wound, black arrows in bright yellow signs pointing out a new turn every twenty seconds.

Alien took a deep breath, trying to relax despite a necessary alertness to her and other drivers' every possible fuckup. Veer left accidentally, across the center line, and she'd hit oncoming vehicles or the rock walls behind them. Veer right and it was into tree trunks. Stare too long at the distant snow-capped peaks and she'd flip over the metal guardrail, fall off the edge of a cliff, or — maximum irony — impale herself on one of the many garlanded crosses commemorating a previous roadside death.

Eyes forward, keeping pace with traffic, no more, no less, Alien led them into Taos.

⟢⟡⟣

Drinks followed. A leisurely lunch facing the tree-lined Taos Plaza, serenaded by two street musicians, a guitar and a double bass. "There's a jail under the plaza," said Piñon.

"Really?" said Alien. "How do you know?"

"I was locked up in there. Back when I was just a kid. I raised hell. Drinking."

Afterward, Piñon ducked into a little shop for coffee. Alien sipped free cucumber water. By the time they turned back, it was half past five p.m.

The ride home was different. Much harder. Taking New Mexico 68, they followed the Rio Grande as it dropped into a narrow canyon. Pepper zipped downhill, but surrounding vehicles seemed faster, closer, and far more numerous.

Alien cringed, braking reflexively at every corner, unable to see what was around a bend until she was upon it. WATCH FOR ROCKS, said the sign fronting high cliffs hemming her in on her right. To her left, oncoming cars and trucks sometimes edged over the center line. Bullying crosswinds over the arroyo seemed to want to lift her up and off the motorcycle as she flashed by roadside cross after roadside cross, bedecked with beads, flowers, photos, and even shiny sequins, reflecting the glare of the orange sun.

It was now ninety-five degrees out. Alien sweated, fingers stiff, shoulders locked. Her arms, unused to long exposure, burned. Cars honked, trapped behind her on the pass. Still, Alien couldn't bring herself to edge over and risk spilling on loose gravel, or speed up from her twenty-, twenty-five-miles-per-hour crawl to the posted limits of forty-five, fifty.

I can do it, she told herself, only half-convinced.

Piñon pulled alongside her as soon as the road widened to two lanes.

"There's a casino ahead," he mouthed. "Stop there."

Hot pink and turquoise green neon lights blinked in the casino parking lot. Piñon dismounted and went into the casino without a word. Alien could tell he was frustrated.

After a few minutes, she followed inside. Alien found him feeding dollar bills into a slot machine, one by one. She sat next to him. "I'm sorry," Alien said. "I don't know why I'm so scared."

Piñon sat looking at the slot machine for a few moments. Then he turned to her. "Your motorcycle is better than mine," he said. "It's not safe for you to slow down while you're turning. You have to get comfortable pushing it. That's what riding it means." He paused before continuing. "Let's practice tonight. Okay, sweetie?"

Alien nodded, helmet hugged against her chest.

The tutorial began at two a.m. in an empty Albertsons parking lot near The Island. Piñon mounted Pepper. Alien got on behind and wrapped her arms around his slender torso.

There was no warm-up. Piñon gunned directly toward the thick concrete base of a towering black metal lamppost. He twisted the throttle, sending the speed and rpm gauges sharply to the right.

Alien locked her thighs and dug her nails in his leather jacket.

She screamed and found herself suddenly crying, begging him, "Stop! Please!" at the top of her lungs.

One foot, two feet, three feet, four — the gray base of the lamppost appeared to thicken as they approached.

At the last instant, Piñon cut left, hard. The bike bowed way over, so that Alien was sure her elbow and ribs were only inches from the asphalt. Tears clouded her vision.

They righted briefly, spun around, and slalomed a wooden power line pole, two silver metal cart-return corrals, and a yellow fire hydrant, before attacking the lamppost again.

"See?" Piñon said in his quiet voice when they were finished. "Your bike is capable of so much. But you have to accelerate if you don't want to fall."

Alien's arms trembled as she took the handlebars once more herself. Sitting behind Piñon, she must have gripped the exhaust pipe with her boot, she realized, for the heel had melted off.

"Okay," she said faintly. Alien took a deep breath. "Yes. Got it."

"Good," replied Piñon, and then he sidled onto the bike behind her. "Okay," he said gently. "Now it's your turn. Take us home."

<hr />

Alien roared out of The Island's ribbon-shaped dirt driveway on Pepper one morning two weeks later, accelerating out of every curve on the way to work. She had nowhere near Piñon's expertise as yet, but with every ride she was getting closer. When she arrived at the lab, someone's gray Toyota Camry had taken her imaginary parking space. Alien laughed. *A station wagon is tough. A bike is easy.* She "invented" a new spot on the other side of the lot.

That afternoon, Jake paid a visit to the mezzanine. "There's a journal with a special issue on gamma ray bursts coming out soon," he told Alien. "Do you want to publish an article about the software you're developing here?"

The buzz was instantaneous. As was her assent.

Alien set to work right away, organizing her ideas until five p.m., when she ran into an unexpected interruption. She was still on the MIT Senior House group email list, which had erupted into a flame war when a sophomore equated Israel to Nazi Germany. As someone taught constantly as a child about the horrors of the Holocaust, Alien couldn't let that pass in silence. Others responded in kind, and she followed the back-and-forth another hour, until it was time again to join the harriers.

On the trail that night, David slipped, sprained his ankle, and was told in the emergency room that he would have to walk on crutches for the next five weeks. When Alien drove the two of them to work the next morning, both old and new imaginary parking spots were taken, and they had to make the long limp together from the overflow lot.

It was a quarter after eleven when she finally got to her computer.

Her login didn't work.

"Does yours?" she asked David.

He nodded.

Alien called IT.

"I don't know what happened to your account," the lady who answered told her. "It's not there anymore."

Alien hung up. She remembered keywords from yesterday's heated exchange.

Terror networks.

Massacre. Subvert. Survival.

Uncle Sam. Israel.

Nukes.

Her connection to MIT was encrypted, but she speculated that the lab's internal security office took the additional step of monitoring everything employees physically typed for certain keywords.

Now someone would have to find her logged keystrokes, read them, and realize Alien was just in a harmless argument with friends before she was cleared to work again.

"Jake?" Alien called her boss.

"What's up, kid?" he asked.

"I'm *missing*," she said.

———✦———

Whatever Jake told the powers that be, by the afternoon Alien's lab account was restored as mysteriously as it had been deleted. Meanwhile, the gamma ray journal deadline loomed. Mid-morning Tuesday, August 12, three days before the due date for submissions, Alien let out a hearty "Hallelujah!" to see an actual available parking space at work. She toted grocery bags of frozen food from her car to the office kitchen, planning to hole up all week, if necessary, until her paper was completed. U.S. GOV'T PROPERTY, FOOD ONLY/NO CHEMICALS/NO RADIOACTIVE MATERIALS, said signs on the white Frigidaire.

Alien wrote at her desk for fifteen hours, ate in front of the microwave for fifteen minutes, and then slept four hours on a clear plastic inflatable couch in a corner of the mezzanine. She woke and wrote, ate and slept, and woke to write again.

As Alien worked early Thursday afternoon, she saw messages on her MIT account from Marie and others on the I/S network security team. A serious new Windows worm—Blaster—was attacking computers across the country. Ten thousand machines at MIT were vulnerable. And infection rates had spiked from two or three systems an hour to one every fifty-five seconds. *Come in if you can!* Marie wrote everyone. *It's all hands on deck to help.*

"This is incredible," Alien said, realizing how stressed everyone must be.

"I know," said David.

He did? How? "Are you talking about Blaster?" Alien asked him.

"No—I don't think so," David said. He'd just checked the news online. "There's a big blackout in the Northeast."

"What city?" said Alien.

"Entire *states*," David answered. "Ohio. New York. Michigan. New Jersey," he read the list aloud.

"*All* New York? *All* New Jersey?" Alien stood. Was it terrorism? The worm? Both?

David shrugged. "All this article says is that it's *spreading*."

Alien scanned his screen, making out scattered phrases: "cascading failure," "widespread blackout," "millions without power." Her parents and many of her friends must be affected.

Power returned to much of the Northeast by late evening, news outlets reported. An alarm system malfunction leading to overloaded transmission lines caused the blackout, they said. But what caused the alarm system malfunction? It might have been Blaster, thought Alien. In any case, the worm had to have distracted authorities during the first stages of the power failure and then complicated efforts to get things back online.

If she were still on the MIT network security team, maybe she could have detected the worm before it got out of hand.

———◆———

Four p.m. Friday, after three straight days in the office, Alien submitted her finished paper. She staggered outside in the dry heat.

She searched for her car and stopped.

It had moved. This entire section of the parking lot. Or, rather, the chain-link fence beside it had. Tuesday morning, the eight-foot-tall barrier had been five feet behind her Volvo. Now, Friday afternoon, it was five feet *in front* of it. Her car was trapped on the other side.

Alien walked straight up to the fence. She peered through the translucent green mesh canvas covering and then up at three rows of razor wire. Alien then followed the brand-new fence perimeter to a brand-new checkpoint protected by four security police in camo.

Metal glinted in their hands. Each held a black assault rifle.

"That's my car," Alien said, pointing. A turkey vulture, visible through the slats in the razor wire, spread its wings and let the wind carry it east.

"May I see ID?" one of the officers asked.

Alien offered him her badge.

"Sorry," he said, checking it. "You don't have requisite clearance."

She could bring proof of ownership or come back under escort by a higher-up.

———◆———

The turnstile was bad enough. Having her car impounded at the place where she worked so hard was too much. Alien was sick of clearances. That night she read an email invitation to a party thrown by her old poker night friends in their apartment and felt a pang of longing to join them.

Eight months earlier, all Alien had wanted to do was escape MIT. Now she told Jake and David that she missed Boston and was going to go home.

Marie would hire her, she knew. And with her talents, there would surely be other options in a high-tech place like Boston.

But she wanted to go back on her terms, and she wasn't the same Alien who had left.

"I'm going to take the motorcycle," she announced to Piñon.

"You're crazy," he told her. Santa Fe to Boston was almost 2,400 miles. "You're still learning how to ride."

"I'll learn more by doing," Alien said.

He shook his head. But as she wrapped up at the lab and moved her things to storage—she'd fly back and get them and her car the weekend of Piñon's birthday, October 22, she'd decided—he helped prep both their bikes. "I'll ride with you," he declared.

"Deal," said Alien. She'd pay for gas and hotel rooms. And afterward Piñon would visit one of his sons, who lived in New York City.

Piñon hedged, however, as the date got closer, saying he wasn't sure. Now Alien was starting to feel nervous. She hoped he would come but didn't want to pressure him.

Sunday, the morning of her departure, Alien woke at seven a.m., ate her breakfast, and then carried a mug of black coffee to the side porch, where Piñon was smoking and replenishing the nectar in a red hummingbird feeder.

"An opening bribe," Alien said, passing him the cup. "Or is this good-bye?"

Piñon drank between drags, typically silent. Then he walked to his room and retrieved a camouflage-patterned heavy-duty travel pack patched with duct tape, which he tossed on the back of his black Yamaha.

"All right!" Alien said.

They rolled off, trailing dust, and onto the open road.

08

A Hackable Heart Transplant

A LIEN RETURNED TO CAMBRIDGE in September 2003 and rejoined the MIT network security team. After Jake's tutelage at Los Alamos and months of work on her project there, she could match UNIX skills and computer programming chops with anyone. Working in MIT's IT department was no longer a temporary gig, a way to cover expenses and complete an interesting research project en route to graduation. Alien now had the authority and responsibility to safeguard one of the world's foremost computing environments.

When she arrived, the Institute was still dealing with the fallout of Blaster and related worms that took advantage of similar vulnerabilities. The expense of cleaning up affected machines and recovering data ran about a million dollars, not counting the collateral costs of computer downtime during the crisis and the irrecoverable loss of many files. As soon as possible, Alien rewrote NetVision so she could see even more with it. Then she reviewed what had happened and began formulating a strategic plan for how the network security team should respond to large-scale emergencies in the future.

As this planning was taking place, new leaders with their own ideas took over Information Services. They merged it with other organizational units at MIT, renamed the new entity Information Systems and Technology, and installed a corporate culture, including a nine-to-five workday and dress code. A rumor spread that soon employees would have to wear branded baseball caps, like fast food workers. Several of the colleagues Alien respected most, people who had worked there for decades, specifically because they wanted to be at MIT instead of a place like IBM, were pushed out or quit. These were people who had constructed extraordinary systems like Athena.

Marie left in 2004. Alien stayed on several more months, until a meeting with her new boss. Success, going forward, would be measured by counting the number of closed CaseTracker cases, he said.

"That's not a real security improvement," Alien objected. "Most of our open cases come from automated warnings—they might be nothing. A better metric would be the number of active cases, and then what's a priority among them."

The man's face turned red. "If you keep interrupting people, one day somebody's going to slap you!" he said.

Alien felt personally threatened—and by the man she was supposed to go to for help if she was harassed. She was sure he would never have said that to someone older than her, or to a male employee of any age.

She quit.

———✦———

Alien started scanning postings for technical jobs. Security-specific listings were rare, but in May 2005 a want ad from the IT department at Mayflower Hospital, building its information security team, caught her eye. Alien applied. When they called for an interview, she was taking no chances. She put on her most professional outfit, a fitted suit and black heels, and prepped by reading a book called *60 Seconds & You're Hired*.

That afternoon, she steered Pepper through Boston city traffic, the tips of her heels barely touching the ground when she drew to a stop in a free space between a couple of parked cars. Alien dismounted, removed her silver helmet, and straightened the suit jacket. Before she crossed the street to her appointment, she touched her index finger to an embossed metal charm tied by its chain to the bike's dashboard, between the ignition switch and the speedometer. It had been given to her by her Santa Fe housemate and fellow circus performer, the fire artist.

BELIEVE, the charm said, below a bald, bug-eyed ovoid figure of—what else—an alien.

An hour later, she had the job.

———✦———

Mayflower was huge—a vast interconnected complex, like a college campus, built up steadily over a century, and now taking up most of three city blocks. In its annual report, the hospital noted that it served more than 300,000 people a year. Yet the entire six-story building in which Alien worked housed no medical equipment, no doctors, no nurses, and no patients.

This was the hospital's IT center, responsible for all its computers and computer networks.

At first, Alien was surprised that a hospital could be as reliant on fiber optic networks as on intravenous tubing. But hospitals, behind their human dramas, ran on data, she came to recognize. One critical computer system, for example, registered patients for admission, discharge, and transfer. Another stored medical records, clinician notes, and prescriptions. A third kept all the imaging: X-rays, MRIs, ultrasounds, you name it.

There were billing systems with patient payment and insurance information. Clinical systems specific to allergy or urology, cardiothoracic surgery or pediatric dentistry. The hospital's internal email system, its remote login system, and shared workstations, just like at MIT.

Alien's position was in information security—often shortened to InfoSec. Their job was not to run any of these systems, each of which was managed by its own team, but to protect them all.

There was pushback, however. As at MIT, people saw security measures as nuisances. Until they needed them.

The first Monday in November, five months into the job, Alien entered through a side door, said hi to the guard, and placed the lanyard holding her employee badge around her neck. Across the street a food truck pulled up, as it did every weekday at nine a.m., emitting the strange fluttering horn that let her know she was late.

When the elevator to the second floor opened, Chris, the leader of the hospital UNIX team, was standing right there, obviously waiting for her. Thirty-two years old, balding but not yet committed to a shaved head, he wore a comb-over and brown plastic-framed glasses, a beige sweater, and wrinkled corduroys.

"You took my servers down this weekend with your AutoAudit script," he said, referring to a program she had written to scan his systems for thousands of known security holes.

Alien pinched her eyes shut in exhaustion. Her natural bedtime was still what others would call the middle of the night. She would never be good at mornings.

"The AutoAudit script wasn't even running this weekend, Chris," Alien said.

Chris glowered. "This isn't over," he said.

"Fine." Alien walked down the hall to her cubicle and logged in to her computer, using her hospital-assigned username, "gk229120." Although she was only twenty-four years old, she already had two stints on the MIT network security team and her period in the nuclear nonproliferation and international security division at Los Alamos behind her. At the same time, the hospital was her first job independent of any MIT connection, and, in that sense, her first in the "real world."

"Eleven years, two months, a week, and four days." Harry, the silver-haired data center manager, stood behind her, offering his daily update of how much time remained until his retirement. He paused for effect before continuing. "And seven hours, forty-four minutes, and eleven seconds."

Alien let herself laugh, as Harry intended. It was a joke between them. *Beigeworld,* they called the office.

"Lunch?" Harry whispered.

She nodded.

Alien typed, toggling back and forth between emailed problem reports and more proactive measures like AutoAudit.

At noon, she saw Harry stand, carrying a heavy winter coat under one arm out the door. As he looked back, Alien nodded, indicating she'd meet him in a few minutes at the end of the employee parking lot. She was just wrapping things up on her computer when she heard her desk phone ring.

I'm going to kill Chris, Alien thought.

The caller wasn't Chris, though. It was another colleague, Amy, from the network team.

"We're having a bandwidth issue," she said. "It's completely clogging the network. And we can't isolate the source."

Alien heard the urgency in Amy's voice. "Be right there," she said.

"Rain check," she texted Harry as her pulse took a pleasing jump.

<hr/>

Amy was a lanky brunette, twenty-seven or twenty-eight, dressed in jeans and a teal pullover. Alien knelt beside her in her cubicle as they studied network traffic information from Internet addresses across the hospital.

"We started getting calls two to three hours ago saying the Internet was slow," Amy told her. "I checked it out, and they're right: some internal address is just *spewing* traffic."

"It's got to be a worm," Alien said. "Can you shut off the port?"

"I could, but I don't know what's plugged into it," Amy said. "What if it's an important machine? I don't want to just cut it off."

"Let me see," Alien said. She stepped up to the keyboard and scrolled back through Amy's command history, double-checking her investigation. Amy was a pro, though: on the basis of the Internet address alone, the closest they could do was trace the worm's origin point to a third-floor hallway in the same building that held the Mayflower ER.

Alien's eyes narrowed. The fatigue was gone.

"Stay here—I'll find it," she said.

Alien ran to the elevator, popped outside, and cut diagonally across the May-flower campus. Seven minutes later, wide sliding doors separated for her at the entrance to the ER.

Alien passed the sick and injured, spread across three large first-floor waiting rooms. She flashed her badge and entered a room of curtained individual treatment areas. Inside, she focused not on the patients but on the array of blinking and humming devices everywhere around them.

A beefy middle-aged construction worker, accompanied by two others in his crew, one still in his hard hat, was hooked to an infusion pump while he waited for someone to stitch his bloodied forehead. A little girl with a swollen arm, her hand on her chest, and a frightened look in her eyes as she was comforted by her mother, was having her heart examined with an electrocardiograph. An electronic respirator delivered oxygen to the mask over the mouth of an elderly man who lay unconscious, as his desolate wife sat beside him. And wired to a vital signs machine measuring body temperature, blood pressure, heart rate, and blood oxygen saturation was a young pregnant woman.

Alien grimaced. Each patient bed had multiple devices beside it. Anything with a plug probably included a computer chip—and almost as likely, Alien thought, a network card. For maintenance, maybe. Or data sharing. Or as an untapped, even unnecessary "feature" about which the sales rep could still boast. If she didn't identify the culprit for the worm quickly, any of these devices could become infected.

Alien rushed forward, past an anesthesiology machine (a computer), two nurses' stations (twelve computers), and around a thick-walled glassed-off area holding a CT scanner (yet another computer). Ideally the hospital would have a complete map of Internet addresses by room and specific port on the wall as well as floor of the building. But that level of coordination was a fantasy even at a technical university like MIT or a military and scientific research site like Los Alamos. Instead, people went online as they could, installing equipment as they went, and IT discovered unregistered machines only when they presented problems.

The one way Alien could hope to track down the infected machine was to head upstairs to the hall she and Amy had identified, check the closet there that held a network switch, and hope the equipment was well labeled.

—⟡—

Amy had called ahead for backup. An IT staffer assigned to this building met Alien at the third-floor elevator and showed her to the right switch. It serviced a long, quiet hallway. By now, Alien had burned almost half an hour. But she was getting closer.

Back out on the hallway, Alien stopped in front of the only door in sight. Doctors and nurses swished past. Alien stepped back, feeling out of place without a white coat or scrubs. When a nurse slowed before the door, however, Alien flagged her down.

"Hi, I'm from IT security," she said, and showed her badge. "I need to get in here."

"Oh." The nurse swiped her own badge and the door clicked open. "I'll have to accompany you," she warned. "This is a restricted area."

—⟡—

The room was warm and dark. Alien could make out a few rows of what appeared to be high, narrow carts on wheels, each with a monitor nearby. It was vaguely reminiscent of a server room. But her entire concern was with the network ports located close to the floor. Alien dropped to a crawl. Using the same Maglite she'd had since her freshman year at MIT, she swept the walls, looking for the guilty port.

Twenty seconds passed. Forty. Sixty. Finally, Alien's beam illuminated a yellow plastic port cover to which someone with a label maker had attached the alphanumeric name of the infected machine.

Alien smiled in triumph and relief. She used the Maglite to trace the black Ethernet cord coming out of the port. It led to a profusion of other plugs and cables entering the back of the machine closest to her.

She'd page Amy, and Amy would alert both their bosses. They'd get the problem diagnosed as soon as possible—before the machine infected anything again.

Alien stood up. She felt the nurse touching her back gently, to get her attention without speaking.

"Turn that flashlight off, please," she asked in a low but firm whisper. It was more a command than a request.

Alien obeyed. She felt a sense of alarm, even dread. Had she done something wrong? Where were they? There weren't any patients in this room, she had thought; it had no beds, only more machines like this one. Her senses suddenly heightened, however, she now heard the sound of slow breathing all around her.

For the first time since her eyes became accustomed to the dark, Alien took a look around the room. On each of the wheeled stands was a tiny pallet enclosed by clear plastic.

The pallets, she saw now, held tiny blankets. And under each blanket was a baby. A tiny one, sprawled out on its back and head turned to one side, all wired up. These newborns were essentially on life support, and fast asleep.

The room might resemble a server room, Alien realized. But it wasn't. It was the NICU—the neonatal intensive care unit.

"Babies," she said to herself.

Alien walked slowly back to Beigeworld, having remembered why she was here.

<hr />

About the same time she started work at the hospital, Alien had moved into a large three-story Victorian house turned commune in western Cambridge called Fireberry Manor, shared by a dozen people, all MIT graduates and their friends. The Sunday night after tracing the worm to the NICU, she led a new boyfriend to her room on the top floor.

At three a.m., just as the two of them were settling into bed, a friend and Warehouse resident called her.

"Did you hear about Frostbyte?" he said.

⸺⬥⸺

Alien went straight to the Warehouse after work on Tuesday. She ducked yellow police tape over the big metal door and walked through familiar, once enchanting rooms, suddenly empty except for broken glass, splintered wood, and scattered clothes. It felt so surreal, and so sad. The light walls and sculptures, custom turntables and speakers, secret freezer and one-of-a-kind furniture—all were gone.

One man called to another on the street below. Alien froze in front of a huge freight elevator, painted in slashing black and bright yellow stripes, ready to run if she heard footsteps. Less than seventy-two hours ago, while she snuggled in bed with her boyfriend, Frostbyte had collapsed during sex. His boyfriend called 911 while roommates contacted friends. Already, though, Frostbyte was dead and the police, who saw the entire site as an underground designer drug lab, had seized or destroyed almost everything. Violently.

The voices passed. Alien walked slowly through the empty halls, hearing only the sound of her footsteps crushing broken glass. All along, the Warehouse had been a squat. After the police raid, anyone who'd lived there risked arrest. Not just a life, but also a community, had been annihilated.

At the open door to the room of the friend who'd called her, she smelled dusty flaking paint. On the floor was the body of an orchid, its green leaves limply spread across broken glass and packed soil.

Alien scooped it up, cradled it in a scarf, and carried it home.

⸺⬥⸺

Eight weeks later, early January 2006, Grant, the InfoSec team leader, surveyed the room at an information security team morning meeting. Five ten, trim, in his late thirties, he wore a black suit and a yellow-and-black-gridded tie. His staff was a short, plump fifty-something woman from South Boston, responsible for all user account setup; a buzz-cut army reserve officer in his mid-thirties, who worked with Alien on UNIX security issues; their skinny Windows security lead, only a year or two older than Alien; and Alien herself.

"In February, the entire hospital is switching from traditional phone service to VoIP"—Voice over Internet Protocol—Grant said. "What's the potential impact?"

The Windows security lead spoke up first. "What isn't?" he said drily.

Because medical equipment was so expensive, hospitals expected devices to last fifteen to twenty years. What was brand-new in 2006 would still be in service in 2021. Once VoIP became the standard office phone setup, they'd have to make sure it didn't break anything else, now and for at least the next two decades.

"Be specific," Grant prodded.

"They fax prescriptions, don't they?" the guy said. "We need to keep those protected."

"Docs use the phones to make transplant orders," said the woman responsible for user accounts. In her Southie accent, "orders" was "awdahs."

"In the wards, the phones are like walkie-talkies," said Alien's colleague on the UNIX side. "Lose them and no one could communicate."

Grant nodded. "And that's just for starters. Well, who wants to look into it?" he asked.

Alien had her hand up for a few seconds before she realized that she was the only one.

⟨⟩

Alien threw herself into the research. Ensuring higher-level security at the hospital meant more than cleaning up messes, or vetting existing systems with AutoAudit. Ideally, InfoSec would test new technology *before* it was put in place. To do that, you had to hack.

Now, she had her chance.

Amy, who had helped Alien track the worm, opened for her presentation a week later. The meeting room was now crowded with the hospital's entire Windows, UNIX, network, and information security teams. "Voice over IP is voice data converted to digital format," Amy began. "It's encapsulated in IP" —Internet Protocol—"packets and transmitted across the network."

Amy continued. "This is what all office phones will be soon, the same way cell phones are replacing landlines. The promise is, now you can change offices, take your phone with you, plug it into a computer, and it will work instantly—just like email," she said. "Adding new numbers is just as easy. And going through the Internet, not phone lines, saves Mayflower a lot of money."

On a wall monitor behind her, Amy showed diagrams of the new phones, using a demo model plugged into the presentation laptop as a point of reference.

"VoIP works by dividing a single network line into separate virtual domains, one for regular data traffic and one for phone data," she explained. "You know which is which because phone data is 'tagged' as such. In theory, then, only other phones can receive it."

Chris, the UNIX team leader, crossed his arms. "In theory?" he said.

Alien took this as her cue and stood. "I'm coming at it from the bad guy's perspective," she said, taking over at the presentation laptop and flicking to a new slide. "VoIP Security," it said. "C-I-A."

The acronym was InfoSec 101. Alien had picked it up at work at MIT. "That's *confidentiality*—can I eavesdrop on calls, monitor conversations in a room, or track phone calls?" she continued. "*Integrity*—can I modify phone calls or spoof caller ID? And *availability*—can I disrupt the phone system, spam people with it, or steal free phone calls?"

She opened a free Windows program called Cain and Abel, described by its developer as a "password recovery tool." Alien clicked once to start its "Sniffer" function—a Mood Ring for the masses in that it secretly recorded network traffic.

"Does anyone have a cell phone handy?" she asked.

One of the Windows team members waved his.

"Here's the phone number," Alien said, passing him a piece of paper.

He dialed. The demo VoIP phone rang and Alien answered.

"Hello?" she said.

"Hey," the guy said awkwardly.

"Tell me you're pregnant," said Alien.

"I'm pregnant," he repeated as everyone else chuckled.

They hung up and Alien showed Cain and Abel's running count of captured packets.

"So, yes, I can record conversations on any phone attached to my computer," she said. "And so could any spyware."

Alien switched back to her presentation, advancing to the next slide. "*Recommendation*," it said. "*Don't use the Access port on the phone.*" Demonstrating, Alien unplugged the phone from her computer, connecting it to a nearby VoIP-enabled wall jack instead.

"Don't worry—we're still not done eavesdropping," she said.

People chuckled again but looked at one another uneasily as Alien ran another free program, Nmap, short for "network mapper." This returned a list of every device online and any open network ports—designated back doors for specific services like email or Web browsing—on each.

"Here," said Alien, pointing to two lines on the wall monitor:

```
PORT STATE SERVICE VERSION
80/tcp open http Cisco IP Phone Conference Station
```

"As you can see, every single phone has a Web server," said Alien. "Let's see why." She opened a Web browser window and typed the address.

"Device Information," "Network Configuration," "Device Logs," the resulting Web page menu offered.

"With the right username and password, anyone, anywhere on the Internet, can log in, change settings, divert traffic, or shut it down," Alien summarized. She paged to the next slide in her presentation. "*Recommendation*," it said. "*Disable Web servers on phones.*"

"Now how about the call manager?" asked Alien, meaning the larger phone system gateway. She returned to Nmap, scrolling through results until she reached the following:

```
PORT STATE SERVICE VERSION
80/tcp open http Microsoft IIS webserver 5.0
102/tcp open iso-tsap?
135/tcp open msrpc Microsoft Windows RPC
139/tcp open netbios-ssn
443/tcp open https?
445/tcp open microsoft-ds Microsoft Windows 2000
   microsoft-ds
1433/tcp open ms-sql-s?
1720/tcp open H.323/Q.931?
2000/tcp open callbook?
2001/tcp open dc?
2002/tcp open globe?
2301/tcp open http Compaq Insight Manager HTTP server 5.3
```

```
3389/tcp open microsoft-rdp Microsoft Terminal Service
5800/tcp open vnc-http WinVNC
5900/tcp open vnc VNC
```

"That's *fifteen* open ports," Alien counted. "Each one needs to be turned off or secured. As is, I can download, delete, or change any phone's configuration file."

"*Recommendations*," said the next slide. "*Turn off unnecessary services. Use secure protocols. Lock the system down.*"

Alien pointed to another laptop plugged into the port next to the one in which she had connected her phone. "This is my own unregistered Linux laptop," she said. "It's never had a phone plugged into it. But while Amy was explaining VoIP to you, I ran another program, vconfig, to tag *it* as the call manager."

Alien opened the laptop and showed everyone a series of short commands typed earlier onscreen. "Here it's saying, 'Hey, everyone—send all your traffic to me,'" she said. Alien demonstrated two more programs, Ettercap and Ethereal. "This whole time," she said, "I've been collecting the stream of data as it comes and picking out the voice traffic."

Last, she ran VOMIT—"Voice over Misconfigured Internet Telephones," Alien decoded the cheeky acronym. "This converts captured VoIP packets to an audio format," she said.

Alien typed again and a recording played on the tinny laptop speakers. It was the Windows team member from a few minutes earlier: "I'm pregnant."

"Congratulations," joked Alien. She continued. "Theoretically, you can turn on speakerphone and record conversations in any room. Reverse the process and you can take over someone's line with prerecorded messages. Flood the system and you get an easy DOS"—denial of service—"attack. Like this."

She typed. The conference room phone rang and Grant reached to answer it.

"Check the caller ID first," Alien interrupted him.

Grant did. "George W. Bush," he read, frowning.

"Busy man." Alien typed again. The ringing stopped.

"Do you have your cell phone?" she asked Grant.

"Yes."

Alien passed him the piece of paper with the assigned phone number written on it. "When you get the voice mail, try to leave a message."

Grant dialed. The demo phone rang again.

"Hello," he said stiffly, a few seconds later. "This is—"

Alien interceded, typing a command to barrage the call manager with thousands of instantaneous messages, to the point where it was overwhelmed.

Grant stopped.

"What happened?" asked the Windows team member who had volunteered earlier.

Grant replied softly, eyebrows arched in a wry expression. "It hung up," he said.

"Say you're a heart transplant patient," Alien said. "There's a donor match, but your surgeon can't get or receive the call."

Thirteen more recommendations followed.

"Jesus," Chris said, taking notes. "This makes everything else you've bothered us about look easy."

Alien smiled. "I'll take that as a compliment," she said.

⬥

The phone presentation impressed Grant, who put Alien in charge of developing the hospital's first formal information security incident response policy. But before she finished it, he summoned her to his office for something entirely different.

Grant waited guardedly for Alien to enter before asking her to close the door behind her. "New case," he said, handing her a manila folder. "Sorry."

Alien opened it, and then looked away instinctively as she paged through a thick stack of color photos printed on eight-and-a-half-by-eleven-inch printer paper.

In the first photo, two very well-constructed nude women were trying on high heels in a mirrored dressing room. In the second, cheerleaders were engaged in a gymnastic routine as lewd as it was athletic. In the third, a famous singer and her boyfriend were making the most of a cove that evidently had been less secluded than they thought.

"A nurse on the cancer wards turned these in," Grant said. "She says their printer is infected. Whenever she reloads the paper in the morning, this stuff starts spooling out. What do you think?"

"This happens repeatedly?" Alien asked.

"Every morning for the past five," he said.

Alien sighed. "How much—er—*material* does it print?"

"Thirty, forty pictures. Sometimes more. Once one hundred," Grant told her. "Why?"

Alien tapped her chin, thinking. "Tell me," she said a moment later, "does it happen *only* when the nurse puts new paper in?"

Grant nodded. "That's the other thing. It's always out of paper when she gets there," he said.

"Give me a couple of hours," Alien said. "I think I know what's going on."

—————

Bordering Beigeworld was a black metal barrier: the entrance to the hospital data center, where fans whirred loudly, circulating air to cool nine hundred computer servers. Alien swiped her badge and the heavy door clicked open. Immediately, Alien felt the breeze press her black velvet dress against her legs above her boots.

Step one: chill-out music. As soon as she had closed the data center door behind her, Alien took out her iPod headphones and scrolled to King Harvest's "Dancing in the Moonlight." The second the electronic keyboard started, she took a nice long exhale.

Locked black metal racks held the computers in groups of twelve to twenty. Standing on tiptoe, Alien grabbed a key from the top of the third rack from the door. She opened the rack and pulled out and popped up a tray with a laptop that monitored and controlled the machines around it. Now to test a new logging system she'd just set up.

Alien poked around the system authentication logs for ninety minutes, looking for anyone who might have accessed the printer the last five days —and nights.

Just as she'd guessed.

—————

"It's not a virus—it's a new night shift maintenance worker," Alien reported to Grant. "Between seven p.m., when the last person leaves, and seven a.m., when the nurse starts work in the morning, he's the only person logged in on that floor."

She showed a graphical chart of the employee's routine, taken from the logs. "Here, around one in the morning every night he's signing in at one of the shared workstations," Alien said. "He goes online and prints porn, more pages of it than there is paper left in the printer. When he gets the 'out of paper' message, he goes and gets his pictures. He forgets about it, but the printer's memory doesn't, even after he signs off. Then, when our nurse comes in and restocks the printer, it finishes printing from the queue."

Alien followed the chart with a lengthy printout, highlighted to show the relevant items in a time-stamped list. "Once I knew what workstation he was using, I grabbed it and pulled the Web-surfing history. Take a look. Everything matches."

It was her first independent network forensics case. And it made her realize how differently people acted when they thought no one else was watching them. What they didn't understand was that everything they did online left a trail.

"Poor nurse," Grant said. "I'll report the guy to human resources."

"Poor guy," said Alien. "There's no anonymity on the Internet."

<hr>

The first week of May, Mayflower replaced asbestos-laden carpeting on the fourth floor of the IT building. Movers came and dismantled all the cubicles and their contents, either shifting them to other floors or stacking them in the conference room. Then everything went back to where it belonged. Except that the head of patient accounts reported that his desktop computer had not been returned to him.

Alien placed an alert on the network; if the machine came online, she'd detect it. Next, she contacted a colleague in physical security and told him where the staging areas for the move had been. "Are there cameras there?" she asked.

"I'll check," he said.

Last, she went in person to see the head of patient accounts. The location of his desk, near one of the building's few windows with a view, indicated his seniority. Fifty or so, round-faced and chubby, he kept nervously fingering the collar of his white short-sleeve button-down shirt, as if seeking reassurance.

"Is there any patient information stored on the computer?" she questioned him.

"Of course," the man said.

Alien paused. "For roughly how many people?"

He thought about it. "Ten thousand patients."

"Ten thousand patients," Alien repeated to Grant afterward. "And right now the computer and its hard drive could be anywhere from Roxbury to Romania."

"It would take a while to get to Romania," Grant countered. "Are you *sure* it's not here in the hospital? Maybe it just got misplaced during the move."

"Let's hope so," said Alien. The new InfoSec policy she'd written used two main measures to rate the urgency and importance of possible information security incidents. One was the *sensitivity* of any system at risk—how critical it was to hospital operations. The other was the *confidentiality* of any data involved—whether it was public or private, for example, or subject to internal Mayflower policies or federal regulations.

Losing this computer hit the second gong hard.

"It's got names and addresses; driver's license and Social Security numbers; credit card and bank information—all totally unencrypted," Alien said. "If you were interested in identity theft, this hard drive would be a one-stop shop. And then there's all the medical information."

Grant didn't wait. Immediately, he and Alien conducted a blanket search of the building—cubicles, closets, conference rooms, and data center—every nook and cranny. Nothing.

Grant paged the other information security team members. He passed out printed copies of the floor plans. They stayed after work, walking through the deserted offices, turning everything upside down again—with no result.

At midnight, following Alien's new policy, Grant notified his boss, Mayflower's head of IT, who called the hospital's CTO—chief technology officer—who alerted legal.

"What now?" she asked Grant at dawn.

"We're investigating" was all he told her.

All week Alien waited for a news report or press release—even a staff memo of some kind—about the missing computer. None appeared. And Grant, when she asked again, made it clear that the entire incident had been taken out of his hands.

"It's a random Dell desktop," Harry tried consoling her at lunch on Friday.

"Someone probably saw the chance to make five hundred bucks, grabbed it, and sold it to a friend."

"And that's fine with you?" asked Alien.

"Of course not," Harry said. "But you don't have to make a federal case out of it."

"But it *is* a federal case," said Alien. "Have you heard of HIPAA?" The acronym stood for the Health Insurance Portability and Accountability Act—a recent federal law that restricted access to private medical information. "Ten thousand patient medical records just walked out the door. We don't know what happened. We need to take this seriously!"

Harry impatiently eyed the sandwich and fries he'd ordered, but Alien continued. "Did you know personal health information can be resold for ten times the price of stolen credit cards? And you know why? Because you can't 'cancel' your medical history and get a new one." She paused. "In the wards, the doctors wear white coats to stop anyone from thinking of blood. The floors are squeaky clean so no one imagines that an infection could be transmitted. If people trust us with their health and the health of their loved ones, we need to take the same care with the security of their intimate personal information."

Alien stood. She couldn't just cross another workday off the calendar as Harry did—not now, she felt, not with a case that really mattered like this one. Medical identity theft affected more than a million Americans a year. Mayflower Hospital had to deal with calls from puzzled and outraged people claiming "I never had that surgery" after someone else had used their health insurance. If your provider was duped by an imposter's fake ID, you might be billed for fraudulent copays or hit your insurance limit before you knew it. And if your medical records were altered in the process, such as having another person's blood type entered in place of your own, the consequences could be dangerous and even fatal.

"Where are you going?" Harry said. "You haven't eaten anything."

"I'm going back to the office," said Alien. "I'm checking the logs to see if the computer came back online."

"It's gone," Harry told her.

"I'm not giving up."

A month passed. Late one night, Alien lay beside Fireberry's house manager, Keenan, in the backyard hammock. Tall and muscular, with dreamy green eyes and a terrific spiked haircut, Keenan attracted a stream of women to his third-floor bedroom, across the hall from hers. So far, at least, Alien wasn't one of them. Yet when Keenan sat up slowly and started massaging her shoulders, she realized how much trouble she was having relaxing. Her mind was still stuck on the missing computer.

Mayflower was hardly alone in confronting a potential data breach. In late May, the U.S. Department of Veterans Affairs reported that a contractor's laptop and unencrypted hard drive had been stolen. On it, too, were names, birthdays, and Social Security numbers, as well as disability ratings. The scale of the information at risk was breathtaking: 26.5 *million* veterans, their spouses, and active-duty military personnel were affected. There were similar revelations from ChoicePoint, a commercial data broker; LexisNexis, the research database giant; Equifax, the nationwide credit bureau; Bank of America; and the U.S. Department of Energy. With this information, criminals could get a bank loan, credit card, or driver's license, obtain medical care or prescription drugs, or even buy a house, all in a victim's name.

"Something happened at work," said Alien. "I can't tell you exactly what. But something went missing and we can't find it. And I don't think they're going to tell anybody."

Keenan moved his hands in a gentle circle on her back. He virtually never spoke but was happy to listen. Confiding in him was a way to think things through for herself.

Alien stared up at the night sky. The moon and stars peeked through streaky white clouds.

"It just seems wrong," she said. "To not tell anybody. How can I take this job seriously if we don't tell people what happened?"

Her job at the hospital had always required compromises Alien didn't like. When the exchange was having to get up early, sit at a desk in a cubicle, and deal with bureaucracy in return for an increasing opportunity to do meaningful work in a new and exciting field, she accepted it.

With this case, the balance changed. Now she felt shut out from and maybe even betrayed by the decision making of the people in power above her—and in her specific area of interest, expertise, and (she had thought) authority.

"Am I just a human checkbox?" Alien asked Keenan. "It feels like I'm here so that the executives can say, 'Yes, someone's job is to try to protect you.' They don't really mean it. They just want to check off a box."

———◆———

Six hours later, Alien climbed off Pepper, passed through the turnstile, and up the elevator into Beigeworld. She didn't want to quit her job. But to continue at the hospital, something had to change, something within her control.

How about herself? In recognition of everything Alien was doing and how much more she wanted to accomplish, Grant had suggested she take some kind of class.

While Chris complained and Harry kibitzed, Alien began an online search. "S·C·A·N," said four large stenciled letters across the top of the website she loaded. Below was the promise: "Secure Computing and Networking."

Alien scrolled down. Information security was growing into a multibillion-dollar industry. SCAN was the new field's foremost training institute. Though headquartered outside Washington, D.C., it advertised regular workshops in locations across the continent and around the world — this week Miami, next week New York, and so on through Houston and San Francisco, London and Paris, Sydney and Singapore, Dublin and Dubai. The instructors were top people who took these gigs for some extra cash and to develop new clients from the companies that sent them students.

"Fundamentals of Information Security," "Advanced Information Security," "Defending Windows," "Defending Linux/UNIX," "Incident Handling and the Hacker Mindset" — Alien halted, curious, and clicked on the last of these class listings.

"The bad guys have to find one opening to succeed. Security has to find all of them," the course overview stated. "Learn EVERYONE who is attacking you, how, and how to stop them in this fast-paced, hands-on workshop designed for incident response team leaders."

Alien read on another twenty minutes and then clicked the button marked "Registration." She focused on a six-day session in July in Toronto. She had also heard of the instructor, Bruce Rich, and his company, Elite Defense. The tuition was three thousand dollars.

Alien took a deep breath, stood up, and walked into Grant's office.

The question was out of her mouth almost the moment she saw him: "What's our funding for professional development?"

Agents and Jedis

Capture the Flag

Toronto. July 2006.

ALIEN CAREFULLY TUCKED A black button-down shirt into black slacks. She laced up low-rise leather boots, looped the lanyard with the laminated SCAN badge over her head, picked up her laptop case and a travel thermos of hot Earl Grey tea, and headed for the hotel elevator. At five minutes to nine this Sunday morning, she entered the conference room where she would spend most of the next six days.

The front wall of the room was covered with a screen, before which was a table holding a projector. Facing the screen were three rows of chairs positioned behind tables meant to serve as desks, underneath which were floor outlets. At the rear of the room was one more table that held a carafe of coffee, pitchers of water, and two piles of spiral-bound coursepacks, ten to a pile.

Alien assessed the nineteen other badge wearers — her classmates — milling about the room. Most were in their mid-thirties or older and wore jeans and a T-shirt. All were guys.

The extreme gender imbalance didn't surprise Alien. By now she was accustomed to it. InfoSec combined two male-dominated industries: technology and security. The whole field originated in hacker groups, on the one hand, and the defense industry, on the other, both of which were boys' clubs at heart. And even at MIT, where women were a much larger minority, she had often been the only woman in a particular class.

People introduced themselves awkwardly. Alien stepped smiling into a cluster of four. "Hi. I'm Elizabeth." She extended her hand to each guy in counterclockwise order, reading the name tags as she shook with them. "And you're Doug? Dan? John? James?" She took half a step back and asked, "Where are you all coming from?"

"Google," the first guy answered.

"Apple," said the second.

The elder of the last two answered curtly for both of them: "We work in government."

The Google guy chortled. "You know what that means, don't you?" he told Alien as these two excused themselves to grab coffee.

Alien guessed. "NSA?" she said.

"Right," the Apple guy answered. "'No Such Agency.'"

Alien chose a seat in the middle of the first row and booted up her laptop. Thirty seconds later, a sudden hush fell upon the room. She looked up to see the instructor enter.

Maybe thirty-five years old, he led with his beard. Bright red and bushy, the size and shape of a saddlebag, his facial hair extended from his gauged ear-lobes to the third button of a green, red, and blue tartan plaid shirt only partly tucked into loose-fitting corduroy pants. Narrow patches above his chin and below his nose were shaved, as if clearing a landing area for his lips, which he formed into a broad, jovial expression that matched his twinkling eyes and Santa-worthy potbelly. He introduced himself—"Bruce Rich"—to the class.

"Welcome," he said in a booming voice. "You're here because you're inci-dent handlers. I'm here"—he raised a woolly eyebrow archly—"to turn you into *defenders.*"

Alien tensed in anticipation. She was tempted to peek back again quickly to see what the other students made of this mission statement. But she'd read everything she could on Bruce before taking the class and didn't want to miss a word he had to say.

In the 1980s and 1990s, almost everyone who broke into and explored com-puter systems was a hobbyist, hacking out of curiosity, for fun or fame, even at the risk of arrest. Government leaders promised comprehensive action to improve security, but failed to deliver, even as the threat became too big to ignore.

Now corporations from Microsoft and Cisco on down had begun hiring hackers of their own to help defend themselves against other hackers. What had been a hobby was quickly professionalizing and splitting into separate, if overlapping, camps. There were *black hat hackers,* who hacked with malicious or criminal intent, for power or profit; *white hat hackers,* who hacked to test, evaluate, and ultimately improve computer security; and *gray hat hackers,* who moved between both worlds.

Bruce and his colleagues at Elite Defense were white hat rock stars: high-priced, rapidly deployed independent global operatives for major businesses, corporations, and government agencies interested in testing their systems against potential attack.

"All of you are charged with defending your assets and responding to break-ins," he told the class. "But to achieve real security, you also need to understand your adversaries." Bruce quoted Sun Tzu: "'To secure ourselves against defeat lies in our own hands, but the opportunity of defeating the enemy is provided by the enemy himself.'

"If you know how hackers think, and the tools and techniques they use, you can beat them," he continued. "Or" — Bruce shrugged and threw his arms wide — "at least you can stop them from beating you."

The class, including Alien, chuckled keenly. Bruce himself, though, shifted to a more solemn expression after a moment's pause.

"Today is going to be hard," he said in a low, serious tone. "Tomorrow is going to be harder. And the next day is going to be harder than both of them combined. I'm here to push you every moment and to bring you to the edge of the cliff. There's a better view there. There's better ventilation. And" — another shrug, eyes sweeping the room slowly, making momentary eye contact with each student — "I will occasionally jettison one or two of you."

Everyone chuckled again, but more nervously.

Alien was hooked. Bruce was so mesmerizing a speaker he could have read UNIX online manual pages aloud and held her rapt.

"This week," Bruce went on, "you're all going to get your hands dirty. If you can go back to work afterward and get promoted, that's great. But even more awesome is if I can put that hacker pathway in your brain."

He powered on the projector. "And here is your final warning," he announced.

With everyone else, Alien leaned forward.

Bruce slipped his own laptop from its case and lifted the machine in the air. "This is my kingdom, my court, my shield, and my sword," he said. "Whether you like it or not, your computer is probably the same for you."

Another pause. "If you have any sensitive data on it, you'd better remove that now."

———⬥———

For the rest of the morning and afternoon, Bruce paced back and forth as he spoke. He never seemed to tire, but when he let them go, all the students were exhausted.

"Rest up" were his parting words. "Tomorrow the perspective flips."

The formal part of the instruction was over for the day, but more remained. That evening, both instructor and class re-gathered to unwind in a bar called Postman's Pub, a ten-minute walk from the hotel.

Ostensibly they were there to enjoy a drink or two in a casual atmosphere. In fact, though, Bruce was holding forth, with students listening spellbound.

Bruce had discovered hacking the way many kids did—in middle school and high school, he said, when he and his friends decided they needed to reverse-engineer the copy protection measures on computer games. From there, for fun, he moved on to dissecting computer worms and viruses. Soon he was present at the birth of the full disclosure movement, when security researchers like him fought to publicize new vulnerabilities.

"Back in the day," Bruce told Alien and her classmates, meaning just four or five years ago, "*everyone* was after us." The computer giants whose product flaws they exposed said the technical findings revealed proprietary business matters, and threatened to sue them. For their part, the FBI and other government agencies claimed the information abetted criminals and terrorists. Some fellow hackers attacked the most prominent white hats as glory hounds intent on giving away hard-won secrets and ruining the fun of hacking for everyone else.

"I remember *my* first SCAN class," Bruce continued. The instructor was a SCAN co-founder. "I was too intimidated to say anything all week. Then we ended up talking in the parking lot." He chuckled. "It turned out that we'd actually been on the same white hat IRC"—Internet Relay Chat—"channel for years."

"Then what did you do?" said Alien.

"We decided to start Elite Defense," Bruce said.

He stood to get a drink. Alien followed. A few feet away from the bar, however, she found her path blocked by a fellow student who had risen suddenly, trying to make it look as natural as possible, as if he just wanted to order another pitcher for his table.

"*Amazing* class today," he said a little too emphatically to Bruce, who nodded.

"So . . . ," the guy offered as an awkward segue. "What kind of firewalls do you think are better?" he said at last. "Cisco or Juniper?"

"Both are like condoms," Bruce said. "If they don't break, I don't care."

"It's where you place them that counts," Alien jumped in.

When Bruce laughed, so did the other student.

"That's what *I* always say," the student added as a follow-up. With nothing more to offer, he went on to fetch his pitcher, leaving Alien alone with Bruce.

"Do you get to travel a lot?" she asked.

"All the time," Bruce said. "I'm just back from Kyoto. I found this amazing hot spring in the woods and soaked for hours with the locals."

"Wow. What did you talk about?" said Alien.

"It's a long story. What are you having to drink?" he asked.

"Sapphire and tonic," said Alien.

Bruce signaled to the bartender. "Another Steam Whistle Pilsner for me," he said, "and we'll have a Bombay Sapphire and tonic for the lady."

———⟢———

The next four days of class were, as promised, even more grueling than the first. Step by step, incident handlers were taught how to transform themselves into hackers.

Monday, Bruce led the class through attacker *footprinting*—gaining information about a target; *scanning*—probing the target's network to identify hosts, ports, and services on it; and *enumerating*—extracting information on usernames, machine names, and settings. To get them into the frame of mind he wanted, he called them "samurai."

Tuesday and Wednesday, they practiced *accessing* and *exploiting*—everything from cracking passwords and capturing traffic to hiding files and remotely running applications.

Thursday centered on maintaining access and covering tracks despite the target's best efforts at detection. Take complete command and you *rooted* the computer and *pwned*—pronounced *poned,* a play on "owned"—your victim. At the moment of triumph, some guys in the class celebrated with whoops and trash talk.

Alien typed on in silence. What was there to be proud of? Bruce had told them exactly what to do. Following his instructions didn't make you a hacking genius any more than transcribing *Paradise Lost* word for word made you a poet.

Friday night she walked beside Bruce and chatted him up on the way to the bar, as she had every evening since Monday.

Halfway there, Bruce pointed up at the sky. "Look," he said. "Jupiter."

Alien searched until her eyes found the pale cream-colored dot, 450 million miles away, amidst a sea of stars. "There's a little perspective," she said.

They watched in silence until clouds obscured the distant planet.

"Do you believe in God?" Alien asked.

"Do you?" said Bruce.

Alien shrugged. "The universe is so old and so big that someone, somewhere must have rooted it," she said.

⋘⋙

The next day, as she and the other students returned to the classroom after lunch, Alien saw Bruce had been busy. A wheeled cart now shared space in the front of the room. On top of it were six computers. As Bruce turned on the projector, he ordered, "Lights off!" and someone in the back row jumped up to hit the switches.

Backlit by the reflection off the screen, Bruce became a bearded phantasm. "So it begins!" he cackled happily. "Capture the flag!"

Bruce had set up each of the six computers to simulate a different server used in most networked office environments: file storage, printing, communications, applications, databases, and domain management (translating machines' names to Internet addresses and vice versa, for example). Each server had a special file, or "flag," at the root of its system. Together, the flags could be combined like puzzle pieces to reveal a secret message.

To get the flags, though, you had to hack into each computer.

"Remember: don't try this at home," Bruce mock-warned them. As they knew, the tools and techniques they were using would be illegal on any machines they didn't own.

Bruce quickly divided the class into five teams, each with four members. Alien didn't know her teammates very well and so relied on their facial hair to distinguish among them. One was clean shaven, another had a carefully cultivated stubble, the third a soul patch. They let her choose their team name: Ziggy Stardust, after the David Bowie album. Their rivals, meanwhile, were the Road Warriors, Alpha Force, Hack Attack, and Pissed Officers. The lineup for the last was the guys from Google and Apple, and the two suspected NSA-ers.

The captain of the first team to finish got a signed copy of *Security by Ferris*, an InfoSec textbook by Bruce's Elite Defense co-founder, Jules Ferris — a legendary pentester, or penetration tester, a professional white hat hacker hired by companies to probe their own systems for security holes.

"Five, four, three, two, one — *go*," Bruce commanded, and twenty laptops flipped open.

For the first twenty minutes, Stubble insisted that he lead Ziggy Stardust. Alien deferred to him. After all, he seemed confident, and the last time she had really measured her technical abilities against other people was at MIT. But then he stumbled trying to type commands. Mr. Clean Shaven took over for ten minutes but missed obvious hacking openings. The teammate with the soul patch, meanwhile, seemed more interested in his cell phone than in the competition. Alpha Force and the Pissed Officers took early leads.

If I'm here, I'm going to play, Alien decided. *And if I play, I want to win.*

She started typing on her own laptop.

Alien recognized right away that computers with the printer and domain servers were both UNIX systems. From her experience at Mayflower Hospital, she knew their vulnerabilities intimately. One after another, Alien grabbed their flags.

Bruce used his laptop to emit a gong noise, announcing an hour had passed: one p.m. On the screen at the front of the room, he projected a running tally:

Alpha Force — 1
Hack Attack — 0

Road Warriors—0
Pissed Officers—2
Ziggy Stardust—2

Five minutes later, Ziggy Stardust pulled ahead, as Alien showed Stubble and Clean Shaven how to make the mail server cough up a list of usernames they could then feed through a free "password cracker" program that quickly tested thousands of common combinations per target until it hit the mark.

At this point, Soul Patch closed his phone, lining up with the other guys like bobsled team runners to look over Alien's shoulder as she steered.

⋯⟨⟩⋯

The next steps were a lot trickier. The applications and database servers were both Windows systems, which Alien had barely touched, so she and her teammates focused on the file server. A port scan revealed that it had a Web interface that allowed users to upload and download data with a simple browser. This Web app was supposed to let you see only your own files, but Alien discovered that she could roam freely if she opened and altered the code for the underlying Web page buttons. This eventually gave Ziggy Stardust their fourth flag.

The gong sounded again: two p.m. Alien looked up. Bruce had projected a fresh scorecard:

Alpha Force—2
Hack Attack—1
Road Warriors—2
Pissed Officers—3
Ziggy Stardust—4

Her teammates cheered. They were leading. Just two flags to go.
Then Soul Patch moaned.
"Shit," Stubble said.
"Tied," reported Clean Shaven.
Alien checked Bruce's updated screen. The Pissed Officers had just grabbed a fourth flag too.

Alien looked behind her, to see the Officers high-five one another. They looked smug and confident, certain of victory.

I don't think so.

⸻

Alien pivoted to the database server. Bruce had spent half the morning on Thursday leading them through a technique called "SQL injection," a venerable database-specific attack. SQL (pronounced *sequel*) stood for Structured Query Language — the language used in database lookups. A SQL "injection" worked by weaving a hacker's own commands into normal queries. Consulting her notes and the coursepack, Alien tried this approach now.

"admin," she typed in the field for username in the database login screen.

"Stardust' or 'x'='x," she entered in the field for password.

The database checked for users with that name and password. "Admin" would be the root account, she strongly suspected, and the "Stardust" part of the password suggestion was just a whimsical placeholder, inserted because something had to be there. But the single quotes and the equation that followed the "or" statement were crucial. Exploiting how the system processed instructions internally, Alien was telling the database, "Let me in if your administrator has the password 'Stardust' — *or* if x equals x." Even if the first part, about the password, was almost certainly incorrect, the second part, containing the equation, was a true statement. So she got in. It was like a test where you could get every question right by adding the same special code word at the end of your answer.

"You did it!" said Soul Patch, amazed, as the system returned the flag itself as output.

"*Shh,*" Alien told him, not wanting the other teams to guess their strategy.

And she already had a trick in mind that she thought might gain them the final flag.

⸻

The only sound in the room now was frantic typing and the low hum of the projector fan. On her laptop, Alien activated a backgrounded window for command line instructions.

"tcpdump -i eth0 -s 0 -w telsniff.log," she entered.

"tcpdump: listening," the system returned.

TCPdump was an all-purpose traffic sniffer. The classroom network had been set up to stop snooping, but Alien had overcome its safeguards near the beginning of the game, when Stubble tried to lead direct attacks. Now she could get complete records of all information sent back and forth by every team. Given that most of her classmates here were far more experienced with Windows machines than she was, it was almost certain one of them would use his knowledge to pwn the application server before she could.

The only question was whether anyone smart enough to grab the flag would be careless enough not to encrypt it in the transfer back to his own computer.

A few minutes passed. Alien typed Control-C to end the listening process. Then she opened the log file she had created in a new program, Wireshark. The screen filled with a long list of captured Internet traffic, broken down by time, source, destination, protocol, length, and content.

"Whoa," she heard one of the guys behind her say.

Alien typed rapidly, telling Wireshark to filter out everything but traffic to and from the application server's address.

"Come to Mama," she whispered expectantly.

Aha. An electric thrill ran through Alien. At least one team—Pissed Officers—had gotten the flag, she saw.

The guys behind her held their breath. Slowly and methodically, Alien carved out the file in question from the mass of raw data, combining it with the other flags to show all six flags together. "Get it?" she asked her teammates.

The flags formed a time-based cipher, using the hours of the day, 1 to 24, to represent the letters A through X. Rather than risk another team's interception this late in the process, Alien translated the message by hand with pen and a piece of paper torn from the coursepack: "W-E-L," it began.

When she finished writing, Alien stood, clutching the ragged edges of the paper with trembling fingers. The other teams were all still working, but she sensed their eyes on her back as Bruce waved her forward.

Alien leaned close, her chin brushing the scratchy outskirts of his beard as her lips reached his left ear.

"Welcome to the virtual world," she whispered.

Bruce paused, regarding her solemnly without responding. Then he smiled, raised the signed book from the table beside him, and presented it to her with a flourish.

"Congratulations," Bruce said, shaking her hand.

Stubble, Clean Shaven, and Soul Patch applauded. The Pissed Officers slumped in disbelief.

———✦———

At five o'clock, all the other SCAN students, now confirmed Bruce group-ies, lined up to thank him, trade business cards, and inquire excitedly about bringing Elite Defense to their workplace. Alien just watched, proudly clutch-ing her signed copy of *Security by Ferris*. She didn't want the chance to hire Bruce or Jules. She wanted to *be* Bruce or Jules.

Now that the capture-the-flag contest was over, all she wanted was to play again — except now for keeps, and as a member of Elite Defense.

It seemed as if her wish would come true immediately. As he said good-bye, Bruce gave Alien his personal email address and phone number. "You should work for us," he said.

———✦———

Alien wrote the next day, and again two weeks after that, thanking Bruce both times for the book and telling him she was interested in discussing a job with Elite. He wrote back both times, amiably, yet with maddening vagueness.

In August, Alien got a voice mail from Bruce. "Hey," he said breezily. "Looks like Jules Ferris and I are coming to Boston next month. We should meet up."

Three more weeks passed without another word. Then, checking her email late Friday night, Alien found a message from Bruce saying he and Jules would be in town *tomorrow* to meet a client. Could she recommend some-place for dinner?

"Dalí," Alien wrote back immediately, naming a lively Spanish restaurant and tapas bar by the Cambridge-Somerville border, just minutes from her own place.

"Very cool. Thanks!" Bruce replied thirty seconds later. "Join us?"

———✦———

It was a perfect warm, clear Saturday night in mid-September. Alien pulled up to the restaurant on Pepper, dressed in one of her black leather motorcycle jackets, a black miniskirt, and high black zip-up boots. Bruce and Jules were waiting outside with the client, who was wearing a suit. When they first beheld her, they did a double take in unison.

"Good evening, gentlemen," Alien said, hugging Bruce and shaking hands with Jules and the client. The three of them seemed to vie to open the door for her until Bruce and Jules let the client enjoy the privilege.

His name was Spencer. He entered after her, already loosening his tie. Bruce followed, nodding his wild beard approvingly at the restaurant's long front bar, stamped copper ceiling, and textured gold-painted accent wall. Last was Jules — clean-cut and cue-ball bald, with frameless rectangular glasses and a semi-permanent impish grin — mouthing his name to the hostess. They passed a table of giddy diners, one of whom blushed as several waiters and waitresses with tambourines and maracas sang "Happy Birthday." The hostess led them past beaded dividers to a dimly lit and less clamorous back room decorated with copper pots and framed photos of flamenco dancers.

"Where did you find this place?" Spencer asked, excited enough to order a pitcher of sangria, a bottle of red wine, and dirty martinis all around.

"Bruce asked Elizabeth," Jules answered.

Alien shrugged modestly. The truth was, she had long heard of Dalí, but had never actually been inside before.

"Good wine, good atmosphere — I'm happy," she said.

Drained glasses and empty plates, bowls, and ramekins covered the table two hours later. Spencer checked his watch — ten p.m. — and sighed.

"Excuse me," he said, standing tipsily, the breast pocket of his suit stained with olive oil. "Thank you for dinner," he told Bruce and Jules. "And thank you," — he bowed to Alien — "for your charming company."

She smiled. After he had left, she turned to the Elite Defense guys. "Let's go get a drink. The night is young. The world is our oyster," she said.

They walked next door, to the Kirkland Tap and Trotter, and took seats at the bar.

"So what brought you to Cambridge?" Jules asked Alien.

"Originally?" she said. "I went to MIT."

"Really?" He looked surprised. "And what did you major in?"

"Electrical engineering and computer science."

Jules looked even more incredulous. It was as if the possibility she could code had never occurred to him. Alien was able to see from his expression that he was recalibrating his presumptions. But simply stating her major wasn't enough. Whereas technical guys assumed another man they met knew what he was talking about until he made an obvious mistake, the reverse was true of a woman. Alien still had to prove she was legit.

She took Jules's hesitation as a chance to seize the moment. "You must get a lot of résumés at Elite Defense. How do you pick who to hire?" Alien asked.

Bruce and Jules spoke reverently about "the Elite culture" and then launched into specific hacking stories. Alien added her own, which surprised them further. As the conversation continued, she made subtle technical references, citing specific Linux varieties and version numbers to further impress on them her experience. The three of them weren't quite comrades in arms, but Alien had made clear her abilities.

If they had a job opening, they would hire her. She was sure of it.

Shortly after midnight, Alien waved good-bye and rode off, and Bruce and Jules waved back as they slid into their taxi.

⟨⟨=⟩⟩

Mid-October, four weeks after the Dalí dinner, Alien checked email late at night at the desk in her bedroom. Her new boyfriend, Tanner, lay in her bed, reading.

Alien was ecstatic. "Bruce wrote!" she said excitedly to Tanner. "He wants to know what salary I want!"

Tanner grinned. Tall and angular, with spiked flame-red hair that accentuated his resemblance to David Bowie (another reason for her Ziggy Stardust shout-out at SCAN), the former Senior House resident made his living as an electrical engineer but spent equal time working as a painter, sculptor, and performance artist. "What are you going to say?" he asked.

"These guys are the best in the business," Alien said. Stay cool, she figured. Start with a nice round number.

"$100K," Alien wrote.

⟨⟨=⟩⟩

Alien woke alone early Sunday afternoon. On her desk was a note from Tanner: "At the studio. Love you." Smiling, Alien flicked on a yellow lava lamp, but natural light from the skylights washed out its spectral glow. She checked email again.

A new message. From Bruce. Five words: "Sorry, that's outside our budget."
No.

⟼⟻

What went wrong? Alien asked herself, reading and rereading the one-line email.

She fell onto her bed crying. Bruce's rejection was unambiguous, Alien thought — and it left no room for negotiation.

That's it, she told herself. *It's over.*

After three months of waiting to get through the door with Elite Defense, the door had been slammed in her face. And *she* had been the one to shut it.

⟼⟻

The tears flowed for ten more minutes. Then, when she could breathe regularly again, Alien picked up her cell phone. Whose counsel could she trust in a situation like this one?

She called.

"Uh-huh, uh-huh . . . ," he said, as she explained what had happened. "Oh, Elizabeth. I'm sorry. . . . No — listen: here's the lesson. In any negotiation, you *always* make them throw out a number first."

"I know that *now*," Alien said. She was near tears again. "But what should I *do*?"

"Relax." The voice on the other end of the line was steady, cheery, and sympathetic. "Just call him."

"Can I?" said Alien.

"Why not? He can say no again. Or he can offer you peanuts. But you've got nothing to lose."

Alien wiped her cheeks dry. "Okay . . . ," she said shakily. *He's right,* she thought. "I'll try it."

"Now you're talking," the voice said. "Go get 'em."

Alien smiled, as calm and confident as she was going to be.

"Thanks, Dad," she said.

⟼⟻

It was one p.m. on the East Coast but ten a.m. on the West Coast — and Bruce lived just outside San Luis Obispo, very close to where he'd grown up.

He answered on the second ring: "Hello?"

"Hey, I got your email," Alien said confidently. "I know you wanted to make it happen, and I do, too. Why don't you just tell me your best offer, and I'll make it work."

Bruce said nothing. Alien counted five long seconds of silence, then ten, and then fifteen.

Shoot, she thought, wincing. He'd have to reject her outright, though, she decided. She wasn't giving up.

Finally, Bruce spoke. "Eighty thousand," he said.

What? Alien's heart surged. She struggled to hold the phone steady. She was going to work for Elite Defense. And they were paying her eighty thousand dollars a year for the pleasure.

"Great," she offered back in the coolest, most casual voice she could muster. Alien fist-pumped. "Sign me up."

10

Check, Please

ELITE DEFENSE WAS OWNED by five partners. Three, including Bruce and Jules, were computer security experts, one was a former Silicon Valley executive, and the fifth was ex-military, a retired air force commander superb at physical surveillance and with an encyclopedic knowledge of technical gear. Thanks to their prior work experience and such current activities as teaching at SCAN, all were good at bringing in business. "If we come in to give you a test, you will have been tested," they promised Fortune 500 companies and government agencies and contractors. "We will pwn you if you can be pwned—and we haven't had a client yet who couldn't be."

Elite itself was a small and loosely organized company. There were only nine people: the five co-founders, two veteran associates, an office manager, and now Alien. The office manager was the only other woman, and no two Elite staffers lived in the same city. They communicated with one another either by cell phone or through a private email and chat system. Since there was no apparent hierarchy among the five partners and they didn't seem to gather regularly as a group, even online, who was in charge of what seemed determined by chance or the whim of the moment. It was a miracle that she'd been hired at all, Alien realized now.

The Elite Defense co-founders called themselves Jedis. Mixing metaphors —or, rather, the *Stars Wars* and *Matrix* movies—they called Alien and the two other associates Agents. Three months after signing on, however, Alien had yet to perform any technical work. Instead, she spent late fall and early winter editing other people's project reports. When she was finally given her first assignment, it didn't require any of her coding and command line skills at all. She didn't know if this was because she was female, or just new, or for some other reason.

The assignment was breaking into a bank.

It was a clear, cold January Monday in Wilmington, Delaware. Alien pressed her hands to the passenger-side heating vents of a gray Ford Taurus — chosen because it was the most boring rental Hertz had on the lot with a closed, lockable trunk. Her outfit was also purposefully nondescript: two-inch black leather heels, a long dark brown skirt, a prim white blouse "borrowed" a few years earlier from her mother, and a long tan trench coat in remarkably good condition considering that Piñon had bought it for her at the Santa Fe Goodwill. Beside Alien, behind the wheel, sat the former commander, a scowling, heavy-jowled man of fifty named Richard. Across the street was the twenty-story glass-clad regional headquarters of one of the country's biggest banks, with over one thousand branches nationwide and $100 billion in assets.

"Six-foot metal side fence," Richard said, pointing out each security feature and its placement. "There's a camera. There's a camera. And there's a blind spot by the corner — see the angle?"

Alien nodded. "Got it." She jotted down the observations in a softcover five-by-eight-and-a-half-inch tan Moleskine notebook. "Castle," Elite Defense had code-named the client, referring to the financial institution's logo, a red castle with two symmetrical turrets.

Richard drove around the block to the rear of the building, which they studied through a small hole in a blue mesh screen covering the employee parking lot fencing.

"Notice the UPS guy," he said, pointing out a brown-clad figure leaving from a side door. "That must be the delivery entrance." The door was propped open with a small wooden block. "I bet they have a freight elevator," Richard continued. "And that looks like an unmanned storage room with an unlocked window."

Alien followed his gaze and then added the details to her notebook, to be integrated later with her own remote reconnaissance notes — information gathered online or via public records, such as the names and positions of local Castle employees and the floor plans of areas for lease. As with hacking computers, a single security flaw was unlikely to give them everything they wanted. But the more they knew and could combine, the more likely it was that they could get in — and then out again with sensitive goods or information.

"Not much movement," Alien said when they were back out front. "Could be tricky to tailgate" — that is, to gain entry by following someone with authorized access.

"Just wait for the smokers' breaks," said Richard. "Or" — a clock outside struck the hour — "lunch."

Alien counted twelve chimes: noon. Employees started streaming out of the building lobby.

"See you tomorrow," she whispered to them.

***

Ted Roberts, Castle's head of security, requested a private booth at the hotel restaurant. A friendly blond forty-year-old man in a business suit, he leaned across the table after dinner and passed both Richard and Alien his business card and a signed one-page note.

Alien skimmed the document, which she had written and sent to Ted, asking him to fill in the blanks and bring it to their meeting tonight. "[Castle] has hired Elite Defense to perform physical security penetration tests and assessments of nine sites in three states," it said. Specific addresses followed, starting here, with the bank's regional headquarters and four branches she and Richard had driven by today, doing local reconnaissance. For the rest of the week, Ted's note authorized, they were to probe the facilities, one by one, to determine if an uninvited visitor could enter, explore, remove equipment or data, or rob the banks. The letter closed with instructions on how to contact Ted if they got caught.

"Your 'Get Out of Jail Free' letter," he said.

Richard harrumphed, but Alien gave her best smile, folding the letter and placing it in her coat pocket. "Thanks," she said, patting the pocket afterward. "I hope we won't need it."

Ted signaled to a waiter for the check. "Good luck — but not too much luck," he said.

***

Tuesday noon, the clock tolled and office workers exited the twenty-story building again. Everyone was bundled up and breathing out steam on their way to lunch. Moving in the opposite direction, Richard entered the lobby to check it out.

Alien watched from the front passenger seat of the car, clutching an empty black laptop case. No—not completely empty. While she waited, Alien reached her fingers into the zippered pocket and checked.

There they were. Beside her "Get Out of Jail Free" letter. Fake business cards she'd printed after dinner with Ted last night.

"Elizabeth Tessman/Enterprise Technology Specialist," they said, to the right of the red Castle logo, above her real cell phone number, a fake Castle corporate email address, and the address of this building, each element copied from Ted's business card.

Alien sighed, shifting impatiently. Then she sat up quickly, seeing Richard approach the car.

"Did you get in?" Alien asked after he had taken his seat and shut the door.

Richard responded scornfully. "There's no way," he reported.

"What do you mean?" she said. All he'd done was try the lobby. What about the freight elevator? Or the storage room with the open window? "What happened?"

"Forget it." Richard turned up the heater and made to shift the car into drive. "It's fucking freezing," he said. "Let's move."

"We can totally do this." Alien unbuckled her seat belt. "Let me try," she said.

Richard shook his head. "You won't get in," he insisted. "There are turnstiles and a security guard watching everything. You'll just blow our cover." He continued gruffly, "Let's try the bank branches first. If there's time, we'll come back here. We found plenty already."

"We're here now," said Alien. "And I won't blow our cover."

Richard could spot a narrow opening in a fence at fifty yards and recite security camera specs from memory. Forthright, credible, and confident, he was, like all the Jedis, terrific at presentations. It was clear, however, that he had neither the patience nor the aptitude for what those in the InfoSec community called social engineering.

Bluntly put, the term meant manipulating people. You might call it charming or, in some cases, scaring them, but it was always about getting them to do what you wanted. Whoever you were, the trick was to assess the other person and figure out how you might talk him or her into something. Perhaps the best name for it might be "human hacking."

Freshman year, for example, getting Alex and Vlad to "help" Alien with her calculus homework had been social engineering. More recently, she had turned her dinner out with Bruce, Jules, and their client into a kind of job interview.

Consciously or not, every child or parent, teacher or military leader, politician or "player" on the dating scene used social engineering. For pentesters or their criminal counterparts, like those who sent phishing emails or persuaded victims to empty their bank accounts, the appeal was obvious. Why bother breaking into anything when you could get individuals to open their doors for you? And because people, especially men, were generally less suspicious of women in this kind of situation, being female could be an advantage.

"It'll be fine." Alien smiled sweetly. "I'll be quick and come right back if there's any problem."

Before Richard could say another word, she was out the door with her laptop case.

<hr />

Alien crossed the gray slate floor of the spacious lobby. Four hip-high stainless steel gateways stood between her and the elevators. Each was equipped with a wedge-shaped black barrier that receded when you placed your badge on a scanner. Then, as soon as anyone passed the gateway, the barrier closed immediately, preventing tailgating.

Next to the gates was a wide marble counter, also gray, behind which stood a white-haired guard in a crisp black uniform, including a matching tie on which were printed diagonal rows of the red castle logo.

She walked toward the badge reader systems, as though expecting to go through. When the barriers stopped her, Alien acted startled, purposefully trying to catch the guard's eye. Then she approached him.

"Hi," she said. "I'm with IT. We have a computer emergency on the seventh floor. I need to get up there." She would be happy to get in anywhere, but knew from remote reconnaissance that this was the floor with the most day-to-day office workers.

Up close, the man looked even older than she had originally estimated—at least sixty-five, Alien guessed, with thin gold-framed bifocals and permanent creases in his forehead. Still, he looked in excellent shape, erect and alert.

"You have to use your badge," the guard said. "Or are you on the list?" he asked, pointing toward a black hardcover binder on the table.

"No—I'm in IT," Alien told him, reassuming an old role. "I'm new—I just started yesterday."

The guard frowned. "Where's your badge?" he asked.

"I don't have a badge yet," said Alien smoothly. "But my name is Elizabeth Tessman. And my boss is Ted Roberts. T-E-D. R-O-B-E-R-T-S. Here's his card."

Alien lifted her laptop case and placed it squarely on the counter between them. She tugged the zipper and took out and slid him one of her new cards as well as Ted's.

The guard entered both names in his computer system. "He's in here," he acknowledged. "You'll need to call him to get added to the list."

Alien opened her phone, pretending to call Ted and leave a message. As she did so, holding the phone against her ear with her shoulder, she undid the buttons of her trench coat.

"Hi, Mr. Roberts," she said. "This is Elizabeth. I'm leaving you a voice mail. I'm really sorry to bother you. They won't let me up to the seventh floor. I know it's an emergency. Can you call me back, please? I'm really sorry. Thanks."

She stood awkwardly in front of the desk, checking her phone and looking fleetingly at the elevators. The guard cringed.

"I can try him again," she said to him. "I'm really sorry to keep you waiting. I know there was a big server crash right before I left and he might be in the data center. I just can't leave without fixing this—I promised."

The guard was clearly conflicted. He looked down, giving her card only a second's glance. Then, though, he waved her forward.

"Look, I know it's important," he said. "I'll make an exception. Just be quick."

"Thanks—I will!" she told him—just as she had assured Richard.

Alien grabbed her laptop bag and stepped forward to the closest gateway.

The guard pushed a button under the counter. The barriers parted with a whoosh.

<hr />

Alien was surprised to feel her heart pounding as she stepped out of the elevator. She'd taken much greater physical risks in college. But she'd never tried to *steal* something.

For now, at least, there was nobody else on this floor.

Alien moved quickly. Most workspaces, she saw, were cubicles containing white desks, separated by six-foot freestanding gray walls. At the perimeter of the floor were the larger individual offices of middle-level managers, with glass walls and doors.

Occupants of the cubicles personalized their space with photos and trinkets—a blue-and-white coffee mug with Chinese characters on it, a squeezable yellow "stress reliever" ball, a Mickey Mouse figurine. On every desk was a black phone and a Dell laptop connected to an external keyboard and monitor.

Alien hefted a few laptops. All were secured with cables.

She decided to try the managers' spaces, starting with a corner office with an unimpeded view of the downtown. It had the same computer setup, though on a larger dark gray desk. She lifted the laptop.

No cable.

Alien heard the elevator ding, announcing the return of the first of the employees from lunch. Two men chatted as they went to their desks, not noticing her. She slipped out of the corner office with the laptop and walked past two more employees. Alien was positive she looked as guilty as she felt, but these employees ignored her too. She ducked into the nearby women's restroom, where she hid inside the stall farthest from the door.

Her heart was beating harder than ever. To a bank, nothing meant more than its reputation for trustworthiness. The machine might have confidential customer files on it, Castle business plans, corporate personnel records, or all of the above. An identity theft ring exploiting that information could make millions. So could shady stock market traders or any of Castle's national and international competitors. And the fines and settlement fees once a big breach was disclosed could run to eight figures. ChoicePoint, the commercial data broker, had paid $15 million the previous year for giving up information on 163,000 people.

In the stall, Alien unzipped her satchel and stuffed the laptop in her case, between the business cards and "Get Out of Jail Free" letter. The laptop was a little too big for the case, and she was very nervous. She told herself to calm down and succeeded in stretching the case over the laptop and zipping it closed.

As Alien was about to exit the stall, she heard two women enter the rest-room. One took the stall next to hers. The other tapped her toes, waiting for Alien or her colleague to finish.

Alien was anxious to leave, but she decided to wait it out. She was afraid that with everyone coming back from lunch, she'd be trapped here for a while. But both women were gone mercifully soon, and she followed immediately.

Alien walked to the elevator as confidently as she could, smiling profes-sionally at others as their paths crossed. Everyone else wore a rigid badge with their name, headshot, and the Castle logo clipped to their shirt or waist-band, so she shielded those areas with the laptop case.

The elevator opened back in the lobby. "Did you get it taken care of?" the security guard asked.

"Yes. Thanks so much!" said Alien, giving him a thumbs-up. She crossed the street, opened the car door, and slipped back inside the Taurus.

"Nada," Richard said in a told-you-so tone.

"I did it," Alien said. She zipped open the case. "I got a laptop."

"What?" Richard's eyebrows rose as he beheld her prize.

"Holy shit," he said.

⟫⟪

At Ted's request, they rendezvoused immediately afterward for Alien to walk him through the heist. They met outside and went back in together, gathering after the walk-through in a second-floor conference room to talk. Then Ted brought in the guard.

The man looked stricken. He was still in uniform. Without the reception counter to stand behind, however, he seemed older and frailer—shrunken somehow.

"This is Elizabeth. You've met her before," Ted said. "She's a professional penetration tester. You let her into the facility. Why?"

The guard lowered his head. "Looking back, I know it was the wrong thing to do," he said. "But I just . . . trusted her." He looked up at Alien. Their eyes met. His were dark brown. He wasn't angry. More ashamed.

Then the guard looked away.

"We're on your side," Alien said to him. Struggling over what to say next, she explained, "Like a doctor—they have to hit your knee to test your reac-tion. It hurts for a minute. But in the long run it makes you stronger."

The man nodded woodenly.

Alien continued. "Let's talk about your visitor verification procedures," she said.

Another wooden nod. No eye contact.

He was forty years older than she was, Alien considered. In a normal world, he'd be giving her advice, not the other way around. Of course he was embarrassed. So was she.

※

Having to face the security guard she'd just fooled was awful, but checking email before bed, Alien found congratulatory messages from Bruce, Jules, and the other Jedis and Agents, patting her on the back. And in her suitcase, she uncovered a present from Tanner.

Alien smiled as she tore off the wrapping paper: a pocket edition of *The Art of War*. In neat black cursive Tanner had inscribed: "I thought it was 'The War of Art.' Maybe 'The Love of War' or 'The War of Love.' How about 'Art Warriors from Outer Space'?

"May our campaigns always be fully committed," he concluded, adding a doodled heart and his initial—"T."

"Thanks, honey! You're the best boyfriend ever!" Alien emailed him. "Guess what? Today I stole my first computer," she told him. "Tomorrow I rob my first bank branch."

※

Late morning the next day, Richard circled the icy strip mall parking lot, head shaking as he and Alien passed the Kinko's where she had made their fake business cards, a Blockbuster Video, a fitness center, a party supply store, and a gyro shop before circling back to the long, low-slung redbrick Castle bank building—the first of the branches in town to be assessed. Again, he didn't see how they could crack it.

"A big office building like yesterday, okay—strangers come and go there all the time," Richard said. "Here, a little bank branch, everybody knows everybody else. They can all see everything that's happening. They're not going to let you just carry out a computer."

"I want to get into the vault," said Alien. "Circle again. Let's check the back of the building. Maybe there's a vent we can climb in."

Richard scoffed. “It’s going to be locked down,” he said.

“We’ll figure it out,” Alien said. Like yesterday. “What would be a good ploy?”

Richard looked at his phone, squinting at an incoming text. He shrugged and said, “My daughter’s choir has a concert tomorrow night. I’m going to switch my flight and head home early. Just give it a shot yourself in the morning.”

Concert or no concert, Alien was surprised that he was giving up so easily. But she couldn’t say that.

“Okay, no worries,” said Alien. “Do you want a ride to the airport?”

Richard checked his watch. “Nah, I’ll take a cab.” He added, “Good luck, but yesterday was a fluke. You’re not gonna get into this place.”

Alien peered across the frost-fringed asphalt, new hope dawning only when her gaze reached the rows of self-service copiers inside the glass-walled Kinko’s.

Time to live off the land.

When Richard had left, Alien strode inside the Kinko’s, grabbing her driver’s license and hotel room keycard from her purse. She made a color photocopy of the headshot from the license, cut it out, and pasted it carefully to the keycard. Then she rented computer time, printed out her name and the Castle logo, and added both to the prop.

Alien held the result to the light, smiling.

There. Her own employee badge, just like the ones she had seen inside regional headquarters—or at least close enough to pass casual inspection.

Alien grabbed a clipboard from the rack of office supplies and returned to the computer bank, loading the Castle logo again and pasting it into a new document.

“SECURITY AUDIT,” she typed. “PART I: QUESTIONNAIRE.”

Shortly before ten thirty the next morning, Alien pulled up in the Taurus and parked just outside the entrance to the same Castle branch bank. “Branch manager: Leon Sanders,” her remote reconnaissance notes reminded her.

Moments later, a middle-aged man in suit and tie exited the building, precisely as he had at half past ten — and then again at half past two — the day before. If the pattern held, she had half an hour, Alien estimated. Then Sanders would return from his break.

She stepped out of the car, dressed as she had been at the regional headquarters, only this time with her new clipboard and questionnaire instead of a laptop case — and the fake Castle employee badge clipped to her waistband.

Alien entered. Straight ahead were teller booths. To the left, in front of the empty manager's office, was a desk for his assistant, a pretty brown-haired woman in her early thirties.

"Hi," Alien introduced herself, holding the clipboard close to her chest. "I'm from central security. I'm here to see Leon Sanders."

"He's out," the woman said, "but he should be back in thirty minutes."

"Hmm." Alien looked at her watch. "I still have still three other branches to do," she said. "How about the assistant branch manager?"

"That would be me."

"Great," said Alien. "I'm here to do a spot check of the branch." This would occur twice a year from now on, she explained. "First I need to ask you a few questions," Alien continued. "Then we're going to do a little walk-through together."

The assistant manager gulped, standing quickly, and then, just as rapidly, sitting down, as she processed Alien's words. Her eyes flashed on the hip badge, but she didn't ask for a business card.

Shame. While at Kinko's, Alien had them print new cards, with a fresh central security title, as she was typing the questionnaire.

⟫⟫═⟪

Black pen in hand, Alien stepped through her questions, beginning with access: "Who opens in the morning? What time do they get here? What's your all-clear signal?" she asked.

"Leon or I open at seven thirty," the assistant manager told her. "Whoever comes in first opens the break room blinds. We check all the areas before opening the others. Then we move that plant" — she pointed to a ficus by the front window, visible from the parking lot — "from the left side of the room to the right."

Alien nodded, outwardly stern, inwardly delighted, and scribbled the answers.

"Do you use bait money or dye packs?" she asked. "Do you have many false alarms? Where do you store your combinations? Are the vault keys locked away?"

More quick questions followed, covering everything from common break times to who settled the ATM. The woman answered them all. Then she opened a locked drawer and gave Alien the log noting any security issues they'd experienced in the last twelve months.

"Can you make a copy of this for me?" Alien asked.

"Of course," the assistant manager said.

They stood afterward and walked together through the facility, beginning behind the tellers, where the woman pointed out the specific details she'd mentioned in her answers to the questionnaire. From there, they entered a rear file room, only to be interrupted by a teller. "Yes, Adam?" the assistant manager asked him.

The guy studied Alien. She stiffened, her heart beating so strongly she could feel her pulse in her neck. Had she somehow been caught?

"Can you notarize a car title?" the teller asked the assistant manager.

The woman nodded. "Excuse me," she apologized to Alien, leaving the "auditor" alone with file cabinets containing the records of the branch's customers: names, addresses, account numbers, debts, assets, and every single one of their transactions.

In other words, precisely the information that could be mined to commit financial fraud, blackmail, or worse.

⊷

"I assume you want to see the vault?" the assistant manager asked when she returned.

"Of course." Alien nodded, acting like it was a question she got daily. But she knew to make it snappy if she didn't want an unwelcome meeting with the manager.

Thirty seconds later—less than twenty minutes since she'd entered the building—Alien stood with her pen and clipboard in a cool, dry, thick-walled room, silent as a tomb.

"Here's the water," the assistant manager said, pointing out a clear gallon jug—there in case someone was somehow locked in. Beside the water was an empty white plastic bucket, for obvious reasons, a flashlight, and a phone.

"Very good," said Alien, running a finger along the rows of safe deposit boxes.

The hard part now was pretending she already knew everything. "So . . . ," she said. "Tell me more about where you store your keys."

⬥

Over the next thirty-six hours, Alien tried her "random audit" ploy on three more Castle branches in the area, now dealing directly with the managers. It worked at every one.

The manager at the last branch was especially helpful. She told Alien about the back door that was hard to close, the location of the security videotapes, and even the combination of the vault. As they left the bank branch file room, Alien saw and took an extra set of building keys. Now, if she had wanted to, she could have treated the branch like her own personal piggy bank.

She returned at five p.m. Friday with one of Ted's actual staffers, Castle's security lead on the East Coast. The manager was mortified. Not embarrassed, though. Just angry.

"I will hate you forever," she told Alien the moment her superior was out of earshot.

The words hurt. Alien tried to shrug them off.

Better me than the real *bad guys.*

⬥

Her plane landed at midnight on Friday. Alien finally got home to Fireberry at one a.m. A scratchy Janis Joplin record was playing and the aroma of a fresh mushroom-and-onion pizza filled the living room. Tanner waited in the kitchen, having opened a wine bottle and made her dinner.

Alien kissed his cheek before cutting and nibbling half a slice. "I have to work all weekend," she told him. "The project report is due Monday morning."

Her mind was still racing from the week's events. In college, in these circumstances, she would have taken G to come down, and then microdoses of acid to work nonstop again once she woke. Now she had FDA-approved alternatives.

Alien filled a cup of water. Upstairs, after changing for bed, she took two translucent orange plastic prescription pill bottles from her backpack. AMBIEN 10 MG TABLET, the first one said. ADDERALL 10 MG TABLET, said the second.

Alien opened the Ambien bottle, washed a little white pill down with water, and climbed up to bed with Tanner.

Right after her alarm went off Saturday morning, she rose groggily and downed a little blue Adderall.

Without changing out of her blue satin nightgown, Alien placed her notebooks from the week between her lava lamp and open laptop. "'CASTLE' BANK—Engagement #1," she typed. "CONFIDENTIAL."

<hr />

Strong winds whipped Alien's hair as she sought the entrance to a cavernous steakhouse a week later. Even in February, twenty-seven degrees was cold for Washington. Inside, it felt like eighty. She checked her trench coat and smoothed her hair. She gave the hostess Bruce's name, and was led to a table deep in the recesses of the restaurant. Jules was also there, along with another Jedi, Hank, a tall and slender man in tan chinos and a blue blazer.

The Jedis wore identical pewter lapel pins. These were in the shape of a tiny bent spoon, a reference to the scene in *The Matrix* where Neo, the hero, is shown how to bend spoons with his mind. The trick, Neo learns, is to realize that "there is no spoon": the physical world people believe they inhabit is an illusion.

Throughout lunch, at their plush cushioned booth, the Jedis jokingly lorded their status over Alien: "Ms. Tessman, can you pass the salt?" "Ms. Tessman, can I have the water?" "Ms. Tessman, I dropped my napkin. Would you retrieve it for me?"

Finally, though, Jules said, "Ms. Tessman, would you please stand up?"

Alien did. People at surrounding tables stared.

With exaggerated ceremony, Jules pinned a pewter spoon on her blouse. "Prepare to be spooned," he declared in mock solemnity.

"Better than forked!" Bruce said.

Alien beamed.

As dessert was arriving, they were joined by another man, showing some of the signs of entering one's forties. His dark hair was receding, he slouched a bit, and his mustache had flecks of gray, but he projected an attractive warmth and geniality. "Flight delay," he explained. "Sorry I'm late."

When the guy unbuttoned his coat, Alien saw he had his own bent spoon pin.

"Agent Tessman," she introduced herself. "Elizabeth."

"Agent Michaels," he replied. "Jim." He reached over the table to shake her hand. "We'll be working together on Castle next week. I'm your new partner."

———✦———

Alien and Jim flew together to a combination check processing facility and Castle back office outside Indianapolis. Driving straight from the airport, they reached a featureless office park late Sunday afternoon and entered a huge parking lot off the highway.

"This is going to be tough," Jim said, pointing out a ten-foot-high fence at the rear of the check processing center and a mantrap-style sealed entrance —two sets of doors, the first requiring a badge, the second requiring a personal identification number—stopping tailgaters cold out front. "We may need something like the stuff you pulled in Wilmington.

"Shit," Jim muttered a moment later, and then Alien saw them: two security guards, approaching from an outer station at the main entrance.

She grabbed a map from the glove box and leaned toward him.

"I think we should have taken a right," Alien said, loud enough for the guards to hear.

"What are you doing here?" one guard asked.

"Oh, we're lost," Jim said, with a tinge of frustration in his voice. He turned to her, saying in a tone that showed he was annoyed, "Listen, honey, I'm sure it's off this exit. I don't need a map."

Alien affected exasperation. "He *never* asks for directions," she complained to the guard.

Jim shrugged as Alien named their hotel and the guard pointed them on their way.

He didn't break character even as they hit the highway.

"I'm sorry I got angry, dear," he said, and they both laughed.

———✦———

Monday morning, the same parking lot was packed. Leaving Jim behind in the rental car, Alien lit a cigarette and walked to the designated smokers' area near a side entrance to the back office building. She tried not to make it obvious that she was casing the place. Guards watched everyone coming through the main door. The side door was unguarded but required a keycard swipe to open. And there was a surveillance camera.

Still, maybe she could tailgate her way inside.

"Morning," a goateed man in his late twenties greeted her as he entered the smoking area.

"Morning," Alien returned. She thought about her last cigarette. It had been part of another world, back in Santa Fe three and a half years ago. Smoking again now, in sub-zero suburban central Indiana, felt like a strange dream. She was cold; the trench coat was not made for a Midwest winter.

"I'm new here," she said to the guy, just flirtatiously enough. "What do you do?" she asked.

"I'm a service tech from Diebold—we run the bank's security system," the guy said.

"*Really?*" replied Alien.

As if to pass the time until they were done with their cigarettes, she asked him questions about his work. Alien soon knew what alarms Castle used, how they tracked alerts, and what times the system went down for service.

"Better get to it," the guy said as he took a last drag on his Marlboro and flicked it away. He turned up the collar of his leather bomber jacket. "Nice talking to you."

"Yeah," Alien said, grinning as she waved good-bye to her new friend.

Alien walked back in the direction of the car. Rather than get in, once she caught Jim's eye she nodded. He nodded back.

Alien headed right, toward the side entrance, figuring it would be a security afterthought, at least until the end of the pre–nine a.m. rush.

A man just ahead of her swiped, pulled open the door, and entered. Alien stepped up and caught the handle of the door just before it could close.

When the man was well into the building, she pulled the door open casually as if it had been shut all the way and stepped inside.

She was at the start of a long hallway. At the end of it, just before a bank of elevators, she saw a second, interior guard station, facing the main entrance doors. Alien held back a moment, joining a sea of Castle employees two and three abreast.

Alien entered the elevator with her group.

Barely breathing, she pressed the button for the tenth—and top—floor.

The cubicle setup, she saw, was like that in the Wilmington regional center, but more densely packed and without any separate offices along the perimeter. The dividers were high enough to afford a semblance of privacy, and would also hide her if she lingered for a moment at a particular desk. Alien had with her a digital camera, equipped with image stabilization and small enough to hold unobtrusively in one hand. It could document any security holes faster and more persuasively than handwritten notes. Given how discreet she needed to be, Alien set the camera on silent and for continuous shot mode.

The security measures in place to prevent an unauthorized person from making it to this floor were reasonably good, if obviously not impenetrable. But if someone did get past them, there was almost zero additional defense against data theft. InfoSec experts called a situation like this the "M&M" security model. Once you penetrated the hard outer shell, there was nothing to stop you from getting at everything inside.

Alien passed a floor map. Emergency evacuation plans. Keys hanging in locks. Open file cabinets with documents marked CONFIDENTIAL and Q4 FINANCIALS and UNITED STATES SECURITIES AND EXCHANGE COMMISSION FILING.

Around the corner was a PREVENT TAILGATING! poster, instructing everyone to "watch your back when you enter a secured entrance."

Good advice.

Many desks displayed unattached keycards linked to the building. At least half a dozen computers had people's usernames and passwords written on sticky notes attached to the monitors. As she had hoped, Alien found a few empty cubicles, their occupants either out for the day or not yet at work. Pausing before the computers in these cubicles, she surreptitiously plugged in thumb-sized keystroke loggers that could track every keystroke typed, website visited, or program run, and send that information to an Elite Defense email address or file server. This could be even better than stealing a computer, because the data would keep flowing and her victims might never know it.

Not that she couldn't do both.

On one unoccupied desk in the middle of the floor was a Dell OptiPlex mini-tower identical to the workstation that had gone missing from the hospital.

Shielded by the cubicle dividers, Alien took out and opened a big black garbage bag. A minute later, she had grabbed the computer and was carrying her prize, wrapped like a present, into the elevator, and down to the first floor.

No one looked up.

———⟨⟩———

The same guard station and card-activated door stood between Alien and the parking lot.

Alien hoped to stroll by the guards and wait for someone to enter through the side door. A guard exited his little booth a moment after she stepped off the elevator, however. Alien heard her heels click and then his footsteps keeping pace exactly behind her.

"Hold on!" he said ten feet from the end of the long hallway.

Alien froze, shoulders tensed. The thirty-pound computer frame cut into her arms.

The guard ran past, placing himself between her and the door.

Which he opened for her with a swipe of his own keycard.

"I got that for you, ma'am," he said. "Have a good day."

———⟨⟩———

Jim opened the car trunk, took the computer from Alien, and placed it gently down.

"That was fast," he complimented her.

"Friendly hosts," Alien said.

Jim left to try his own skills. When an employee in front of him swiped at the side entrance, he hustled forward to grab the open door, as Alien had. Then, calm and courteous, Jim held the door open for a Castle staffer *behind* him before proceeding.

Fifteen minutes later, he returned, pockets emptied of his own keystroke loggers, wheeling a sixty-gallon blue plastic shred bin.

Alien was impressed. She peeked inside. Documents intended for shredding filled the receptacle to the brim. Every one was stamped CONFIDENTIAL.

"I love shred bins," Jim said. "This way, *they* gather up the secret stuff for us. And then we just roll it out."

"How'd you get it past them?" asked Alien.

"Rolled it into the elevator and out the front door." Jim chuckled. "After all, the side door was too narrow."

"And?"

"A guard yelled at me: 'Hey!' I thought, 'Shit,' and turned around and said, 'Yes, sir?'

"'Next time you need to take that down a *freight* elevator,' he said."

⟞◆⟝

Jim and Alien had an hour before their local Castle contact could meet them, so they drove around a bit to celebrate and decompress. When Jim saw a small lake ahead, he pulled into the parking lot by its beach.

Ice floes covered the lake like a mosaic. "It's beautiful," Alien said, still high from the successful raid. She left the car and clicked away with her camera, capturing the deep blue sky, glassy ice, and snow-flecked trees.

"Here." Alien handed Jim the camera. "Will you take my picture, so I can show my friends?"

Alien ran from the parking lot and hopscotched out onto the ice, slipping and sliding a bit in her boots and black wool pants. In the middle of the lake, she vamped for the camera, smiling, waving, and striking a bodybuilder pose.

Then she heard the crack.

Alien scrambled to shore, but just before she got there, the ice gave way. She sank twelve inches until her boots found lake bottom. Alien felt the freezing water around her feet and ankles.

As she stepped out, Jim pulled her to shore with a strong grip.

"I guess you can break into anything," he said.

⟞◆⟝

The next day, Alien and Jim scoped Castle's central corporate security offices in Chicago, which filled three lower floors of an unlabeled fifteen-story building at the western edge of the Loop. The only apparent way in was through the revolving front door, behind which was a guard stand with a computer and telephone. Next to the stand was an airtight badge-controlled system like the one in Wilmington.

Jim drove them into the building's parking garage, whose entrance was around the corner from the front. Maybe that would offer another way in.

It didn't.

"Let's try their front door. How about an appointment pretext?" suggested Jim. "Or a vendor delivery?"

"Hey," said Alien. "Have you seen *Sneakers*?"

⎯⬧⎯

The movie Alien was referring to involved characters played by Robert Redford and River Phoenix. They need to break into an office building whose front entrance is protected by a zealous security guard. Alone, it's unlikely either can accomplish the task. Together, though, with Redford impersonating an impatient office party guest and Phoenix a stressed-out delivery guy, they befuddle the guard with simultaneous demands for help.

Now Alien would play a variant of the Redford role, she and Jim decided, and he a variant of the Phoenix one.

They approached the main entrance five seconds apart, Jim in the lead, rolling his black hard-sided suitcase behind him. He walked straight to the guard.

"I have a delivery to make," he said. "United Airlines." He gestured to the suitcase. "One of your guys left this at the airport." Jim went through the motions of checking the tag.

"Zack Bennett," he announced.

The guard typed the name into his computer system. "I'm sorry, sir, I don't have him in the computer," he said.

"Well, the tag says this is his address," Jim said. They began to bicker.

Alien walked by the two of them to the badge-activated barriers. She swiped with another fake badge. Nothing happened.

"It's not working," she called out, shaking the badge in one hand and her laptop bag in the other. She was dressed in her best MBA ensemble: heels, skirt, blouse, and trench coat.

The flustered guard looked up from trying to find Zack Bennett in his system.

"Look, I really need to drop this off, and someone has to sign for it," said Jim, insisting on attention. "I don't have time to wait around."

Alien pouted impatiently. "Excuse me?" she said loudly. "I'm late for a meeting."

"Hey—is he in there or not?" Jim demanded of the guard.

"Hold on!" the guard said. He wavered briefly between the two, and then —just like in the movie—hit a button to let Alien through.

—◆—

Alien did a little victory pirouette when she met Jim back at the car.

"*Two* stolen computers," she announced, handing him her laptop case and a bulging black garbage bag. "We just have to take photos of them."

"Let's go." Jim drove the car back to their hotel and led her up to his room, where they plopped their swag on top of the bed. "Do you want to pose with them for the report?" he asked.

Alien cuddled up with the silver laptop and black desktop, blowing kisses while her partner clicked.

—◆—

By nine the next morning, they were at their last stop. Castle headquarters was a sixty-story steel-and-glass skyscraper two blocks from the corporate security offices, crowned with the red logo.

Alien tailgated in with little difficulty and rode one of a vast bank of elevators to the second floor. She walked into a finance staffer's empty, unlocked office and took an armload of important-looking files. Minutes later, she met Jim at a downtown parking lot and put the files in the trunk.

"Now what?" she asked him. "This is easy pickings. I could go back and hit another office."

"Nah," he said. "Better leave room just in case I nab another shred bin."

He left. Alien looked up, taking in the building she'd just looted with a proprietorial air. Below the Castle sign, she noticed, were glinting double-height windows for three floors of top executive office suites.

Could she get into one of *those?*

—◆—

Alien tailgated again into Castle headquarters. She hovered by the elevators marked 40–60 until she saw a smartly dressed older woman stop and swipe her keycard. Broad in the chest and hips, she wore her hair in graying black bangs unnervingly similar to Alien's mother's.

The woman adjusted her purse while she waited for the elevator to arrive. The door opened, the woman entered, and Alien followed. The woman pressed the button for the fifty-ninth floor, and then, on an adjacent keypad, typed a special four-digit access code she blocked from Alien's view with her body.

"Can I *help* you?" she asked, when Alien didn't press any buttons herself.

Alien smiled. "I'm from IT," she said, drawing her empty laptop case higher, as if it explained everything. "There's an infected computer on the fifty-ninth floor," she confided.

"Oh no," the woman said.

"Yeah, it's attacking other computers," Alien said. "My boss sent me over to find it. I don't want to interrupt anybody, though. Do you know whose it might be?"

The woman looked alarmed. "It could be Mr. Wallace's," she said. "There's nobody else up there right now. I'm his secretary," she explained.

"Oh, okay." Alien nodded sympathetically. Wallace, she knew from remote reconnaissance, was the name of Castle's chief financial officer.

"Well, it will only take a moment to diagnose the issue," said Alien. "I know how important he is and I promise I won't take up very much of your time. It's just that this virus on his computer is attacking other computers and it's interfering with bank operations, so we need to get it taken care of *immediately*."

The elevator whisked them up.

⊷

Alien gaped when they reached the fifty-ninth floor. The area where she'd been earlier had a linoleum floor and fluorescent lighting. Here there was plush emerald-green carpeting beneath a vaulted ceiling and brilliant chandeliers.

"Knock, knock," the secretary whispered before an open door in front of them. "Come in," she told Alien a moment later, leading her into an apartment-sized office whose floor-to-ceiling windows offered a sweeping view of Grant Park and Lake Michigan.

The CFO, Wallace, was a tall, thin fifty-five-year-old with glasses. He studied something on his computer behind a massive mahogany desk.

"Sorry to bother you, sir," said Alien, handing him a fake card. "I'm from IT. Your computer has a virus on it. I know there are top executives here, so we didn't want to shut off your network connection. But I need to clean it off quickly before it spreads."

Wallace frowned. "Again?" he said. "Let me close and back up my files."

Alien waited while the copying took place, checking out framed family photos on the desk—a young wife and three children between two and ten years old.

"Cute kids," Alien said.

"Thanks," Wallace responded.

"So . . . ," Alien asked him. "What's it like being CFO of a big bank?"

Wallace looked surprised but answered frankly. "You know, it's not all it's cracked up to be," he said.

"Really?" Alien stared out the picture windows, watching the people and vehicles pass on the street below like little ants. "You don't like it?" she said.

"I'm not really sure," he ruminated. "It's nice being up here. But I feel like I don't have time with my family. That makes it hard to enjoy the view." At this, he pulled his chair away from the computer. "All yours," Wallace said.

"Great," said Alien, moving forward. While Wallace fidgeted with his tie just a few feet away from her, she knelt to install a keystroke logger on his computer and copy his files to a USB stick.

Why not go for the grand prize?

"Hmm," Alien muttered audibly. "I can't get the virus off," she said, turning to Wallace. "I'm going to need to take your computer back to IT."

He sighed, but he didn't protest. "Sue!" he called in the secretary.

When she arrived, he told her, "IT needs to take my computer. Can I work from yours?"

"Of course."

"What's your password?" Alien asked him. "Just so I can get everything open again after we shut it down here," she explained.

Wallace started to answer: "Jamie one-nine-nine-six—"

Before he could go further, his secretary interrupted him. Her voice had a new sharpness to it.

"Where are you taking it?" she asked Alien.

"Oh," said Alien. "To corporate security." She gave the address, to bolster her story.

"Are you going to *carry* it out?" the secretary asked.

"Yeah . . . ," said Alien. She scratched her neck, blushing. "Or I could call somebody."

The secretary studied her. "What's your name again?" she demanded.

"Elizabeth Tessman," answered Alien.

"Let me look you up in the system," the secretary said.

Alien hesitated. Then, perhaps too quickly, she said, "You know, I'm new and may not be in the system yet."

At these words, Wallace looked her in the eye. He wasn't happy.

"Stay right there," he said.

⟐

Alien presented Wallace with her "Get Out of Jail Free" letter. His secretary called Castle security. Security called Ted Roberts.

Back in Jim's hotel room, Alien told him the whole story. Jim sat on the edge of his bed, facing the desk, where Alien had pulled out a chair. He found it all very amusing, both how far she had gotten and that she had been discovered.

Alien winced. "I was this close," she said, pinching her left thumb and index finger together. In her mind's eye, she returned to what had happened in Wallace's office after his secretary checked the database of company employees and found that she wasn't in it.

"They were *so* freaked out that I got up there," said Alien. "Afraid, I mean. Wallace—it was like he thought I might be an axe murderer or something."

Jim laughed out loud. "No one cares that you got caught," he reassured her. "They care that you got in. Remember, Castle forecloses on people's houses. All they need is some angry guy showing up on the CFO's doorstep. Now that you got up there, they're contracting for a thirty-thousand-dollar follow-up engagement just to look at the security of the senior executive floors."

"Oh." Alien stared at her hands. In her single-minded focus on getting in and out with the most valuable materials, she hadn't considered that Elite was after bigger game.

Jim stood, grabbed a bottle of Perrier from the minibar, and unwrapped two film-covered plastic cups. He poured them both drinks, and then sat opposite Alien again to deliver hers. In the exchange, his fingertips grazed Alien's—their first physical contact, not counting when he'd helped her out of the lake two days earlier.

In three days of working closely together, they had been avoiding any touch, Alien realized. No handshakes, no back pats, nothing. She felt herself flush involuntarily. Why?

Alien glanced up. Jim was looking into her eyes.

"You're good at this," he said.

11

Up in the Air

THE BUZZ FROM THE Castle assignment lingered even after Alien and Jim filed their report. Having proven herself, Alien expected new assignments right away, and she couldn't wait. So she was puzzled when the Jedis put her back on writing or reviewing reports for work done by others. It was even more confusing — and disappointing — when they hired two new Agents, both men, to whom they immediately gave technical pen-testing jobs of the kind she wanted and knew she could handle: researching new network security holes and trying to break into computer systems to find their vulnerabilities. After all, Alien had impressed Bruce in the first place by demonstrating exactly these skills in his course at SCAN. Her predicament was probably typical of other women in InfoSec, but, given that the work was top secret and she was the only female Agent or Jedi at Elite, there was no one else she could ask. She didn't know where she stood.

Alien was further frustrated when the Jedis told her that she was on the team, along with Jim, Jules, and the two new Agents, for a particularly interesting new project. The client was the U.S. Department of Defense, which had hired Elite to study hidden flaws in computer memory that let an interloper see and steal important passwords. The DoD even gave Elite permission, when the project was over, to present its findings at SCAN Capital, the training institute's largest and most important conference of the year, held every April in Washington, D.C. Alien's co-workers never shared any specific project details with her, however, let alone asked her to do anything. The one instance in which she *was* contacted was when one of the new guys saw her name on an email chain and sent her an angry message asking why she was late in processing his time sheets.

"I'm an Agent—I don't process time sheets," Alien wrote back bluntly. "You need to send this inquiry to Melinda," the Elite office manager.

Afterward, Alien decided to ask Bruce directly for more assignments that would use the expertise she'd spent the last half decade building at MIT, Los Alamos, and Mayflower Hospital. "I have a degree in computer science and electrical engineering," Alien reminded him. "I'd like to do technical work."

"I hear you. You're right," Bruce replied. But he thought that before she took on technical cases, she needed more training. He suggested she take another SCAN class or two. Not as a normal student, though. Alien could be a "facilitator," with Elite paying five hundred dollars instead of the usual three thousand dollars a class in exchange for her assisting the instructor. Bruce would pull strings to make sure she got the appointment.

Alien accepted gratefully. The first five days at SCAN Capital she spent as a facilitator in an advanced digital forensics class. Then she rounded out the week with a two-day Web application pentesting crash course.

The final evening, Elite's presentation on its DoD project was the headline event.

Alien slipped late into the packed hotel auditorium and had trouble finding a seat, even way in the back. Jim and Jules, the two project leaders, were already onstage. The session would have been far too technical for almost any other audience, but this group was as eager and ready to take it all in as a bunch of superfans at a rock concert.

Alien watched from a distant corner. She wanted to be up there with her colleagues. Not for the limelight but for the respect it meant. Give her the opportunity and she knew she too could contribute to cool research. But they had never given her a chance.

Forty-five minutes passed as Jim walked through examples of their techniques in action.

"Login! SSH! IM! Email! TrueCrypt! Root!" Jules announced each captured password in turn.

The crowd roared.

After the session, SCAN executives joined the Elite team for drinks at a big circular table in the center of the hotel bar. It was the evening scene at SCAN Toronto all over again, greatly magnified in both size and prestige, as wide-eyed admirers approached, shaking hands with Jim and Jules and asking questions about their project.

The conference higher-ups traded industry gossip with the Jedis. "Symantec bought @Stake. Who's buying Elite Defense?" one of the former asked.

Bruce answered for everyone. "A samurai never sells his sword," he said.

When Alien took a seat next to Bruce, she saw someone point at her and whisper to a buddy, "Who is she?"

Alien's eyes narrowed. Being the only woman in a boys' club might have a certain cachet. But it wasn't clear that she was actually a member.

⟺

Soon after she returned from D.C., Alien finally got onto a technical project. Jason, one of the new Agents, led the effort from his home in Austin. When his report was overdue, Alien was asked to help him. She worked from a bright orange armchair in a crowded Somerville café full of mismatched furniture, a cup of Earl Grey tea at her elbow and her cell phone pressed between her right ear and shoulder.

The client was a global airline. The assignment was a remote pentest—trying to break into computer systems via the Internet alone.

"How about I ride shotgun?" Alien suggested to Jason. "I'll verify and document what you discover."

"Sounds good to me," Jason responded in his Texas drawl.

"Let's get you in," he continued. "SSH as 'test' on their reservation system." SSH stood for *Secure Shell*. The program used encryption to let you log in and execute commands on a remote machine over an untrusted network. First, however, you needed the name of a valid user account—in this case, Jason's instructions implied, "test."

Alien entered the command in a terminal window on her laptop and took a sip of tea as she waited.

"I'm there," she reported, as a prompt—"Password:"—appeared onscreen.

"Lowercase a-b-c-1-2-3," Jason said.

Alien, shaking her head in disbelief at such a common password, typed as instructed.

"$," the terminal returned a moment later, showing a standard UNIX command line.

"It worked," Alien said. Exactly like in the capture-the-flag contest. Only this wasn't one of Bruce's simulations. It was a real airline's reservation system, for actual passengers in actual planes.

"Okay," Jason said. "Type 'su -l.'"

Alien did so, shaking her head again. That Elite had found and cracked the test user account was bad enough. Pivoting from there via the su command to "superuser" status would be a much more dramatic accomplishment. Normal users could see and modify only their own files and programs. The superuser, or root, had full access to *everything*.

"Ready," Alien told Jason when she saw the new prompt for a password.

"Capital A. One. Lowercase r-p-l-a-n-e," he said.

Now she groaned. As if password crackers didn't try basic letter variations. Alien entered the characters, one by one, and hit Return.

"#," the command line said now—the sign that she had, indeed, become superuser.

"Oh my God," Alien whispered, to herself as much as to Jason. "I've got root on a fucking airline network." *And it was so easy.*

"What now?" she asked.

"Knock yourself out," Jason said. "Look around, see where you can go. Take screenshots. We'll talk later and then put it in the report. Bye."

Alien didn't say anything but just sat there as Jason disconnected the call from his end.

She looked around the café. Just another morning in Somerville. People were reading, doing crossword puzzles, typing, and chatting as they sipped their drinks and nibbled on scones. There were Picasso prints on the walls and notices for Iyengar yoga classes, piano lessons, and improv comedy on the bulletin board.

And soon, with maybe a few more hours of exploration, Alien could change or cancel the tickets of any or all of the airline's customers, and reschedule any of a thousand flights, wrecking travelers' itineraries and throwing airports everywhere into chaos.

And so could anyone else, anywhere in the world, with Internet access and the skills at her command.

Alien ran ifconfig, netstat, and other diagnostic commands in the system, just to get the lay of the land. Yup. She could do just about anything she wanted.

Her heart was beating as it had when she had made her way inside Castle. Alien didn't trust her own fingers.

Log out, she told herself. *Don't risk hitting the wrong key.*

She hurriedly took several screenshots and exited the reservation system.

<hr />

That night, following an Ambien, Alien dreamed she was boarding an airplane. She buckled up and put on an eye mask as the safety presentation started. Soon they were in the air. Alien slipped headphones over her ears, plugged in her iPod, and scrolled to select a playlist. Brian Eno, *Music for Airports.* She could vaguely hear the pilot's announcement: "Ladies and gentlemen, we're at cruising altitude."

A piercing rattle followed. Flickering lights. A sudden stomach-lurching drop.

Alien threw off her eye mask and looked out the window. The wings were on fire.

She bolted up in bed beside Tanner.

Alien rubbed her eyes. *It's just a dream,* she told herself.

She reached for the bottle of Ambien. Alien washed a fresh pill down her throat with water and waited for the pull back toward unconsciousness.

<hr />

The plane crash dream recurred several times a week for several weeks. Alien had trouble shaking the fatigue and disorientation from bad sleep, so she relied more on Adderall for energy and focus. She sped through work impressively, but couldn't turn her mind off afterward. So more Ambien. And more Adderall. And a lot more assignments for Elite.

At the end of April 2007, the Jedis sent Alien on the first major forensics job of her own. The client, code-named "Cheeseburger" and headquartered in Seattle, was one of the country's largest fast-food restaurant chains. One of its computer systems had been compromised. She was to assess how, and how badly.

Alien proudly affixed her bent spoon pin to the jacket of a fitted suit. As she entered Cheeseburger's bright and airy lobby, decorated with framed quadruple-life-sized images of every one of the chain's diet-busting menu items, she pulled her equipment behind her in a rolling suitcase.

The Cheeseburger contact, an Asian American man in his late twenties named Dexter, led her to their data center three stories underground. "We noticed the first file transfers yesterday," he said. "I don't know if it's a virus, or we've been hacked, or both."

"And the target was your credit card processing system?"

Dexter nodded. "Yep, we're concerned about PCI"—payment card industry —"compliance."

"Makes sense," said Alien. Cheeseburger franchises served hundreds of thousands of customers a day, and more than half of them used credit and debit cards. If the cashiers couldn't take plastic, the places might as well not open.

Dexter showed her to the machines in question. Alien sat down and started unpacking hard drives and cables from her equipment suitcase. "We'll get the analysis started as soon as I finish the data acquisition," she said.

Dexter thanked her and shook her hand. As he was leaving, he turned and asked, "Anything I can bring you?" He smiled. "The company test kitchen is right upstairs."

———◆———

Fueled by waffle fries and test-kitchen-only "bacon" veggie burgers, Alien worked three straight sixteen-hour days. While the enormous amount of data was being copied, she met with Dexter to discuss larger issues that might have caused the vulnerability. For example, she'd discovered that Cheeseburger had missed several security updates, or patches, on almost every machine.

"Where do you think you need more resources for patch management?" she asked him. "Is the issue with your funding for equipment, or funding for staff?"

"We have the equipment," he said. "But we don't have the staff to keep everything up to date."

Alien opened a new Moleskine notebook. "I'll highlight that in the report as one of my recommendations."

Dexter, who had been consistently tense and somber, seemed to brighten and loosen up.

"That would be fantastic," he said.

———※———

Alien got home and worked all weekend on the Cheeseburger report. As soon as she submitted it, the Jedis sent her to three more consulting engagements in quick succession. With all the travel, the only house chore she could perform was Fireberry's weekly group grocery shopping. Since she was on the road so much, when she woke each morning Alien had to remind herself what city she was in. But at last she was a real Agent.

In early June, Bruce asked her to work side by side with him on a big new case. An emergency: a breach in the computer systems of a southeastern state government.

He told her they needed to get there right away, to book the first flight available, regardless of cost.

After a quick search, Alien had her flight picked. It left in three hours. The ticket cost $1,200. In order to pay, she typed in her credit card number.

CARD DECLINED, her screen shouted at her.

Alien sighed, but there was no time to waste. She found her purse on the floor, returned to the ticket purchase page, and gave her backup credit card information.

Ten seconds of hope. Then the site crushed it. CARD DECLINED, it repeated.

Tanner messaged her. "Do you want to get dinner before poker night?" he asked.

Shit. She'd said she'd be there tonight. "I have to go out of town," Alien typed.

"Again?" Tanner wrote. "Already?"

"Sorry!" Alien told him. The sound of gunshots echoed downstairs, succeeded almost immediately by happy hoots. Friends and housemates in the second-floor lounge watching *Bonnie and Clyde*.

Alien pawed through her desk drawer for her old khaki-colored traveler's money belt. She unzipped the pouch and extracted her backup backup credit card, holding it to the light of her screen.

Alien typed in the numbers, expiration date, and security code.

She waited. More gunshots sounded.

TRANSACTION COMPLETED, the website said at last.

Alien grabbed her suitcase and then SSH'd back into her Elite Defense account. "Dear Jedis," she emailed the founders:

> I find I am fronting the company $800–$4,000 before reimbursement. Often these expenses are large and on very short notice. For example, my last plane flight was $1,000, hotel was $1,400, and car rental was $700. Would it be possible for me to have a company credit card to use?

Alien packed in fifteen minutes. Afterward, she checked her work email. One reply to the credit card request.

"No," Richard had written. "Agents don't get company credit cards."

⸻◆⸻

State and local governments were prime hacker targets. First, they frequently used outdated hardware and software, with weak security settings, and thus were easy to footprint and scan without detection. Second, they held vast quantities of sensitive information. Various agencies stored the names, addresses, birth dates, and Social Security numbers of public employees and vendors, welfare and worker's comp recipients, children in foster care, and members of the National Guard, for example. Identity theft rings could have a field day with such data. There was so much to choose from, they could even develop specialties, selecting certain kinds of victims. Using the Social Security number of a child, for instance, was an increasingly common way to establish a fraudulent line of credit, because the minor might not have any other financial dealings for years.

The state's department of information technology was in a two-story red-brick building eight blocks from the capitol. Bruce explained the situation. "Five weeks ago," he began, "IT changed firewalls"—the part of a computer network restricting outside access. As a rule, firewalls were configured to block *everyone*. Then you added each trusted point of contact, one by one. "During the shift," Bruce said, "the 'Deny All' rule was accidentally removed." Now the entire Internet could walk through the gate.

Elite Defense was hired to learn who got in—and what got out—in the month before the problem was discovered.

Jedi and Agent worked together for five days, meticulously examining the firewall, performing vulnerability scans, and checking event logs. Every day, Bruce taught Alien—and then entrusted her with managing—more of the operational details and logistics.

"With limited time and a large network like this, you want to make sure your scans aren't getting hung up," he said. "First, ping the systems you're scanning"—that is, send a timed request for contact—"and find the average roundtrip time of a packet."

In Nmap, Bruce explained, there were options to set the minimum and maximum times the program waited to get results. "Don't just accept the default. When you have the average, you can set reasonable numbers, but you're not going to wait around forever."

He offered an analogy. "It's like mapping a cave," Bruce said. "What do you use? Probably echolocation. The sound waves go out and they bounce back to you." In surveying an unknown network, you started by sending packets. "They go out, and they bounce back to you. You're waiting for that system to respond."

Alien felt privileged to have the tutorial. Bruce was as great as a one-on-one mentor as he had been in the classroom.

Once they knocked off for the day, well into the evening, Bruce dedicated himself to researching and choosing which upscale restaurant they'd eat at, a new one every night. Although there were only two of them, he ordered half the menu so that they could sample as much as possible. He didn't know the meaning of downtime.

"We've been on-site all day," said Alien the second evening. "We have to be up early tomorrow morning."

"C'mon. Work hard, play hard," Bruce said.

———◆———

As the sun set on their final day, Alien watched the dying light out a second-story conference room window with physical longing, wishing she could feel its heat on her body for even a few seconds, rather than endlessly recycled air conditioning. She turned back, though, as Bruce cleared his throat. "Ms. Tessman will bring you up to date," he said.

Alien nodded, first to Bruce and then to the state's chief information officer—a poised middle-aged woman—and the four men who made up her IT leadership team. The government employees prepared for the worst.

"We found evidence that the systems were penetrated over a period of three weeks by attackers who spoke four different languages," said Alien. "The intruders appeared to come from addresses in Vietnam, Egypt, Thailand, Turkey, and Estonia. We know this based on logs that happened to remain on certain host systems. However, because the firewall was open and not logging, there is not enough evidence to determine what, if any, data they may have transferred."

The CIO pursed her lips. Her staffers slumped. Bruce nodded encouragingly, however, signaling Alien to continue. As the natural light from outside diminished, fluorescent bulbs overhead gave everyone's face a sickly pallor.

"There was no central server collecting or retaining logs," Alien went on. "So, for the Windows systems, at least, we have no way of telling when anyone logged in, when they logged out, where they were coming from, or what they did on the systems. Because local system logs were retained only for thirty days, we don't know precisely how or when this all began. We worked with Steve"—she gestured to one of the IT staffers—"to see if we could recover logs from backups of the systems. Unfortunately, after attempting a test restore, the backups do not appear to be working."

Steve looked at his shoes. The CIO frowned.

Alien wrapped up. "We also examined several Linux servers," she said. "These did have logs stored on them, and we were able to confirm that they were accessed by unauthorized users. In one system, we found Social Security numbers, health information, and other records. So it is likely that many state residents have had their information compromised. I've shared the important log files with your team, and all of the details will be in our report."

She stopped. No one said anything for a moment. Alien glanced out the window again. It was totally dark. The glass reflected her own gaze back like a mirror.

"Excellent work," said Bruce, sweeping in. "Ms. Tessman is a very thorough investigator," he told the others. "Do have any questions?"

The CIO spoke. "The governor is being considered for an ambassadorship," she said. "Discretion is very important."

Alien didn't wait for Bruce. "I recommend consulting with your legal counsel and your PR team," she said. "Legal will make the decision on who needs to be notified. We'll have the full forensic report ready for you in two weeks, and you'll have the opportunity to review the draft and let us know if you need any changes. It's been a pleasure working with you."

The IT managers filed out. Bruce excused himself to take a phone call, leaving Alien alone with the CIO. While Alien packed up, the woman asked her, "Have you been enjoying your visit?"

"Oh, yes," Alien replied politely as she zipped up her laptop case. "It's been lovely."

"Any interest in staying?"

Alien looked up.

"If you want a job with us, we'd love to have you," the CIO said.

Alien considered it. Warm weather year round. The power to help ordinary people. Weekends to herself. But go back to sitting in a cubicle?

No way.

Bruce reentered the room.

"Thank you very much, but I'm happy where I am," said Alien. "Perhaps Elite Defense can consult with you on proactive measures, and I can visit you again soon."

In mid-June, Alien and Tanner broke up. Her work schedule wasn't the only problem, but it was a big one. Any personal cost seemed a fair exchange, however, when Bruce called again.

"The Pentagon booked us to do a security briefing July ninth," he said. "Interested?"

"Really?" Alien's voice rose in excitement.

Bruce chuckled. "I'll take that as a yes. And one more thing." His voice turned serious. "You have to get great evals," he warned her. "Over nine"—on a zero-to-ten scale—"or you won't get a gig like this again.

"And before that," Bruce went on, without waiting for a reply, "we want you to do a wireless network assessment for an outfit outside Los Angeles, code name 'Neptune.' They're a big defense contractor. It'll be a good warm-up for DoD culture."

Tuesday, July 3, Alien flew to LAX, rented a car, and drove south. Neptune's head of IT, Rafael, was, like Alien, from New Jersey. "Would you like me to give you a tour?" he asked after they shook hands in the company's carpeted lobby and reception area.

They walked down a flight of stairs from reception to a guard station, and then through a door to the Neptune manufacturing plant, a white-painted, almost windowless concrete box the length and width of a football field, with tall, shiny metal exhaust towers like a cruise liner.

Inside, Alien passed men and women wearing thick protective gloves and goggles. They worked with industrial-sized lathes, drills, saws, and other equipment, which produced impressive sparks en route to tall stacks of shaped metal. Behind the stacks, other employees, using much smaller tools, including lasers, performed careful detail work. A third set of employees tracked everything produced with low-beeping handheld barcode scanners, with most of the remaining floor space taken up by a gigantic tub of water.

"What's that for?" asked Alien.

"Testing," Rafael said. "Almost everything we make has to work underwater."

They left the fabrication area and returned to Neptune's offices, passing sales, human resources, IT, and upper management before ending at a tidy closet, secured with a badge-activated lock, for Neptune's network equipment. "Great," Alien said, checking color-coded cables labeled by use and location. The more organized IT was in a hub like this, she had learned from experience, the greater the odds the network was secure everywhere else.

At the end of the tour, Rafael set Alien up in a conference room. She booted her laptop, plugged a six-inch black wireless antenna and special-purpose Wi-Fi-monitoring network card into the USB ports, and ran a free software program called Kismet. Unlike with the company credit card, Richard had been happy, even enthusiastic, to outfit Alien for this assignment, promising, "This is the top-of-the-line gear."

And he was right.

Within seconds, a list appeared of nearby wireless access points and their respective clients, traffic, signal strength, and encryption, if any.

"How can I help you help me?" Rafael asked.

Alien turned and looked out a window to the parking lot.

"I'm going to take my laptop for a walk," she said.

As Alien circled the Neptune building, she kept adjusting the antenna. Every few yards, the names of new access points appeared on her screen—some from Neptune, some from neighboring buildings, including ones she couldn't see. Whenever she detected a Wi-Fi network, Alien checked to see whether it was using an outdated encryption standard called WEP (Wired Equivalent Privacy); if so, she tried to crack it. Once she completed her initial walking tour, she sat down on a bench outside Neptune's main entrance, paused Kismet's packet capture feature, and checked the length and file size of the results.

When she got back to the hotel that night, she'd produce a map that showed the relative strengths of access points that were available from each location.

Alien looked up. Blue skies. The sun shone, its heat tempered by a gentle breeze. She smiled as she walked past the parking lot, along the tree-lined highway access road, testing how far away she could get a signal, until the ocean came into view.

⟫

Alien met Rafael back in the conference room. "I have to go through and analyze the results, but I was able to get into your barcode scanner network and manufacturing equipment network from all the way down the street," she said. "Pretty close to the highway."

"No kidding." Rafael tugged his shirt collar.

"I have a pretty nice antenna," Alien said. "But anybody can order it on Amazon. And your manufacturing network is still using WEP encryption."

"I *know*," he said. "We can't upgrade to WPA"—Wi-Fi Protected Access, the new standard. "Our vendors don't support it."

"Well, I captured a bunch of packets," Alien said. She swiveled her laptop to show him the raw data. "If you want, I'll do a live demonstration for your execs and then they can decide if they want to invest in security."

"That would get their attention," Rafael told her. The factory and its physical contents weren't Neptune's most valuable resource. Its plans and data were. With them, a competitor could save itself hundreds of millions of dollars in research and development costs. Worse, America's foreign adversaries could leap a generation in their own military capabilities. What did a water tub test matter if an enemy stole Neptune's technology and used it against the United States?

"*Really?* The highway?" Rafael asked after a lengthy pause.

She nodded.

"We're *leaking,*" he said.

"Everyone is," Alien said.

⟿

Alien got home from California the afternoon of Wednesday, July 4. Her only meaningful mail was a cluster of credit card statements indicating overdue payments. Tents and sleeping bags, camp food and cooking gear filled the Fireberry living room. A dozen friends and housemates ran up and down the stairs, adding to the heap before a camping trip to Maine.

Eddie, her old friend since college, was with them. As he gave Alien a hug, the sleeves of his V-neck tee tightened around his biceps. "I'm so excited," he said. "It's going to be the best weekend ever! You're beautiful! Come with us!"

Alien laughed. It felt so good to see Eddie again. And she really wanted to join them.

"I can't," she said wistfully. The Pentagon presentation was Monday morning. In the meantime, she had to write the Neptune report and prepare.

⟿

Alien spent Sunday afternoon rehearsing for her presentation. When she heard raindrops pitter-patter against her skylights, she thought of her friends and their camping trip.

Where are they? They should have been back hours ago.

Looking forward to hearing their stories of the trip, she'd chosen the latest flight to Washington she could.

At five p.m. Alien called her housemate Kinza, who didn't answer.

Alien called Eddie but got his voice mail greeting. "Have a beautiful fucking day and don't hold nothing back!" he said.

Alien smiled.

⟿

Seven p.m. came and went. Alien had to head to Logan. *Maybe they stopped for dinner.*

She was lugging her suitcase down the stairs when her phone rang. It was Kinza.

"What's going on?" asked Alien. "Where is everybody?"

"You didn't hear?"

Alien waited, afraid to answer.

"Eddie's missing," Kinza said.

⟞⟝

Alien hated herself for flying to D.C. instead of driving straight to Maine to join the search party. "Can I move up my return ticket?" she called and asked a customer service rep at one a.m., after checking in to her hotel.

"I'd be happy to assist you," the woman said. She typed. "There's a two p.m. flight this afternoon," she reported. "The change fee is a hundred and fifty dollars."

Alien pictured her pile of credit card bills, plus the additional line item for this hotel room. "You don't have a bereavement fare?" she asked.

"I'm very sorry for your loss," the woman responded. "May I ask the name of the deceased and the telephone number of the funeral home?"

"My friend is missing—not dead," Alien told her.

"Oh," the woman said. "The bereavement fare is only for after someone has died."

Alien opened her purse and paid the regular change fee with her backup backup card.

He's still here—he has to be.

After hanging up, Alien tried Eddie again. The same message answered. His voice mailbox was full.

Alien stayed up all night. She called Eddie again and again, until it was time to shower, down an Adderall, and get dressed.

⟞⟝

Alien tried and failed to smile as a Pentagon police officer took her picture the next morning. He printed a barcoded fluorescent yellow laminated badge and told her where it had to be displayed, directly above her bent spoon pin on the jacket of a new brown-striped black skirt suit. To the right of the photo, Alien saw, was her name, the Pentagon Force Protection Agency logo—an eagle, wings unfurled over the iconic five-sided building—and, in all caps, ESCORT REQUIRED.

Under that was printed the name and phone number of her escort, Melvin

Harris, of the Information Assurance Branch of PENTCIRT—the Pentagon Computer Incident Response Team.

"Welcome," said Harris, who carried himself like a soldier but was dressed in dark blue civilian trousers and a crisp white short-sleeved shirt and blue and red rep tie. "We're going four rings in, two stories down, six corridors over," he told her. "Should take about twenty minutes."

Alien grimaced, already regretting her choice of two-inch stiletto heels. "Lead the way," she said.

They walked, stopping multiple times at checkpoints for badge swipes or ID verifications. Alien complied automatically, meanwhile examining her surroundings. Access control equipment varied from door to door. *Wonder if they have a consistent procurement policy for their security systems,* she thought. Then, well into the windowless bowels of the building, a gift shop appeared, selling coffee mugs and challenge coins, Iraqi "Most Wanted" playing cards, and a T-shirt with red, white, and blue sequins in the shape of the Pentagon.

Her feet screamed.

At last they reached the basement auditorium: four hundred black-backed seats and a gray stage fringed with black velvet. Flags surrounded a podium behind which Harris loaded Alien's PowerPoint slides on his own secure laptop. Her talk title—"Defending Yourself Online"—appeared on giant mounted flat-screen monitors to the left and right.

The gist of her presentation—on encrypting email and hard drives, installing firewalls, and avoiding viruses, keystroke loggers, and other malware—was the same as it would have been for almost any client. Keeping military information safe, however, involved much higher stakes than even the highest-profile corporate or government case, since the worst possible outcome was not just lost time, money, and trust but deadly warfare. Meanwhile, everyone was a potential adversary, from what InfoSec professionals called "script kiddies"—inexperienced and juvenile (in both senses of the word) hackers—to well-funded offensive hacking experts in the service of other nation-states.

People filed in, some in suits, some in military dress, some in normal work clothes, all with ID badges.

"Ready?" Harris whispered after an A/V guy clipped a mic to her. It was a few minutes to nine. The presentation, including the Q&A, was scheduled to last two hours.

Alien nodded. She felt nothing now — not fear, not excitement. She wanted to finish this and get back to Cambridge.

While she was being introduced, Alien glanced down at her left wrist. At work, she always wore a Raymond Weil watch with gold hands and a small, easy-to-read white face her mother had given her as a college graduation present. It wasn't there. She must have left the watch in her hotel room, Alien realized.

"Everyone — please remember afterward to fill out feedback forms," Harris said.

Alien opened by thanking the audience.

"What a privilege to be here," she said.

The normally bustling Fireberry was empty. Lights out, no music. This gave it a haunted quality. Alien carried her bags up to the third floor. She shed her suit and heels and threw on shorts, a T-shirt, and sneakers. She ran to Star Market, filling the Volvo with apples and bananas, cereal and granola bars, cheese and tortillas, soup and sliced bread, peanut butter and jelly. It was just like one of her usual grocery runs, but without the return trip home.

She drove alone to Maine.

Her friends waited, crammed three or four to a room, in an Econo Lodge in South Portland. With them were Eddie's mother, father, and sister.

Alien hugged them, one by one.

They all played cards after dinner. "What happened?" Alien asked.

"We walked around the lake Saturday afternoon," Kinza told her. "We were nearly back to camp when Eddie wandered off on his own. He had taken some acid. The rest of us started a fire. He never came back."

"He's fucking with us," said Alien. "It's Eddie."

Kinza smiled. She bit her lip to keep from crying.

"When Eddie does come back, I'm going to kill him for this," Alien said.

Finding Eddie was a forensics case, Alien told herself.

First thing the next morning she visited the campsite, turning from a wide tree-lined lake to the start of the forest trail where Eddie had gone missing. With several friends, she combed the twisting path, calling, "Eddie! Eddie! *Eddiiie!*" If he was out here in the woods, however, he'd hidden himself too well.

Uniformed state police officers visited the hotel that evening. Their leader, a fit fifty-year-old sergeant with a crew cut and a mustache, passed out copies of a topographic map. "The dots mark everywhere we've looked," he said.

Eddie's mother saw the marks for the campsite, forest trail, and surrounding mountains. "But why are there all these dots in the lake?" she asked.

The sergeant spoke gently. "Those are dive team locations," he said.

⟢⟶⟶⟵⟶

They searched and waited two more days. Friday morning, Alien inventoried Eddie's backpack, making a careful list in one of her Moleskine notebooks she used for Elite Defense work. Afterward, Alien folded Eddie's clothes. When she finished, her hands smelled like the smoke of a campfire she had never seen.

That night, the state police arrived at the Econo Lodge looking for Eddie's parents. The rescue team leader asked them to come to his cruiser. Alien and the rest of her friends watched from the room where they'd been sharing a pizza.

The trooper spoke quietly, then opened the front door of the cruiser and took out a clear plastic bag that he showed them.

Eddie's mother began to cry and fell into Eddie's father's arms.

Alien's heart sank. She stepped forward anxiously.

In the bag was what looked like one of Eddie's Crocs.

Alien and the others soon learned that a kayaker had found it, floating in the middle of the lake.

It was a recovery operation now.

⟢⟶⟶⟵⟶

Alien's eyes were red from crying when she got home. Alone in her room, she checked her work email mechanically. Half her inbox was a message chain with the subject line "Re: Pentagon."

Alien swore. She'd run out as soon as possible after the Q&A, leaving Harris, her host and escort, to collect the evaluations. She didn't care what they said.

Alien opened the earliest message from her bosses, bracing for the blow-back.

"Congratulations, Agent Tessman!" Bruce wrote, with a cc to all the other Jedis. "You averaged 9.8 on your evaluations. The Pentagon wants us back two more times this year."

⊰——⊱

Eddie's body was recovered three weeks after he disappeared. The first Sunday of September, his thirtieth birthday, friends and family gathered in a park near Fireberry for his memorial service. Later in the month, Alien flew to New Mexico to see Piñon.

Mace. Frostbyte. Eddie. "Why does this keep happening?" she asked Piñon over lunch at a tiny Mexican restaurant on Airport Road.

Alien and her friends encouraged one another to push limits and do daring things on their own. But they were also supposed to watch out for one another. Eddie's death made her realize anew how difficult it was to do both at once.

"Let's make a pact," Alien said, only half-joking. "I'll go to your funeral if you go to mine."

Piñon lit an Eagle. "I'm not coming to your funeral," he said.

Alien was hurt. "Come on. I'll come to your funeral," she teased. "I love you."

Piñon puffed. "I love you too, sweetie," he said. Then he changed the subject. "Have you been riding your motorcycle?"

"Lots," said Alien. "I'm not scared anymore."

Piñon didn't say anything, but she saw satisfaction in his single nod.

He seemed sadder and a little mysterious when it was time to drop her off at Jake's house, where Alien was having dinner and crashing on her old boss's couch. It was a pricey neighborhood, and Piñon's self-maintained blue Subaru beater contrasted sharply with the sleek new luxury vehicles in surrounding driveways.

"I'll miss you," he said quietly.

"Oh, Piñon." His words sounded so final. Alien hugged him. "We'll be friends a long time."

She hopped out and shut the car door. It closed with a thud.

⊰——⊱

In early October, Alien flew to North Carolina to help a hacked video game company. The week after that, Castle had contracted for a new round of physical pentests in and around corporate headquarters.

Her first day off in between, Alien rushed through a series of errands. She was in front of a pet store, on her way to buy crickets for a new pet frog, Pterodactyl, and lizard, Nancy, when her cell phone rang. Alien saw a Santa Fe area code.

It was the fire artist from the Island commune.

"Hey—I just wanted to let you know," he said.

Alien's shoulders shook at the next sentence. Her eyes stung. She buckled. "How?" she asked.

"A heart attack in his sleep."

Alien struggled to sit down on a step in front of the pet store. She lowered her head between her knees and sobbed.

———◆———

Alien spent seven hundred dollars—fuck the bereavement fare—to fly back to New Mexico.

Standing the next morning in the middle of the Rio Grande Gorge Bridge walkway, Alien couldn't reconcile the feeling of warmth from the sun and the cold of the wind. She was with Piñon's two ex-wives and two grown children.

The high-pitched chirps of American dippers and dusky flycatchers echoed off the canyon walls. The vast steel bridge trembled a bit whenever a vehicle crossed. Clouds swelled overhead, making shadows pass and play.

The family members handed the urn from one to another, each reaching in to scatter Piñon's ashes to the white water coursing 550 feet below.

I thought Eddie would stay young forever. And I thought Piñon would never die.

"I travel with you to play in the nine rivers . . . ," Alien read aloud from *The Pocket Tao Reader:* "The sky will darken soon; / But wanting to stay longer, / I forget about going home."

———◆———

The Castle return engagement started two days later. Alien and Jim succeeded at every site but the last, though it wasn't their fault. They went to the address they had been given of a data backup and disaster recovery center on Chicago's South Side. To their trained eyes, it looked like an abandoned brick building.

"Is this it?" Alien asked.

"Well, this is the address," Jim said.

Sleet began to fall. They peeked as best they could through filthy windows and saw piles of old newspapers. No servers. No people.

"Are you *sure?*" asked Alien.

Jim called Ted Roberts. "He says it's the right place," he reported.

They circled it a second time. "There's no indication of any activity," said Alien. "Not any for a while."

"Maybe they want their DR site to be undercover," said Jim. "Should we try the lock?"

With frozen fingers, Alien took out the same lock-picking tools she'd had since freshman year. Jim had his own. One at a time, they halfheartedly tried to pick the rusty back door lock.

Nothing budged.

"I'm soaked." Alien hugged herself, teeth chattering. She peeked in another window. Behind it, a little black wire ran to a box above the door. "At least it looks like it's alarmed," she said. "But I'm getting the willies. Can we just go?"

"Yeah." Jim nodded. "Okay."

The call came fifteen minutes later, as they were approaching their downtown hotel. "Uh-huh," Alien heard Jim say. "Well, no harm, no foul."

He hung up. "Wrong address."

⟡

Alien showered and wrapped her hair in a towel in her hotel room. From her suitcase, she changed into flannel polka-dot pajama bottoms and a gray cotton Route 66 tank top emblazoned with the legendary highway sign.

A seven-beat knock. *Shave and a haircut—two bits.*

Alien opened the door.

Jim was there, holding a bottle of wine.

⟡

They sat on opposite sides of the bed, knees up and backs against the headboard, watching a movie. Two plastic wine cups, appropriated from Alien's bathroom, sat in easy reach on the two night tables. About forty minutes into the movie, Jim inched closer to the middle. Without a word, Alien recipro-cated. Soon they were side by side, eyes on the screen.

The movie ended.

Alien rested her head on her partner's shoulder.

Jim studied her. He took a strand of hair that had fallen across her cheek and tucked it back behind her ear.

He put his hand gently under her chin and lifted her face to his.

⟪⟫

Early gray light filled the hotel room the next morning. "It feels so good to hold you," Jim said.

They snuggled, murmuring happily. But Alien felt guilty.

"Are you going to tell your wife?" she asked.

Quickly, gently, he said, "I wasn't planning on it."

Alien turned over. Jim pulled her back. They kissed.

Bad, thought Alien. *So bad. For both of us.*

12

Europe on Five Hacks a Day

ALIEN AND JIM WERE like two cops assigned to work a beat together. They were partners. They had experiences together—intense experiences, like something out of a movie. They made each other laugh. They impressed each other. They respected each other. They saved each other's butts. And one day, it seemed to Alien, they simply realized that they were in love.

Whether that was true—or if it mattered—only time would tell.

Over the next six weeks—late October, November, and early December 2007—Alien spent an average of six out of every seven days on the road for Elite Defense. Three times she and Jim were scheduled for the same conference or engagement. At first Alien thought it was a coincidence. Then, after they gave a talk together in Detroit almost identical to the one she had done alone at the Pentagon, she asked him, "Did they *need* two people here?"

"I told my contacts I thought it was important to have you here as well as me," Jim said.

Alien kissed him. He *wanted* her, and was talking Alien up to others. But she still felt uneasy about two of them being sent when one would do. And, as she buckled up for the plane ride home, another, more intimidating thought occurred to her. Both she and Jim were Agents. But he obviously held more sway at Elite Defense. If he could get Alien assigned to anything, he could probably also get her unassigned.

And she would never know.

In mid-December, Melinda emailed Alien with a new assignment. The following Monday, she was to lead a security awareness seminar in Silicon Valley.

"Jim is presenting with you," the office manager wrote.

Sunday morning, Alien took a five a.m. cab to make her flight out of Boston, but snowstorms held her plane on the tarmac for hours. By the time they took off and flew almost seven hours to San Francisco, the runway was jammed and the gates were full, so the plane circled the city until ten p.m. local time, more than twenty hours after she had gotten up.

Alien dragged herself to the taxi stand, holding her rolling suitcase upright in front of her like a walker. She didn't get to the hotel until close to midnight.

The door to room 1219 opened before she could even knock. Jim, whom she had called from the cab, had been listening for her footsteps. He swept Alien up by the waist, sank his face into her neck, and began undoing her belts and buttons.

Alien had barely enough strength to step back. "I'm exhausted," she said.

"Oh . . ." Jim paused. "We don't have to," he said. But his eyes begged otherwise.

"No . . . we can." Smiling, Alien stroked his chest. "Just slowly. I'm so tired. And so happy to see you," she said.

Alien paused in the middle of brushing her hair in the bathroom the next morning. "I have an idea for a research project on recovering deleted evidence from hard drives," she told Jim. "It would be a perfect conference presentation. Want to help?"

"Sure," he said. Jim entered, holding her coat. "Fill me in on the drive."

An hour later they stood side by side in front of thirty programmers and their bosses. The client was a fast-growing dot-com too busy building their platform to think about its vulnerabilities. Alien loaded the slides she'd prepared for them. Jim made the introductions. "Hi—I'm Jim Michaels. I'm a senior consultant with Elite Defense," he said. "And this is my colleague, Elizabeth Tessman. She's a junior consultant."

Junior? Alien looked up in surprise.

Jim had arranged things so that he and Alien had almost a whole free day together following their presentation. Back at the rental car she said, "I'd appreciate it if you'd introduce me as a consultant or senior consultant too. It's hard for me to have leverage with the client as a 'junior' consultant. Besides, I'm another Agent, the same as you."

"Sorry. You're absolutely right." Jim patted her knee.

They drove to Half Moon Bay. Still unsure how he really thought of her, Alien followed up about the research project. "You know what would be cool?" she said. "I bet I can make it all boot from the SD card in my phone."

Jim said nothing for several seconds. Then: "You'd need three partitions," he said.

Alien nodded enthusiastically. "Say five hundred megabytes for the usual cell phone stuff, sixty megs for a RAM dumper, and the remainder for whatever else we can rip."

It was raining when they reached the beach. Nevertheless, Alien pulled Jim after her, over and into the dunes.

During the rest of December 2007 and January and February 2008, Alien pursued her research project with Jim as best she could. They still saw each other in person every two or three weeks, but the collaboration—like every other aspect of their relationship—took place via email far more than through any live exchange. The hours she spent programming were on top of her already intense work schedule, whether on the road or back in Cambridge, for Elite and its clients. This meant she was up well into the night, her phone or a test laptop half-disassembled in front of her for easy access to the memory and storage units.

The exhilaration she felt when she sent Jim her latest code, or reviewing what he sent her, more than compensated for the lost sleep. Alien imagined them presenting their findings at a packed session of an important security conference and then meeting back at the room later to celebrate.

The killer effort was worth it. But it was still killer. And the requirements of her job could always push everything else aside.

On the Thursday after Presidents' Day, one of the Jedis called Alien. A multibillion-dollar U.S. bank, code-named "Diamond," had bought a French competitor—"Bastille." In the wake of the acquisition, some Bastille executives and employees left to start their own new financial institution. Diamond believed that they had been poaching clients all the while, and planned to sue. To prove the charge, however, they needed evidence.

In secret. From Paris. This weekend.

Enter Agent Tessman.

⟐

Alien's flight was slated to leave Logan Airport for Charles de Gaulle at eleven p.m. At eight thirty p.m. she was just pulling into the parking lot of Micro Center, Cambridge's computer supply superstore. She grabbed a shopping cart and hurried to the aisle for external hard drives. Alien swept the shelves clean. In ideal circumstances all the drives would be identical, but she had to take what was available.

Next came power strips, extension cords, USB adapters, and French electrical outlet adapters. Then gaffer tape, a label maker, rolls of label tape, and Sharpies.

The cart teetered. A Micro Center staffer, a tall, thickset bald guy in a dark blue shirt and tie, approached. "Can I help you?" he asked.

Alien counted her present haul: fifteen hard drives. "Do you have more in the back?" she said. "I'm ten hard drives short. I'm looking for external hard drives," she said. "Or extra SATA drives would do in a pinch. And do you have anything better than fifty-four hundred rpm?"

The Micro Center employee looked down at her. He was at least six two, a foot taller than Alien. "Well, little lady, let me tell you something about hard drives," he said. "You don't care about speed—you care about storage space."

Alien took a deep breath. "Thank you so much for your help," she said as cheerfully as she could muster. "Do you have any seventy-two hundred rpm drives? Also, do you have any more of these SATA-to-USB adapters? There were only two."

As expected, polite persistence was more effective than a lecture.

"I'll check," the man said, heading in the direction of the storeroom.

Alien wheeled toward the register, preparing stoically for the hit to come to her credit cards. Between tonight's hardware buy, the deposit on her Paris hotel room, and her plane ticket, the total was around ten thousand dollars. What was her alternative, though? Pass on an international corporate espionage case?

Maybe I'll get the reimbursement before the credit card bill, she lied to herself.

Alien sighed.

She unloaded her shopping cart and opened her purse.

⸻

Bastille Bank headquarters was a four-story white stone neoclassical building with Doric columns in front and heavy mahogany doors with brass fittings. The client contact—Mitch, a tall Diamond American security executive in his mid-fifties, dressed in a trench coat—unlocked the ornate doors for Alien and her gear suitcase after the last employees had left Friday evening at six p.m. "The janitorial staff won't come until Sunday night," he said. "If anyone else enters unexpectedly and asks questions, you're an auditor."

"I'm not great at French," said Alien, suddenly getting flashbacks to seventh grade.

"Even better." Mitch handed her a keycard necessary to open other doors inside.

The first three stories of the building each had dark glass-topped desks for fifteen to twenty employees in a modern open office layout, with a ten-person conference room on both the second and third floors. The top floor held three executive suites, another, larger conference room, and the Bastille data center. While they waited for others on the engagement to join them, Alien walked the entire building with Mitch, making detailed notes on the setup of every desk and workstation in a Moleskine notebook and taking photographs with her digital camera—better to reassemble later everything they were about to take apart.

Over the next two hours, Mitch let in the entire team. First to arrive after Alien was a mustached man in suit and tie, contracted as legal counsel. "Al," he introduced himself. Following him were six trusted French tech staffers, hired after the acquisition, who understood English and were ready to receive orders. Last came Bruce, the only Jedi on-site, toting a brick-sized black Tableau Forensic Imager, used to make precise disk copies at very high speeds, among other functions.

By eight p.m., everyone had gathered in the third-floor conference room. But Bruce, standing back, holding the Tableau, made no move to take charge.

"Let's set up in the conference room," Alien said. "Move the tables off to the side," she directed the local staffers. "Make a ring. And then can you guys get us ten workstations that we can use to do the imaging?"

While they worked, Alien ran power cables and adapters taken from her suitcase, and then unpacked four of the external hard drives. She carefully labeled each of them, using the label maker.

"There are seventy desktops in the office — some with forty gigabytes, most with eighty gigabytes," Alien told Bruce. "Each external hard drive is two hundred and fifty or five hundred gigabytes — I wasn't able to get all the same size drives. So each drive can store images of at least three desktops."

They returned together to the first floor, carrying the label maker and a set of tiny screwdrivers. Alien and Bruce opened the physical frames of desktop computers. Inside each, where no one else would notice it, they affixed a small white label corresponding to the matching external hard drive they were taking back to the United States. That way, too, they could be sure they were reinstalling the correct drive on the correct computer on the floor plan when they finished.

When she and Bruce were done with the first floor, Alien booted the workstations the other men had brought into the conference room with a CD running Helix, a computer forensics toolkit. To each workstation she connected one of the first batch of ten desktop drives she and Bruce had removed, and one of the external drives. She ran a checksum program, MD5sum, a kind of digital fingerprinting tool to make sure nothing was inadvertently altered in the disk duplication. Finally, after she started the imaging process, Alien typed "while true; do ls -l; sleep 10; done" at the command line.

"Now it will give a file size update every ten seconds," she told the local guys. "Wait a few minutes and then extrapolate to how long forty or eighty gigs should take."

Bruce turned on the Tableau and said, "Different drives will end copying at different times. We'll have to babysit them."

Alien nodded. She flipped her notebook to a new page and drew up a schedule of shifts and breaks.

———◆———

At dawn Saturday, walking to her hotel to crash briefly, Alien calculated when the last hard drive copy would complete. Using the workstations, each forty-gig drive took approximately four and a half hours to image. An eighty-gig drive took approximately nine hours. Working all weekend, even with the Tableau, they'd barely be half-done. That left Monday, Tuesday, Wednesday, and Thursday nights, seven p.m. to four a.m. And her return flight was at seven a.m. Friday, after which Diamond expected analysis to start in the States.

Alien winced. It was going to be tight.

She looked up to cross the street. Five women in their mid-twenties tumbled out of a cab in front of their hostel off the Boulevard Saint-Germain, dressed in heels and miniskirts, laughing after a night on the town.

C'est la vie.

<hr>

Thursday night at seven p.m., Alien and Bruce made a final pass through the Bastille offices, comparing every detail with her earlier notes and photos. "Good?" Bruce asked, screwing shut the last desktop computer frame.

Alien checked. "Perfect," she said.

They walked to a metal door at one end of the fourth floor. Alien typed a six-digit keypad code and pressed her keycard to a reader. The door beeped and opened, revealing the bank's data center.

Machines whirred—servers in racks. In the middle of the data center's white-tiled floor were four laptops, each connected to a labeled black external hard drive. "Copying complete, checksum correct," Alien verified. Bruce returned the laptops to their original place in the room while she added the gathered hard drives to neatly stacked piles.

Another beep. Mitch, the Diamond security executive, joined them, trailed by Al, the attorney.

"Knock, knock," Al said.

Bruce and Mitch exited the data center to talk in a darkened hallway.

"All set?" Al asked Alien when it was just the two of them alone.

"Just one thing," Alien said. The lawyer's presence made her think. Every time they signed in, Bastille employees viewed a short notice, in both French and English and in twenty-four-point capitals, advising that all activities on the corporate network were subject to certain terms of use and might be monitored. Few realized, however, that a digital forensics specialist could reconstruct the products of their clicks and keystrokes, going back *years*.

"Are you sure this is okay?" she asked hesitantly. "Doesn't Europe have strict laws about exporting private information?"

"It's fine," Al said. "I'll sign off on it."

"But these drives don't just have work documents on them," Alien said.

"They have people's Web browsing, photos, and personal email and voice mail."

Al smoothed his tie between the thumb and fingers of his right hand. "It's fine. *I'll sign off on it,*" he repeated.

Alien opened her mouth once more, but the lawyer interrupted her.

"Here's the rule: if it's the company's computer, it's the company's data," he said.

By now, Bruce had returned to the room. "Al's the attorney," he said. "It's fine."

<hr />

Hard drives covered the bed in Bruce's hotel room. Alien encased each one in bubble wrap, as she had done for the trip over, loaded them in her gear suitcase, and strapped down the pile. The elastic side pockets, designed for toiletries, held the remaining office supplies. She threw out a power strip to fit in the Tableau.

"Can you hold the suitcase shut so I can zip it?" Alien asked Bruce at one a.m.

He turned from his laptop, grinning broadly. "I'm going to Amsterdam," he said.

"What?" she said. "When?"

"Now," Bruce said. "Well, the first flight out. Come with! You need a vacation."

"I can't," Alien said. "Chain of custody. I have to drop the hard drives off in the U.S. tomorrow morning."

"C'mon—Mitch can take the hard drives back himself," Bruce insisted. "And I bet I can get you a ticket. It'll be really easy. Let me just try to change the flights."

Alien watched, speechless, as he called the front desk. "Yeah," Bruce said. "Can you connect me to the Paris office of KLM? *Merci.*"

He waited thirty seconds. "What?" Bruce cupped the receiver of the hotel phone. "*Voice mail?* How is a major airline not picking up the phone? Fucking France!"

Bruce hung up.

<hr />

Mitch accompanied Alien to Charles de Gaulle Friday morning. They would fly to Boston and await instructions. At the airport security screening in Paris, he cut to the front of the line and pulled two guards aside, speaking softly and showing them some kind of letter pulled from his trench coat.

Alien waited. Then, to her surprise, she was waved forward with her gear suitcase and two others — no X-ray necessary.

Mitch flew first class. Alien and the hard drives and related evidence rode coach. She hoped to get a little sleep, but it was difficult to relax with everything in the bin above her.

At U.S. customs in Boston, Mitch strode forward and showed another letter.

"Bring your bag around, ma'am," the officials said.

"Wow," Alien said, facing the exit doors of the airport a few minutes later.

Mitch shrugged nonchalantly, as if there were nothing unusual about what had happened. "See you tomorrow."

They shook hands. Alien dug to find and turn on her phone.

The second the welcome screen appeared, it rang.

⊰⊱

Richard was waiting impatiently when Alien pulled up behind him at the side of the foggy, freezing New Jersey Turnpike five hours later. Elite Defense was assembling a stateside team to pore over the gathered evidence, he'd said by phone. Work started this weekend in Diamond offices outside Philadelphia. Since he was already there, and had received the necessary clearance to enter before her, Alien should hop in her car and deliver the goods to him at the closest open stretch before the exit to Diamond on the turnpike.

"This everything?" the Jedi asked when they'd transferred the last hard drive from her Volvo to his silver Audi.

"One minute." Alien was blind with fatigue but groped about in an outer suitcase pocket for the Tableau. "There," she said. "Unless you want the label maker."

They signed chain-of-custody forms. Richard paused before leaving, however.

"Book yourself a room at the DoubleTree and then meet us on-site tomorrow morning," he said. "Seven a.m. We have to get the images pulled onto the system ASAP."

—◈—

Alien had already spent a week in Diamond's employ, but their office security procedures made it clear she was a stranger until proven otherwise. Pulling in at seven a.m. sharp on Saturday, Alien provided her driver's license at a front guard's station before being escorted to another station, where she was photographed, fingerprinted, and handprinted.

Here Alien signed in and got a swipe badge and a sticker with her name and headshot printed on it.

"The colors change based on the time of day," the guard explained. "By seven p.m. it'll be covered with red and blue lines. That means it's expired."

Sticker in place by half past seven, Alien moved with her gear bag through a narrow guarded turnstile at the entrance to an eight-story redbrick operations center. Inside was a central courtyard with a fountain surrounded by chairs and tables. Alien turned right, as the guard had directed her, and swiped her badge at the inner door there, her entrance captured by surveillance cameras. The next door she wanted was in the middle of a long carpeted inner hall. To get inside, she palmed a handprint reader.

Low, wide, thickset tables, as in a science lab, filled the windowless room. Spread out across the tables for sorting and examination were the labeled hard drives. As Alien entered, Richard and Jason, her fellow Agent, looked up from workstations running EnCase and FTK—multi-thousand-dollar commercial data recovery programs.

"Hi," she said, walking over. It took effort to summon the energy to smile, but Alien wanted to show that she was alert and ready.

She read the labels of the hard drives they were studying. "Are these the images from the Bastille executives who left the bank to form their own firm?"

Richard grunted. "Affirmative."

"Find anything?" said Alien.

"Zeros," said Jason, shaking his head.

"You mean they wiped them?" said Alien. "Isn't that suspicious?"

"Could hurt the case, if the judge gets it," Jason said. "Bruce said she's not very tech savvy, though."

—◈—

Three and a half weeks passed in Philadelphia. They worked continuous four-teen-hour days, seven a.m. to nine p.m. Supervised by Richard, Alien and Ja-son read Bastille employees' email, reconstructed their Web browsing, copied their documents, and restored what had been deleted, bit by bit.

During her absence from Fireberry, Alien scrambled to find friends and housemates to water her plants, feed her pets, and do her weekly food shop-ping for the residents. She didn't even bother looking at brochures in the hotel for Independence Hall or the Philadelphia Museum of Art. She couldn't see them, she knew, any more than she could have seen the Luxembourg Gar-dens or the Louvre when she'd been in Paris. Soon, any sense of the outside world receded, though she still worked with Jim via email to complete their research and pitch a presentation on it to different conferences.

"Good news," he wrote her one day, two weeks in. "We got a speaking slot at SCAN Capital."

Alien couldn't wait.

Near the end of March, Elite subcontracted with a new SCAN instructor, Elliot, to help the case. He was a bearded redhead, a onetime military medic with a broad jaw and burly linebacker's build that made it appear as if his Clark Kent glasses were props.

Late in the morning of his third day, Elliot slipped half a Ghirardelli dark chocolate bar across the lab table to Alien when Richard and Jason weren't looking.

Alien smiled briefly, pocketed the treat, and focused on her work. Every hour they were in the office, she knew, Elite billed Diamond two hundred dol-lars a head.

Stealing a few minutes for lunch two hours later, they shared sandwiches in the courtyard.

"Favorite Linux tool?" Elliot asked her.

"Emacs!" Alien said. "*Obviously.*"

Elliot clasped his hands to his heart. That night, he trailed Alien back to her hotel room. Elliot sidled close. "May I have the honor of offering you a foot massage?" he said.

Alien rebuffed him as gently as she could. "SCAN Capital is this weekend," she said. "I have to get ready."

The next night, nine thirty p.m., Richard, Jason, Alien, and Elliot gathered for dinner with Jules Ferris at a dimly lit downtown Philly steakhouse. By now Alien had the menu memorized, having come here with the guys at least a dozen times. "House salad," she told the waiter.

"Bone-in rib eye steak—rare—shrimp and grits, and a twenty-one-year-old Macallan," said Elliot. "And"—in a wry, plummy voice—"bring the lady a cabernet."

The drinks arrived. Elliot tipped his glass toward Alien. "To your talk," he said, as Jason and the Jedis poured themselves pints from a pitcher of beer.

"Thanks." Alien strummed her fingers on the white tablecloth. "Hey, I could really use a little time to polish the presentation," she told Jules. "I haven't had a day off since Paris. Not even on a weekend. Can I go home for a day before SCAN?"

Jules turned to Richard, who shook his head without lifting his eyes from his porterhouse.

"We need you on-site," Jules said, with an apologetic shrug. "Your presentation is a voluntary commitment you made."

The waiter returned. "Your salad?" he said, delivering Alien's plate.

"Good news," she overheard Jules say to Richard with obvious pleasure. "Diamond wants us here through May."

Alien sighed, thinking about all the chores she hadn't done. And she also realized that the bills for her maxed-out credit cards would arrive before her next paycheck.

Richard gloated. "This project is paying for my daughter's college education," he said.

Alien stabbed lettuce as the Jedis clinked glasses.

⊸⊷

Alien squinted as she stepped off the podium following her SCAN Capital presentation late Saturday afternoon, captured by flashing cameras and a videographer.

"Are the techniques you just demonstrated real-world issues?" a reporter questioned her.

"Deleting data doesn't erase it," Alien said. "If you haven't used DoD-approved standards to destroy any unencrypted data, assume that someone else can read it."

I know, she thought, *because I was up late last night undeleting the last ten years of a French bank officer's emails.*

Other members of the overflow audience approached. "Can you share code?" the first one asked.

"Not yet," Jim said, stepping between them and Alien. "We're waiting for the green light from one last vendor that's about to release a fix," he told them. "In the meantime, users have been warned."

"But we are planning on releasing it as an open source project," said Alien. "Stay tuned."

She handed Jim the presentation laptop to carry. "I go back to Philly tomorrow afternoon," Alien whispered.

"Meet you in your room at nine," he said.

⟨━◆━⟩

Alien threw a bathrobe over the television screen in her hotel room. She showered and changed into a purple satin negligee. More out of compulsion than need, Alien checked her laptop for any Diamond updates. At eight p.m. she ordered room service for two. The food came at nine.

Nine thirty p.m. No Jim.

She texted. No answer. She called. Voice mail.

Ten p.m. No longer hungry, she wheeled the room service cart into a corner of the room. Alien showered again.

Midnight. Knocking. Alien closed her laptop and opened the door.

"Can you share code?" her partner joked as he hugged her.

Alien pushed Jim away.

Her eyes and cheeks burned. Tears.

"Is this"—she waved back and forth between them—"just for fun?"

Jim paused, startled, before answering. "Of course not," he said finally. Then, as if to cover up the delay, he reached to clasp Alien's hands.

"I'm sorry," said Jim. "It's my wife's birthday. She was upset."

Alien rubbed her temples. Her head hurt, listening to him.

I'm an idiot, she thought.

Where is this going?

⟨━◆━⟩

Somehow, he talked her into sex. What was once so electric—to hold Jim, and be held by him—now felt terrible. Alien felt used and dirty afterward. When she woke up the next morning, she was naked and alone in the bed. The clock radio said nine a.m.

Jim stood by the hotel room window, showered and dressed. He fidgeted with the blind, apologizing to someone on the phone.

"I'm sorry," Alien heard him say. "I know it's important. I'll be back—soon."

She sat up, rustling the comforter. Jim turned, startled, said quickly, "I have to go," and hung up.

"Who was that?" asked Alien. But she already knew.

Jim gathered his things. "I'm sorry," he said. "I have to go home."

Alien sat up in the bed, her arms around her knees. "Me too," she said.

Seven a.m., the Monday after SCAN, Alien began cataloging emails again in the Diamond forensics office, but kept an eye on the door.

Richard entered shortly before nine a.m., still on a phone call. Alien approached him anyway. "Can we talk?" she mouthed, exhausted.

Richard put her off with a raised palm.

"Please," begged Alien.

He cupped the phone. "Later," Richard said.

"How about lunch?"

He nodded.

Alien waited until noon before trying again. She was talking to Elliot, waiting for a fresh hard drive scan to finish, when she saw Richard walking out.

"Wait!" Alien called, following him to the courtyard. "Now?" she asked. "Five minutes?"

Richard didn't even slow. "*Later*," he repeated. "I'll find you."

Alien tried again, texting Richard mid-afternoon. No reply.

She called Bruce.

"I don't feel well," said Alien. "I need a break."

"Talk to the Jedi on-site," he said.

At five p.m. Richard was busy at his laptop, trying to finish a report on a different project. She couldn't wait any longer.

"Richard?" Alien asked.

He waved her off. "Not now."

I can't stand it.

Alien grabbed her things. Then she walked up to Richard, interrupting him.

"I'm working normal business hours today," Alien announced, staring the former air force officer square in the eye. He was clearly startled. For an instant, he looked almost scared.

She turned and left, exiting the stale air of the forensics lab, rolling her bag through the carpeted security office, out the main hallway, through the turnstiles, out the front door, and into the cold gray evening, her trench coat flapping behind her. She took a deep breath, enjoying the first thin sliver of sun she'd felt in weeks.

Alien had never felt so free.

⟞⟝

She was still sitting in her Volvo in the parking lot, breathing hard, watching her headshot sticker molt, when Bruce called twenty minutes later.

"Take a couple of days off," he said.

"Cool," Alien answered. "Thanks so much."

She drove home to Fireberry, stopping only once en route, at Star Market, to pick up groceries.

Late Wednesday morning, her phone rang. Alien, in the middle of making an old-fashioned mix CD for friends, reached to check it: Bruce.

"Hello?" she said.

"Hey," he said tersely. "Melinda is on the line with me."

Alien tensed.

"Your position at Elite Defense has been terminated effective immediately," Bruce said. "Thank you for your work. We wish you the best. Melinda will fill you in on the next steps."

⟞⟝

As she listened to Melinda, Alien checked her Elite Defense account.

Her password didn't work.

Shortly after she got off the phone, the doorbell rang. Alien walked downstairs.

Outside, a FedEx guy awaited her, white truck idling behind him, empty cardboard box in hand. "Elizabeth Tessman?" he asked.

"Can I help you?" Alien asked.

"I'm here to pick up a computer." He looked down and handed her the empty carton with a destination address of the Elite Defense P.O. box. "You ordered this?"

Alien took the box and smiled grimly. *Go fuck yourself,* she wanted to say. But it wasn't his fault.

"*I* didn't order it," she said.

Alien closed the door.

———✦———

The phone rang. It was Melinda. Alien ignored it. Then it rang again — Bruce. She turned the phone off. Alien trudged upstairs.

Her lava lamp bubbled beside her laptop on the desk where she worked. Above were bolted remnants of hydroponics equipment Tanner had set up while they were dating. Clothes, CDs, art supplies, and Go set pieces littered the floor.

Alien sat there for five hours without a break. She organized the Elite Defense data by client: Castle, the airline, Cheeseburger, the state government, Neptune, the Pentagon, Diamond, and so on. Alien transferred these from the laptop to an external hard drive on the desk, the one spare from the Paris trip. Then she wiped the laptop seven times, per U.S. Department of Defense InfoSec standards, reinstalled the operating system, and transferred back the client files, encrypted so that only the Jedis could open and read them.

The result was the same Agent's computer it had been before Bruce's phone call, only this time with every trace of the former Agent herself eliminated.

Alien wiped the backup drive. To the laptop she taped a sticky note with the login password.

Her last act for Elite Defense was emailing Melinda from her personal account.

"Feel free to reschedule your pickup," Alien wrote.

⟨⟩

It was six p.m. when the white van drove off again. Alien opened her top-right desk drawer. She took her bent spoon pin and tossed it inside.

Alien cried. She was twenty-seven years old and her dream career was over. She pictured Bruce at the bar at a SCAN conference, talking to another guy. *She had potential,* he was saying, *and we gave her technical work. But she couldn't cut it.*

Hours passed. At four a.m., Alien went down to the Fireberry living room. After sitting on the sofa for twenty minutes looking at her shadowy reflection in the window, she felt for her phone in the pocket of her fuzzy pink bathrobe. She scrolled up and down her contacts. There were Bruce and Jim, Tanner and other boyfriends, Eddie and Piñon.

Alien found the contact she was looking for and hit the bright green button to dial.

"Hello?" a man answered. "Elizabeth, is that you?"

And then a woman, in the background: "Ask her if anything's wrong."

"Mom? Dad?" Alien said in a small voice. "I failed."

PART IV

Owner's Manual

13

The Bartender

Cambridge. July 2008.

AFTER LOSING HER JOB at Elite Defense, Alien felt like a Navy SEAL who had been dishonorably discharged. True, she could find another position in her field, but she had no interest in anything that did not provide the same variety of cases and clients. Or the thrill and challenge of finding ways to break into supposedly secure places, without leaving a trace.

At the same time, Alien experienced something akin to PTSD. She knew how little it would take for an attacker to shut down the computer systems for basic services like water, power, and public transit, and felt as if she were being watched whenever she made a phone call, cashed a check, went to the doctor, or booked a flight.

She had good reason to think so. From 2004 to 2008, the number of Internet users had doubled, to 1.5 billion. Facebook, YouTube, and Twitter launched, followed by the iPhone and App Store. People no longer "went online"; they carried the network with them, in their pockets and purses by day, and on bedside tables at night, relying on it for a host of functions such as shopping, banking, connecting with friends, and finding love (or at least a lover). Her InfoSec work had shown her that each innovation was also another step toward a world where everything you said or did could be captured, controlled, sold, or rewritten by someone else. Every day, hackers discovered new vulnerabilities and virtual sieves through which information could leak.

Alien still stayed up late, but now it was to pursue an old dream of becoming a writer. She started a blog focused on security and privacy, supporting herself in the meantime with unemployment insurance. After the demands of being an Agent on the Jedis' terms — and the shock, shame, and insult of her abrupt termination — controlling her own life again and letting her ideas flow into words was exhilarating. The problem was that, whatever its satisfactions, blogging did not offer an income, especially at first, and maybe never.

A way to make a living while still leaving time to write seemed to offer itself one afternoon in early July when she passed a bulletin board near the MIT campus covered with paper fliers. On one of the fliers, a smiling woman slid a triple-olive martini along a highly polished wooden surface.

"Boston School of Bartending," the flier read. "One-week night classes. Get certified and GET A JOB."

⟫⟪

Alien signed up to take the bartending course, which began the following week. The "classroom" was a tiny storefront with a red awning between Chinatown and downtown Boston, a few blocks east of the Common. She plunged in with her characteristic intensity.

Manhattan... Margarita... Tom Collins... Gin and tonic... Cape Codder... Kamikaze... Their final evening together, the instructor, a South Boston native in his late fifties, drilled Alien and six other twenty-somethings, her fellow students, on all their recipes.

Alien turned behind the room's fully stocked wooden counter, grabbed the right glass and ingredients, and made each drink in turn. She felt comfortable, reminded of her mother's restaurant supply store in Hoboken, which sold bar equipment. Helping out as kids, Alien and her sister had sat on barstools behind a counter. And she liked slinging drinks. *No getting up early. No airplanes. No computers. And I get to make things and hang out with people.*

Above all, it was simple. Customers ordered, she gave them what they wanted, they were happy, and it was done.

Instant gratification.

"Perfect," the instructor said each time he reached her position and took a sip.

When this last class ended and everyone was filing out, he gestured for Alien to stay. "I have a good job lead for you," he said. "A buddy's got a place, and he's looking for help."

Given her instructor's recommendation and her restored self-confidence, Alien hoped she'd get the bartending job, but the position didn't open until late August. She arranged an interview for the middle of that month. Alien was pleased, but hadn't figured out just what she would do with her remaining freedom.

Later the same evening, when she checked her email, she saw a message from Amy, her former colleague on the Mayflower Hospital network team.

"Hey — Hubby and I are going to the HOPE conference in NYC this weekend," Amy wrote. "Let me know if you'll be there!"

HOPE? Alien looked it up online and found a Web page with white text against a black background. "HOPE is the seventh Hackers On Planet Earth conference," the page announced:

Join the rest of the hacker community from around the world July 18 to July 20, 2008 for this momentous occasion at the historic Hotel Pennsylvania in New York City.

There will be three days and nights of speakers along with all sorts of activities to keep you entertained and enlightened. We have a tremendous amount of space for us to make use of and it's all right in the middle of the city, across the street from Penn Station. You still have time to get involved in this historic event, whether by attending, volunteering, speaking, or creating something new that none of us have thought of yet.

Alien was positive she was done with InfoSec as a profession, but this sounded like a fun party. The DIY vibe suggested plenty of potential blog fodder. And there were sure to be some interesting guys.

"I'll be there," she told Amy.

For the first time in more than three months, Alien set her alarm.

Alien caught the eight fifteen Amtrak at South Station the next morning. Before she stepped out at Penn Station in a rose-print dress, she stuffed her flats into her backpack and strapped on her Rollerblades. As she glided through the subterranean concourse, Alien noticed several IF YOU SEE SOMETHING, SAY SOMETHING security signs.

Creepy. She understood the presence of such instructions in a post-9/11 world, but the way everyone was being recruited to keep a suspicious watch on one another made her uneasy.

By the time the escalator reached street level, the temperature topped ninety degrees, with humidity to match.

Alien gazed ahead and then angled her eyes up.

Cameras. Surveillance cameras everywhere.

They were set into white metal utility boxes, mounted fifteen feet high on the lampposts along the lineup of yellow taxis. The cameras themselves consisted of wide glass spherical "eyes" — lenses with a 360-degree scope behind protective plastic. The utility boxes were equipped with network fiber cables, wireless transmitters, or both. Each box carried an NYPD emblem.

What was law enforcement tracking? Who had access to their information? And would they be any better at keeping this information secure than all the banks and hospitals, defense contractors and government agencies that had been hacked, some by Alien herself?

Alien pictured an anonymous office building, packed with people who sat behind computer consoles monitoring endless bytes of video — both Big Brother and high-tech sitting duck.

She snapped a series of photos with her phone. Something to think and talk about.

The WALK sign came on. Scooting around pedestrians, Alien moved as quickly as she could along Thirty-third Street to the other side of Seventh Avenue and into the hotel.

⇥⇤

The Hotel Pennsylvania had seen better days, but those days were pretty wonderful. Entering the lobby was like stepping into 1924: maroon fixtures and furniture, and a peach-colored marble floor. The place was now worn and dingy, but it had been full of fashionable people, flocking to hear jazz gods Duke Ellington, Count Basie, and Glenn Miller, all of whom had performed at the Pennsylvania. Miller had immortalized the hotel's phone number — "Pennsylvania 6-5000" — in one of his hits.

Now it was getting by as a second-tier convention site, thanks to the ridiculous prices of top-of-the-line New York hotels. HOPE attendees loved the buzz of the city, but most of them were independent aficionados of limited means, not corporate employees on expense accounts.

The conference was a bargain. A single SCAN class cost thousands of dollars to attend. HOPE was an all-inclusive eighty bucks. The badge alone was almost worth the price of admission. It included a dog-tag-sized metal strip equipped with a small circuit board and watch battery.

"What's this?" Alien asked.

"It's a trackable RFID tag," a skinny guy behind the registration table told her. He passed her an explanatory flier.

"The tracking technology, known as RFID, is fast becoming an unseen part of everyday life," it said. "For the very first time, the general public will be able to participate in the transparent operation of a major RFID tracking program."

RFID stood for radio frequency identification — radio waves that broadcast a person's or object's presence to automated readers. New inventory control systems used the technology. So did contactless "smart cards," increasingly common on transit networks and in high-tech buildings. HOPE attendees could always take the battery out to turn the tracking off. But the entire point of the badge for this crowd was to serve as the basis for the kind of security games they loved to play, in many cases for real.

"Players will seek ways to protect their privacy, find vulnerabilities in the tracking system, employ data mining techniques to learn more about other participants, and choose how much personal information they will disclose in order to play," Alien read.

"Cool," she said. She was as creeped out by technology like this as she was by the NYPD camera network, but here it was out in the open, something to be examined and questioned. Everyone saw the data dragnet at work. And probing the system for vulnerabilities would be rewarded rather than punished as some kind of criminal act.

Alien rolled on, passing low-budget vendor booths and packed contest and activity areas. If most people saw hacking as the ultimate antisocial activity, the hundreds of happy nerds around her, talking enthusiastically to one another, suggested the opposite.

There was Segway racing, a maker space for electronic tinkerers, and a giant Lego sculpture garden. Free public Internet access terminals and a "phone phreak" playroom with old rotary phones and pay phones, their innards exposed. A capture-the-flag competition like the one she'd won in Bruce's class at SCAN. A live-streaming online radio station. Robot-backed punk bands, art created from old Commodore and Nintendo games, and trippy computer-generated videos patterned with data from on-site packet sniffing. The scene reminded her of MIT Rush.

And the male-to-female ratio was ten to one.

"Alien!" a voice called. She spun around, wondering who here would call her that. Alien spotted a familiar face, another of the few women at HOPE. She was a striking figure with a shaved head and square earrings made of tiny LED lights displaying an animated Ms. Pac-Man munching power pellets.

"Rpunzel!" Alien greeted her old MIT Coffeehouse Club companion.

Rpunzel stood before her own small booth. She was selling custom kits for making electronic jewelry and other novelties.

"Check it out," she said, handing Alien a kit to turn a kids' metal lunchbox into an LCD projector.

"Awesome!" said Alien. While she fiddled with the package, a good-looking guy nearby with gelled-back black hair caught her eye. Alien did a double take. His wrists were locked behind him in a pair of shiny steel handcuffs.

A crowd of young men surrounded him in a half circle, calling out in unison how long it was taking him to get free.

"Fifteen seconds!"

"Thirty seconds!"

"Forty-five seconds!"

The guy twisted his right hand back toward the cuffs and jammed a flat metal strip, cut from an empty Tecate beer can, between the locking mechanism and the teeth of his restraints. He simultaneously squeezed the cuffs tighter and pushed the metal strip down hard with his thumb.

"Open!" he declared with a broad grin just before the minute mark.

His buddies high-fived him. Alien made plans with Rpunzel to catch up later and walked over to the escape artist. He reached out his uncuffed hand.

"I'm Aaron."

"Alien," she said, as they shook with mock formality.

Aaron dangled the handcuffs. "Want to try?" he said with a wry smile.

Alien laughed warmly. "I prefer things the other way around."

"I'm with TOOOL," Aaron said, gesturing over his shoulder, where the same guys had regathered to time someone else. "The Open Organisation Of Lockpickers."

Part education and advocacy group, part social club, TOOOL ran one of the conference's most popular activity areas, consisting of several tables littered with pick sets, training locks, and other gear to tinker with. Dim the lights and it would be like Alien was back at one of Zhu and Rex's practice lock-picking sessions in the Bemis hallway. Another similarity to MIT roof-and-tunnel hackers was that the TOOOL crew had their own explicit code of conduct. "First rule of ethical lock picking: do not pick locks you do not own," an old hand told a newbie.

They said they picked locks to *improve* security, contradictory as that sounded. "Security is achieved through openness," one of the group's leaders had asserted at a 2005 talk. "Take things apart and play with them. . . . Exposing bad security is what protects us all."

Alien, who had learned to pick locks as a freshman hacker at the giant playground that was MIT, was well past the point where she had to be introduced to the subject, but she was glad people were having fun with it. And Aaron was cute. She accompanied him to a private party in a hotel room rented by TOOOL, and Friday ended at dawn with the two of them making out in the hallway outside Alien's room.

She slept in—alone—on Saturday, but rejoined Aaron for a very late lunch with a fellow TOOOL member and his girlfriend in a classic New York diner, à la *Seinfeld,* across the street from the hotel. Then she had drinks with Amy and her husband. Returning to the Pennsylvania shortly before nine p.m., she soon found herself facing the biggest celebrity at HOPE. In the main hall, Alien saw a dark-haired, slightly sunburned mid-fortyish man in a V-neck tee beneath an unbuttoned black dress shirt. He was patiently receiving dozens of admirers trying to introduce themselves, shake his hand, and pose for photos with him.

"It's *Mitnick,*" she overheard someone telling a friend in a stage whisper.

Kevin Mitnick, to be exact. The world's most famous (former) hacker. Following his release from imprisonment for breaking into Digital Equipment Corporation servers and copying the company's operating system software, Mitnick had proceeded to crack Pacific Bell. During his two and a half years as a fugitive from the FBI, he continued to use hacking, particularly social engineering, to stay ahead of the law. His arrest, in 1995, had made the front page of the *New York Times*. Mitnick never tried to profit from what he'd taken, but served five more years in prison, emerging as a kind of folk hero in hacker culture.

Now he was a successful white hat, hired by the kinds of companies he used to bedevil. As Mitnick shook hands, he handed out business cards for "Mitnick Security Consulting."

"Thanks," said Alien, taking one.

The "card" was a keeper. It was the conventional size, but instead of being a piece of stiff paper, it was a thin sheet of die-cut stainless steel whose upper half included a detachable five-piece lock pick tool set. Alien slipped it into her wallet.

"Elizabeth?" she heard a raspy male voice calling. Alien turned. He was a middle-aged guy in jeans and a red plaid shirt.

"Bill Rogers—Antidote," he introduced himself, reaching out his hand. "I recognize you from SCAN. How's everybody at Elite Defense?"

Alien wasn't going to tell him that she'd been fired. And she wasn't going to lie.

"I'm not with them anymore," she said. "I'm on my own."

"Oh?" Rogers pressed his own business card on her. "In that case, would you like some subcontracting work?" he asked. "We're always looking for good people."

Alien glanced down the hall, seeing Aaron and other TOOOL members waving for her to join them. She looked back at Rogers.

She had decided to do something else with her life. But rather than explain that, it was easier to let him assume otherwise.

"Sure." Alien gave him her contact info, figuring it didn't obligate her to do anything if he emailed or called. She pocketed his card without a second thought.

⊷⊶

Aaron lived on the West Coast, in Portland. After HOPE ended, he and Alien kept in touch, and he invited her to join him at another conference, DEF CON, held two and a half weeks later in Las Vegas. Given her positive experience in New York, and her interest in seeing more of him before she started bartend-

ing, Alien enthusiastically agreed. With the growth of the information security industry, HOPE, like SCAN, was now only one of dozens of hacking and
counter-hacking trainings and conventions. Each con had its own culture:
some were corporate, some political, some military, some punk. She knew
DEF CON, the largest and oldest conference, had originated at a hacker's early
90s farewell party, and was famous (or infamous) for its raucous nonstop fes-
tivities.

Alien's flight to Vegas landed the afternoon of Thursday, August 7. While
most of her fellow passengers headed for the eye-popping new luxury resorts
and casinos opened over the past two decades — among them the Luxor, New
York–New York, and the Bellagio — Alien grabbed a cab to the DEF CON
venue, the Riviera. Originally opened in 1955, it was a relic of the Vegas of an
earlier era, now situated by a shopping plaza with all-you-can-eat sushi, Indian buffet, and Korean barbecue restaurants, as well as an artificial-turf-encir-
cled concrete booth advertising discounted show tickets and Grand Canyon
bus tours. In its fallen state, the Riviera was as affordable and unpicky in its
convention guests as the Hotel Pennsylvania.

Passing through the sliding doors of the Riviera's entrance with an oversized suitcase stuffed to bursting with flashy dresses — puffy, skimpy, sequins,
leather — Alien found herself almost immediately hemmed in by thousands
of geeks. They crowded together, shoulder to shoulder, boisterously swap-
ping stories and exchanging hugs, handshakes, fist bumps, and high fives.
Nearby, DJs spun techno, vendors sold keystroke loggers and surreptitious
laptop camera activation apps, and a projection screen had been turned into
an ever-growing "Wall of Sheep" — a list of usernames and passwords nabbed
from passersby clueless enough to go online without encryption in the vicinity of the world's largest hacker convention.

Alien was glad she hadn't brought her laptop with her. Do so and you
risked getting an InfoSec education the hard way — as everyone else's enter-
tainment.

Alien found Aaron in a room intended for two but already occupied by
seven male TOOOL members, including him. Skirting beds and sleeping
bags, backpacks and pillows, she threw her suitcase open in the bathroom
and claimed the bathtub as her spot for the night. If during the wee hours one
of the guys had to take a leak in the toilet while she was sleeping in the tub,
so be it.

The rest of the afternoon and evening, Alien prowled the conference. In the vast mass of black T-shirts, a woman rocking heels, a dress, and red lipstick stood out like a snowman on the Las Vegas Strip. While she attracted their attention, few of the horde of men surrounding her expected that Alien might share their interests, or that her technical knowledge might equal or exceed their own.

"I'm a hacker," guy after guy introduced himself.

"Really?" she asked with feigned awe.

That night, drinking by the pool, Alien and the TOOOL crew brainstormed ways to break into safes, suitcases, ATMs, and elevators. Next to them was a guy sketching circuit diagrams on a scrap of paper for another guy, someone setting up a shortwave radio antenna atop a cabana umbrella as others gathered, and another nerd who thought the way he turned the hot tubs purple with industrial dye was the funniest thing ever, though a bikinied woman in one of the tubs, a regular tourist who had made the mistake of booking a stay here during DEF CON, begged to differ.

"Wait until morning," Aaron said. "By then, all the lobby furniture will be stacked in the elevator." He laughed. "And the elevator display for what floor you're on will show some dude's area code"—a shorthand tag for the location of one's "home" hacker group.

It was all hacking, all the time, even when hacking wasn't officially on the agenda. Alien felt like a kid at summer camp, one with few rules and no counselors. At two a.m., a stout bearded TOOOL member named Deviant led the gang on an expedition to crash a Microsoft-sponsored party with an open bar. The cab ride from the Riviera, at the north end of the Strip, to the Luxor, where the party was located, on the south end, took almost twenty minutes. Even in Vegas, the Luxor's size and shape—a thirty-story gleaming black pyramid—made it one of the city's most visually arresting structures.

The lock pickers and Alien made their way through the lobby and casino to a two-level nightclub whose décor somehow resembled a cross between a Gothic nave and a medieval dungeon. The entrance was a mix of webbed metal and blood-red lights. In front of it was a milling crowd of disappointed would-be partygoers.

"You have to be on a list to get in, and then once you're in, they stamp your wrist and you can go in and out as many times as you want," reported a gangly teenager with a neon-green Mohawk who'd been turned away.

Alien and the others lingered outside the club, trying to talk people up, until Deviant recognized a friend.

"Hey, Blivet!" he called.

He quickly learned that Blivet was on the list. His special status was due to the fact that, while he volunteered as a DEF CON "goon"—the official term for convention staff—his day job was chief information security officer, or CISO, for an important Microsoft customer. Big and beefy, Blivet wore combat boots, camo shorts that revealed thick hairy legs, a black T-shirt, and a goon-only version of the conference badge. His carefully cultivated don't-fuck-with-me scowl was transformed into a boyish grin as Deviant explained his plan.

He was a goon, but he was their goon. Which offered an opportunity for some social engineering.

After conferring with Deviant, Blivet entered the nightclub and returned right away, stamp ink still fresh on his right wrist. As they had arranged, Deviant pressed his left wrist down on Blivet's wrist, and then again on his own right wrist. Now the stamp design showed there, too, if only faintly—until he quickly darkened it with a Sharpie. It was far from perfect, but in the crazy lighting it was good enough.

Deviant transferred the "stamp" to Alien, Aaron, and the rest of the lock pickers the same way. And then to the Mohawked teenager and a half-dozen others who'd been waiting with them on the outskirts.

"Drinks on Microsoft!" one of the hackers cried as Alien filed in behind him.

———

Alien's bartending interview was scheduled for the Friday after DEF CON. Checking email around five p.m. the night before, however, she was surprised to find a message from the Antidote executive, Bill Rogers. Black hat hackers had just broken into the website of an upstate New York newspaper, infecting online readers with malware—malicious software deliberately written to damage or disable system functions, steal information, or give outside forces control of their computers. The newspaper had hired Antidote to help investigate and respond to the incident.

"Are you available tomorrow?" Rogers asked.

There was no deliberation. Only an adrenaline jolt, as if Alien were about to step from a great height without knowing if she would fall or fly.

She sensed immediately that she was going to do it. But feeling burned —and burned out—by Elite made her aware of the risks. If Alien went back into InfoSec, she would have to do so on her own terms.

She called not Rogers but Elliot, the subcontractor on the Diamond bank case who'd offered her a foot massage. "Hey," he said warmly.

"Hey," she answered, and cut to the chase. "You're an independent consultant, right? I have my first potential client. How much should I charge?"

"Uh . . . that depends," said Elliot.

Alien explained the situation. "Does two hundred dollars per hour sound right?"

"Oh, sure. Totally," Elliot said.

A moment later Alien was on the phone with Rogers. Although she now had a figure in mind, she didn't want to repeat the mistake of her Elite Defense job negotiation, when she had named a number first.

"What do you usually pay?" she asked.

"One hundred dollars an hour, plus expenses," Rogers said.

"Hmm, I usually do one hundred and fifty. Why don't we meet in the middle? How about one hundred and twenty-five?" Even if it was less than what Alien had discussed with Elliot, the rate was ten times what she had made just a few years earlier as an MIT student employee. A week of consulting paid more than a month of pouring drafts and mixing mojitos. And if it didn't work out, she could always find another bartending gig.

"You're hired," Rogers answered.

<hr>

On the floor in front of Alien a few hours later were her laptop and gear suitcase, packed anew with external hard drives, cords and cables, a label maker, and other Micro Center purchases. CD cases held various system boot software and forensics programs. Last were two printouts: an evidence acquisition log and a chain-of-custody form from Antidote.

She pulled her brown-striped black skirt suit out of the closet for the first time since April. There was a tiny hole in the lapel where the Elite spoon pin had been. Alien fingered it for a moment, inhaling deeply.

Leave now and she would make it to her hastily booked hotel room at three thirty a.m. The newspaper expected her on-site at seven thirty.

Half an hour later, Alien was in her Volvo, moving rapidly westward through the darkness along the Mass Pike.

⟢

Framed copies of a century of historic front pages — the U.S. entry into World War I, VJ Day, John F. Kennedy's election, and the fall of the Berlin Wall — lined the walls of the conference room where Alien met the newspaper's CEO, legal counsel, IT director, and public relations chief the next morning. To judge by the bags under their eyes, their slumped posture, and their wrinkled clothes, it looked as if no one had slept — or changed — since the day before.

"What happened to our computers?" the CEO asked anxiously. "And what do we tell our customers?"

Alien eyed her gear suitcase but reached first for old technology: her Moleskine notebook and a pen. A laptop would make the situation less intimate and interfere with her ability to build trust and bond with the client. To listen carefully and reassure them that they were in good hands. That everything was going to be okay.

Alien clicked the pen open. "Let's back up. Start with what happened," she said, using her most therapeutic voice. "Tell me who discovered what, and when. Then we'll help you recover and come up with a plan to prevent it from happening again."

⟢

Legal huddled with the CEO in the conference room afterward. PR drafted a statement to subscribers. Alien had instructed the IT director to reset local administrator passwords and copy any firewall logs for later examination. Those tasks completed, she followed him in her car to a warehouse-sized building fifteen minutes across town. This was a colocation facility, or shared data center, run by the newspaper's Internet service provider, with separate rows of secure server racks for different large customers in the area.

Alien entered to the familiar sound of cooling fans. She plugged the first of her external drives — wiped, formatted, and labeled, exactly as she'd done for the Elite Defense assignment in Paris — into a computer in the server rack for the newspaper. Next, Alien inserted one of her CDs and found the keyboard that controlled the rack.

She typed at the command prompt:

```
dd conv=sync,noerror if=/dev/sda of=/media/NEWS-0345-
    001/0345-001_WINSRVWWW-02.dd
```

The imaging took almost fifteen hours. Alien "babysat" the process, checking on it periodically to make sure it was moving along. While she was waiting, she worked on the report. Forms filled out and hard drives stacked and packed at last, Alien called Rogers to check in.

Late that night she rang Aaron from her hotel room. She was even more excited than she had anticipated to be back in action, and wanted to tell someone about her day.

No answer.

Alien thought for a moment, and then tried Elliot.

He picked up on the second ring. "How'd it go?" he asked without saying hello.

"The client's servers were all Windows machines," Alien told him. "And I had to do a live image"—copying the computers while they were on and being used. "But the most stressful part was knowing I couldn't call Bruce or anyone else at Elite Defense if I had a problem."

Elliot cleared his throat. "You can always call me."

Alien liked the sound of that. "Just maybe I will," she said.

⤙⬦⤚

Alien was eager to nail her first assignment as a freelancer, both out of professional pride and so that it wouldn't be the last. She returned the next day to Cambridge, where she scanned the imaged server, identified the malware and how to remove it, and ran a file system timeline to determine what had been affected on the server in the interim. Alien called the newspaper's leadership team to share the basics and then started on the rest of her report, listing specific recommendations about changing passwords, tightening firewalls, blocking ports, and updating software to improve security going forward.

After work every night, she chatted by phone with Elliot. He traveled all the time to teach SCAN classes, but made his home in Parkmont, Colorado, a town of sixty thousand set against the west slope of the Rocky Mountains.

"Come visit!" he urged.

The day after submitting her report, she was browsing Boston-Denver plane tickets in her bedroom. Rogers called. "Nice job on the newspaper case," he said.

"Thanks for the opportunity," Alien told him.

"If you want another, we've got a social engineering assessment," Rogers said.

People across the country were being hit by "phishing" attacks from criminals pretending to be working for well-known companies, such as banks, brokers, and online shopping sites. The scammers combined fraudulent emails, websites, and phone calls to garner passwords, credit card numbers, and other valuable information. News reports focused on individual victims. But if a victim was an employee of a large company, the entire business might have been exposed to a major theft, a devastating data breach, or both. Now a rural bank—code name "Barn Door"—wanted to see how vulnerable its own staff was to phishing.

"Can you do that?" Rogers asked. He offered a flat fee of eight hundred dollars—exactly half, he told her, of what the bank was paying Antidote.

Alien grabbed her laptop, still open to the Web page listing flights to Colorado. She imagined Richard and the other Jedis chuckling derisively at such small fry. If she took this job, though, the pay would be enough to visit Elliot *and* buy new hiking boots when she got to Parkmont. Plus, if past experience was any indication, successfully breaking into one bank client could lead to a lot of other business.

"Send me the contract," she said. "I'll squeeze it in."

⟺

One thing Alien had learned from her time with Elite Defense: trying to work in the same room where you sleep ruins both.

That night, in search of a convenient space, she entered a vacant bedroom with a high ceiling off the Fireberry kitchen. Inside was a ten-foot-tall blue-and-black cylindrical metal robot her housemate Keenan had "rescued" from an MIT lab and was planning on fixing up. Nearby was a plastic folding table and chair.

Alien set up the table and chair in the robot's shadow and then plopped down and plugged in her laptop. Barn Door's website was BarnDoorBank.com. Using a program called Wget, short for "World Wide Web get," she downloaded the site's underlying HTML code—the online equivalent of copying someone's business card or company letterhead.

But what should her decoy be?

At the command line, Alien typed, "whois BarnDoorBankPoll.com."

"No match for 'BARNDOORBANKPOLL.COM,'" her display answered.

She smiled.

⟨⟩

Alien registered BarnDoorBankPoll.com as a domain name, selecting a Web server in Parkmont run by an amenable friend of Elliot's—the head of his local Internet service provider—as her host site. Because of their connection, the friend let Alien record his ISP as the official site owner so that it would be completely anonymous, or at least untraceable to her. In addition, she set up a firewall so that only she—and, later, the people she was targeting—could access the site. Google, government agencies, and others who wanted to see inside would be shut out.

On the real Barn Door site, Alien found an "About Us" page with headshots of the bank CEO and president. Using these and the same page's fonts and logos, background color, and set of links as a template, she coded a new Web page, titled "IT Poll."

"Dear employees," the page began in boldface type. "Barn Door Bank is conducting an important poll. Please help us plan and budget resources for next year."

Now came a three-item questionnaire: "Do you use Microsoft Office software?" (Yes or No.) "How important is your computer to do your job?" (Very important, Important, or Not important.) "Would you like the option to work from home?" (Yes or No.)

Its brevity would get employees answering quickly, Alien figured. And almost everyone who came to the page would answer "Yes," "Very important," and "Yes," setting a positive mood for the final fields to fill before a Submit button.

Still, some people might be wary. From a shopping site on the Internet, then, Alien copied the red-and-black check-mark "VeriSign Secured" logo, as well as the boilerplate promise "Your access and use of this system is validated and protected using Secure Socket Layer (SSL) and all communication to and from this system is encrypted for your security."

None of that was true, of course. But *they* wouldn't know that.

"Username" and "Password," Alien asked last—the only information she actually wanted.

⟫⟪

Now the emails. How to get people to *want* to participate? And to respond right away?

Alien went into the kitchen, filled a teakettle with water, and put it on the stove.

How can I get them to bite? What are people really excited about?

As she waited for the kettle to boil, one of her housemates came into the kitchen to grab a USB charger he'd left behind.

"New iPod," he said, showing off his music player. "One hundred and sixty gigs."

Bingo.

She hurried back to the borrowed desk. "Subject: Employee Poll—Win an iPod!" Alien drafted an email.

"Barn Door Bank is conducting a quick internal poll. If you are one of the first twenty employees to help us by responding, you will be entered into a random drawing for a new iPod. Thank you for your participation—and good luck!"

In moments, she had added colorful iPod images, followed by a link to the poll page, the name of Barn Door's head of IT, and his email address, modified to be @barndoorbankpoll.com rather than the real @barndoorbank.com.

As Alien sat back in her chair, she noticed for the first time the kettle's loud, impatient whistle.

⟫⟪

All week Alien coordinated with her Barn Door contact, making sure he understood and approved her plan. She was to attempt her email phishing scheme on all fifty of their employees, and then follow up with ten of them by phone, trying to get them to download and open a potentially malicious file on their computer. In between those two steps was the Web poll she'd devised.

Click, track, call—con.

Each stage of the scam offered a different category of potential phish. "Cold," "warm," and "hot" phish, Alien termed them.

Everyone Alien was targeting started as a cold phish. A cold phish would become a warm phish if he or she clicked the email link and visited the fake website. Last, a warm phish would become a hot phish if he or she completed and submitted the poll form online.

To prime them for the phone calls that would follow, hot phish would be redirected to another Web page decorated with additional iPod images.

"Thank you!" it said. "A caller will let you know shortly if you've won."

To make her own work easier, Alien wrote a computer script to send the initial cold phish emails out, taking as variables her subject line, message body, purported sender, and list of employees to contact. As the script ran, each email added a unique identifier to the poll link. Now her website could track individual warm phish by name whether they submitted the form or not. Further scripting recorded visitors' Internet addresses and what Web browsers they were using, information added to running warm phish and hot phish logs.

Or at least that was the plan.

Teacup in hand, dressed in her pajamas, Alien launched her attack at ten a.m. the Tuesday after Rogers had called, three days before the flight she'd booked to visit Elliot.

"tail -F warm.txt," she typed in one screen, calling up the bank's warm phish log. "tail -F hot.txt," she typed in another, calling up the hot phish.

Alien watched nervously, counting the seconds since her script had started. Would anyone respond?

Fifteen seconds in, the first warm phish entry appeared onscreen: a Barn Door HR staffer, logging in from the corporate network, using Internet Explorer. At seventeen seconds, a loan officer, working remotely, using Firefox, swam into the net.

By thirty seconds, there were four employees on the site. By forty-five seconds, there were seven. By a minute, there were seventeen.

It worked!

Meanwhile, the first hot phish appeared: a branch manager. "Tue, 02 Sep 08 10:00:32," the log reported, followed by the guy's email address and poll answers.

He'd submitted his username and password too, but—unlike a real criminal—Alien did not actually transmit or collect the latter. The point was confirming she could have. And her social engineering assessment still had one more step.

Alien grabbed her phone. She found the branch manager's number on her employee list, blocked caller ID, and started dialing.

"Hello?" he answered.

Her heart pounded. A familiar rush. How long until some employee called Barn Door's actual IT department and word spread that it was a scam?

"Hi, this is Elizabeth in IT," she said. "Congratulations! You've won an iPod for participating in our poll! I'm going to direct you to a site to download an Apple Store gift card."

"Oh!" The guy sounded shocked. "I never win anything! I can't believe it! Wait—"

Alien paused.

"Can I get the iPod at an actual *in-person* Apple Store?" he asked. "Or does it have to be online?"

"Oh *no*," she riffed. "You can *definitely* get it at the Apple Store in person. Just print the gift card and take it in and they'll scan it for you. You should see a bar code.

"Stay with me," she continued.

The branch manager had already entered his username and password. But the masterstroke would be getting him to put whatever she wanted on his computer, because it would mean she never even needed to log in to probe or attack the bank.

"Open your Web browser." Alien directed the manager to a final BarnDoorBankPoll.com Web page she'd created, titled "You've Won!" When he got there, a button let him download a "gift card" file: gift-card.exe.

"Got it?" she said. "Hit 'Run.'"

"Uh . . . I got a pop-up," he said a second later. "Is that okay?"

"Yeah. Click 'Okay,'" said Alien.

"I did . . . ," he reported. "Nothing happened."

Alien grinned. She'd set the file up that way on purpose. But if it were an actual computer program, it could have done anything she wanted it to do, like copy, transfer, edit, or delete files, send email or instant messages, or explore the corporate network. All she needed, however, was its presence on the manager's machine. This would prove to Barn Door that her ploy had worked, without risking any real damage.

"Hmm," said Alien, pretending to be puzzled. "I'll email you the gift card. What's your address? And what's your phone number? And do you have an employee number, just in case I need it?"

He told her everything.

"Great, great," she said. "We'll get that to you by the end of the day."

"Thanks!" the manager said.

"You're welcome." *Score!*

The feeling was like taking a flag in the SCAN class competition. Except this time the flag wasn't a computer file—it was another human.

The call ended. From the other side of the door, Alien could hear and smell sizzling bacon—one of her housemates making breakfast. She looked up at the giant blue robot staring down at her, and then back down to her screen.

Alien paged forward to the next phone number on her hot phish list.

One pwned, she told herself. *Nine to go.*

14

The Best Around

ALIEN WAS IN BUSINESS. Over the next three months, Antidote subcontracted with her to provide twenty-four more social engineering assessments for corporate clients, phishing their employees by email, Web, and phone. As Jake had taught her at Los Alamos, she streamlined her procedures for maximum efficiency. Alien standardized her call script and fine-tuned her computer code to the point where she could quickly compare security vulnerabilities from company to company, branch to branch, with clinical precision.

Her first report, for Barn Door, became a template for those that followed: describe the phishing strategy, generate tables and charts with the number and percentage of employees who fell for each stage, and then suggest appropriate responses. Warm and hot phish should receive additional security training, for example. Cold phish who stayed cold could be rewarded with a genuine gift card raffle. And the entire company would benefit from follow-up assessments annually or even quarterly.

Soon she was running by herself what was essentially a large scamming operation, except that she was working for the employers of the very people she was scamming. And she was doing it all from the spare bedroom of a Cambridge commune.

Until she wasn't.

Alien and Elliot fell hard for each other during her September visit to Parkmont. They went backpacking, soaked in a remote natural hot spring, and camped, talking InfoSec and trading UNIX jokes under the stars. Elliot was definitely Alien's type: both an art major in college and the only person she'd ever met who had read the three-volume *TCP/IP Illustrated* reference books cover to cover. Subsequent visits, Elliot to Cambridge as well as Alien to Parkmont, raised the question: Since she could plug in her laptop and work from anywhere, why not move in with him?

Over the years, Alien had often wavered about whether she wanted a permanent partner, husband or otherwise. But she had always known she wanted kids. Now she was twenty-seven, and in love. It was time.

In late November 2008, Elliot flew east and packed a U-Haul trailer they hitched to the Volvo and drove west together.

⟞⟝

Moving to Colorado and thinking about starting a family forced Alien to consider her priorities. She was determined to be able to provide for herself and any future children, no matter what. Once, working had been a way to hack. Now, she saw hacking as a way to work. Stability mattered more than novelty. As soon as she got to Parkmont, Alien hired a local lawyer and incorporated Tessman Security Consulting. The same day, she rented an office in the city's pretty little downtown.

The space, on the fourth floor of a six-story 1920s-era yellow brick office building, was twelve feet wide and eighteen feet deep and cost three hundred dollars a month. Alien now ran things from a black swivel chair behind a heavy wooden desk that faced a wooden door inset with a classic frosted glass window and shiny brass mail slot. She set a microwave, mini-fridge, red velvet armchair, canvas lamp, and square black side table against the long wall to her left. On the opposite wall were a whiteboard, two wide wooden bookshelves, and a bedraggled plant left over from the previous tenant, a psychiatrist.

Next door on either side were an acupuncturist and a young attorney.

During one afternoon in Alien's first week in the new digs, fat snowflakes fell outside, piling up on the street below, causing minor traffic delays as area skiers flocked to the surrounding mountains. Alien opened a care package from her mother: foil-wrapped latkes, traditional Hanukkah potato pancakes.

"I'm sorry these are cold," the accompanying note said. "They take a while to get to you. If only you lived closer, they might still be warm."

And then her phone rang. Bill Rogers. Alien had told him that she was opening a "Rocky Mountains" office.

"End of the year is always crazy for us with people trying to check off their security assessment," he said. "Do you do remote pentests?"

Alien didn't hesitate. She'd tracked online security holes at Mayflower Hospital and won the capture-the-flag contest in Bruce's SCAN class, ridden shotgun on the Elite Defense airline pentest case and helped write the report afterward. Yet leading a remote pentest—trying to break into a client's systems using only your own Internet connection and computer—was the kind of assignment she'd wanted but never gotten at Elite. Now Rogers was handing it to her.

So what if she had never done it before?

"Sure," she said.

"Great!" Rogers responded. "I'll send you the specs now. I need it in forty-eight hours—close of business December seventeenth. And it's twenty-four hundred dollars."

For that paycheck, she was happy to pull back-to-back all-nighters if need be.

"I'll get it done."

As soon as she received from Rogers a signed contract and the addresses to be tested, Alien removed a thick orange three-ring binder from her desk drawer. It held the most recent contracts, statements of work, and other records for each job she had undertaken for Antidote. Given how many assignments she had now, she'd abandoned code names like "Castle" as impractical. Instead, as at MIT, everything had a number, each piece of work being identified by a unique four-digit client code, followed by a three-digit project code.

For example, 0424-003 described her third project for client 0424—Barn Door Bank.

The front page of the binder, which she updated with each new project, summarized the contents of the volume in a six-column grid: client name, project description, contract dollar amount, and the dates on which she had submitted her report, invoiced Antidote, and received payment. The whiteboard on the wall listed the same information for active projects.

Everything else she'd brought was still packed except her black ThinkPad laptop and boxy gray space heater. The former was on the desk, the latter on the floor beside it.

Alien fired up both.

The client, ironically, was another cybersecurity company: Knight Watch. It wanted a penetration test of its primary website, which had a login page to let customers and employees upload, download, view, or edit sensitive files. Alien's goal was to see if she—and anyone else online—could do the same.

As the sun set, she gave the company code number 0811, added the job to her binder and whiteboard, and started a port scan of Knight Watch network addresses.

In less than two minutes, Alien nabbed the address and port of the company Web server.

Common login flaws included the ability to trick the process into running database or scripting commands, as in Alien's SQL injection attack at SCAN, or poor management of the connection between the individual browser and Web server, which might be susceptible to retrieval, reuse, or hijacking. Before trying any of these approaches, however, Alien checked the website's underlying HTML source code. First, she used an automated tool to "spider" through the site, systematically visiting every page, before downloading the entire thing with Wget. Then, with custom command-line scripts, Alien searched for any instances of "password," "admin," and other keywords.

Nibbling on a cold latke, she read through the results briefly—and then she leaned forward.

Whoever set up the login portal had left an enormous opening in the password verification system. They'd permanently fixed the administrative username and password, and written them into the source code for the page. Both were listed in a common computer code called Base 64, right in the HTML—like the captain of the guard leaving the key to the palace under a mat at the main entry.

"echo YWRtaW5LVwo= | base64 --decode," Alien typed at the command line. "echo cGFzc3dvcmRLVwo= | base64 --decode."

"adminKW," it returned for the username.

"passwordKW" was the password.

And this is a security *company?*

Alien logged in. *"Woo-hoo!"* she shouted.

Alien roamed as she pleased through the files stored on the Knight Watch Web portal, taking screenshots. If KW's competitors copied her moves, they could see all of the company's customers. Amateur hackers could deface the website, like graffiti taggers. Pros could sell the information inside, hold it for ransom, or use it for blackmail. And hacktivist groups like WikiLeaks or Anonymous could go public with what they found, exposing everyone— Knight Watch, its clients, and the clients' clients as well.

Before taking any further steps, Alien phoned Rogers, even though it was after ten p.m. where he lived on the East Coast.

"That was fast," he said.

"I found a critical vulnerability," she said. "I thought you and Knight Watch would want to know immediately."

"I appreciate it," Rogers said. "And I'm sure they will too."

Alien worked well into the night to make sure every detail was exactly right on the report, and then sent it before she went to sleep. The next day, she filled out the invoice and submitted it to Antidote. With no small satisfaction, she updated her binder and whiteboard tallies accordingly.

"$3,500, $800, $1,500, $1,600, $1,000, $4,500, $1,800, $4,000, $1,200, $2,400," read the last ten entries in the binder's "Amount" column. And there were several more above them.

"Happy Hanukkah," she said aloud to herself.

In her first quarter as a freelancer she was going to make fifty thousand bucks.

———✦———

Hacking was half the job for Alien. The other half was managing her relationship with Antidote and the clients it provided. And her schedule. InfoSec was a seasonal industry. Most pentests were booked between October 15 and December 31, to meet end-of-year deadlines, with long lulls the remaining months. To keep up her own bottom line, Alien called Rogers two or three times a week, chatting with him, charming him, soothing his own anxieties, and soliciting additional work through the winter, spring, and summer of 2009.

The reward was a new roof over her head. In early September, little more than a year after her first assignment as an independent consultant, Alien went house hunting with Elliot, upgrading from his one-bedroom bachelor pad on a busy street to a three-bedroom home on a maple-lined cul-de-sac. The good news, in terms of making the hefty down payment and monthly mortgage, was that she was netting two and a half times her old salary at Elite Defense. The bad news was that she was dependent on Antidote for every penny. By the terms of her contract, Alien couldn't even tell clients that she was a subcontractor, much less ask for direct engagements from them for TSC.

As she was pondering this dilemma, Alien got a call from the head of her local Internet service provider, stalwart host of all her phishing sites. "A kid just came to my office," he said. "He asked if he could hack my network."

Alien smiled. "What did you tell him?"

"'Sorry, no.' But can I send him your way?"

Alien agreed. Soon after, the kid—Luke, a Parkmont College senior—met her at a coffee shop two blocks from her office. Five eight, medium build, with mussed light brown hair and long swooping sideburns, Luke wore black Nike sneakers, blue jeans, and a black button-down shirt redolent of Abercrombie & Fitch Fierce cologne.

"Thanks so much for meeting me. I really want to do pentesting," he said. "And I've done it at the college."

"Done what?" asked Alien.

"I work with the security team," Luke explained. "I scanned the network there and found lots of vulnerabilities. I keep reporting it to my bosses, but nothing happens. Anybody at the college could steal all the student records."

His frustration was obvious to Alien. When she nodded sympathetically, he leaned forward. In a whisper, he added, "Like last week—my friend Gus and I were in lecture, and we totally hacked our professor's computer and made it so that there were sheep walking across his boring PowerPoint."

Alien laughed. "Cute," she said. "If you're going to be a professional, though, you can't mess around anymore. No more hacking your teachers. Got it?"

Luke's expression turned serious as he nodded. "Got it," he said solemnly. "Just show me. I'll work for free," he pleaded.

Rather than jump at it, Alien recoiled at his proposal. She found the idea of not paying people for their time unethical. But she had no idea how employing someone would work either, especially when every contract from Antidote came on such short notice, and with no certainty of more to come.

Still. She remembered her own earnest pursuit of Bruce and Elite Defense. *He wants to learn, and maybe I could teach him. And maybe it would help me.*

Alien took a deep breath.

"I'll give you a tryout, and we'll see. And I'll pay you," she said. "How much do you make now?"

"Ten dollars an hour," Luke responded.

"Deal," Alien said.

An employer in another industry would have seen Luke's youth and classroom hacking hijinks as liabilities. In information security, they were assets. Alien couldn't think of a top white hat, from Kevin Mitnick on down, who hadn't broken the law—or at least the rules of one institution or another—to learn the tricks of the trade. That Luke wanted to explore and break boundaries was part of what qualified him as a potential pentester.

Nevertheless, she wasn't going to take unnecessary chances with her clients' privacy and security, or her company's reputation. She'd have to train Luke carefully, and keep a close eye on his work.

Since Alien wanted her own independent space, she moved up a floor in her building, renting two adjacent offices—one for her, one for him—and drilling a hole in the wall between them to share phone, power, and Ethernet. They needed central file storage, she decided, so Alien purchased a Dell PowerEdge server she set up on the MIT Athena model, including strict access controls and encryption. Now Luke could see and do only what she chose to allow. Finally, Alien asked the same attorney who'd helped her incorporate her business to draw up a nondisclosure agreement and other employee documents. These signed, the paid internship, as they called it, officially began.

Elite Defense had made Alien furnish herself with almost everything she needed to do her work for them. She wanted Luke to feel more supported. She purchased an ergonomic office chair for his workspace, sliding it behind a faux-wood desk donated by her landlord. Atop the desk was a telephone and a refurbished ThinkPad, wiped clean and running Linux, connected to a keyboard, mouse, and external monitor. A few feet away, on a long folding table, the file server whirred noisily. Her biggest purchase was a $2,500 black dishwasher-sized commercial shredder, capable of pulverizing a sheet of paper into more than 1,500 impossible-to-reassemble bits, located directly under the whiteboard.

But the main mission was transforming Luke's aptitude into ability. "I'm going to be setting up a phishing site," Alien greeted him when he arrived on his first day. "Watch me."

"*Yes!*" He was even more enthusiastic than when she'd offered him the job.

"Sit down," said Alien. It was essential to make clear her own professional values and how they translated into specific methods she expected him to follow.

As her opening instructions, Alien repeated what Jake had told her at Los Alamos: "First, always take the time to get your environment set up right. It's worth it to invest the time you need at the beginning."

He nodded, but she wasn't sure he fully got it. She felt she should explain further. "Hacking takes *work*. Yes, you have to be cool winging it. But you won't get any better unless you master your tools and then build up from there."

As they proceeded, Alien quizzed Luke on his Linux command line skills, which seemed rudimentary but promising. They moved to the text editor.

"This is Emacs," she said. "Learn all the shortcuts so you can move around as fast as you want. Practice until your fingers can keep up with your mind."

At first, examining a sample file, Luke inched forward or backward slowly, one character at a time, using the right and left arrow keys. "Control-E—move to the end of the line," Alien instructed him. "Control-A—move to the front." The drill continued through a dozen more common Emacs shortcuts: page down, page up, split window vertically, split horizontally, cut, copy, paste, search and replace, and so on.

"Good," said Alien. What he didn't know, Luke was picking up quickly. "Excellence comes from planning and practice," she told him. "If these shortcuts save you five minutes every hour and you work thirty hours a week, that's one hundred and fifty minutes"—two and a half hours a week, ten-plus hours a month—"you're working productively instead of wasting time.

"The same thing is true on a project level," she continued. "A lot of hackers shoot from the hip. It's true that you need to be flexible. But planning and practice will give you the best results. Line up each domino perfectly beforehand so, as soon as you touch the first, the others fall down in exactly the way you want them."

Luke rubbed his hands together. "I'm ready," he said.

On her own laptop, Alien loaded the website for client 0497, another bank, and explained the poll and iPod prize ruse.

"What Web page do you want to mimic?" she asked.

Luke browsed a minute before settling on one with a group photo of smiling employees. Together they chose a fake domain name, one letter off from the one the bank was actually using.

"Great." Alien switched to the command line, typing one quick instruction to grab a copy of the website, and then another to register the new domain. "It has to be registered for at least five days before the engagement," she told Luke. "Sites that are too new are called 'Day Old Bread.' They get filtered first by spam blockers."

Another nod. Luke's eyes narrowed, locked onto the screen. He sat up straighter, ignoring the end-of-day chatter in the outer hallway as surrounding offices let out.

"Okay." Alien explained as she entered new commands, fingers flying: "Now we need to change the DNS"—domain name system—"so it's pointing to our Web server.... Now we're going to SSH in.... Now we're going to Apache to set up a new virtual domain.... Now we're going to configure Postfix so we can send and receive email.... Now we're copying the Web page we downloaded, renaming it, and replacing the text with our poll template."

Together these steps gave the new domain name a working Web address and server, email access, and a set of bogus poll Web pages based on the website of the actual bank.

They decided on a new final poll question—"Would you be able to perform your job better with a company smartphone?"—changed the giveaway item to an Amazon gift card, and updated the accompanying photos, all with a few more keystrokes from Alien.

"{INSERT CLIENT NAME}," the poll template said, among other variables. "Fill those in with search and replace.... Save.... Change file permissions," Alien told Luke, demonstrating from Emacs and the command line. "Restart Apache."

Alien scooted forward. "Let's test it," she said.

Alien added Luke's new company email address to her target list. With two more commands, she opened the Web server firewall and launched the phishing script. Then Alien slid him the laptop.

"Check your email," she said.

Luke did. "Employee Poll + Amazon Giveaway!" the top message subject said.

"Open it," said Alien. "And follow the link."

Luke clicked. *Poof*—like magic, the new website loaded, exactly like the original bank's, but with Tessman Security Consulting's new poll questions and the Amazon gift card images above the smiling employees. Simultaneously, Luke's email address and other information appeared on the warm phish log onscreen.

"Whoa!" Luke said. He double-blinked.

Alien smiled. What had taken her a week to set up for Barn Door now took five minutes. "Win first. Then do battle," she quoted Sun Tzu.

"What now?" Luke asked her.

Alien patted the desk and pointed up at the whiteboard. "Your turn," she said. "Do the next one. I'll sit with you and walk you through it."

———※———

Luke brought fresh energy to the office. He loved learning from Alien, eagerly taking on new tasks. As he got up to speed with each one, she could delegate routine assignments to him and spend more time negotiating and reviewing contracts. By the end of 2009, there were so many current projects the company needed a second whiteboard.

"Can you hire my friend Gus?" Luke asked Alien. "He's super-talented."

Alien thought about it. The slow season would start again soon. Who knew if she would have enough work to pay even one intern? But she also wanted TSC to conduct and present original research projects, like Elite Defense, and run its own hacking conference contests, like TOOOL. In both cases, keeping up with—and then one-upping—current trends was a way to stay at the leading edge of the industry. And having an influential audience of other insiders hear them speak, or play a contest they designed, was the best possible form of self-promotion.

"Okay," she said. "But you have to help me make a place for you guys to test new hacking ideas."

"You got it," Luke said.

———※———

In January 2010, Alien rented the former break room of an insurance company across the hall that had gone belly-up. She dubbed it the TSC "Playlab," and she and Luke set about rewiring her business to integrate the addition.

They created a network map for the lab, together cramming in close to twenty old desktop computers and other eBay purchases they could use to simulate—and then attack—almost any home or workplace setup. Together they cooked up ToneDef, a pun-filled, story-based, seven-part hacking challenge, to pitch as a DEF CON contest.

Soon after, Alien interviewed and hired Gus, a husky blond junior from Colorado cattle country, and another undergrad, Cheryl, a freckled redhead and accounting major, as interns. Punctilious Cheryl treated the position like a test she'd fail if she ever stopped studying. Gus and Luke, though, who shared a mischievous streak, started "icing" each other—hiding individual Smirnoff Ice bottles, which, when found inadvertently (say, atop the paper stack inside the printer), had to be opened and drunk immediately.

Hustling back and forth between configuring software in the Playlab and answering client email on her work computer one evening in mid-April, Alien heard "You're the Best Around," the mid-eighties synth-pop song made famous by the final fight sequence of *The Karate Kid,* blasting in Luke's office.

And then it played again. And again. And again.

She walked over and found Gus seated on a big beige beanbag chair, surrounded by a half-dozen Smirnoff Ice empties.

Gus was holding his head in his hands. He moaned softly and then spoke with slurred words. "My head hurts . . . "

Luke stood between the printer-copier and a full-sized refrigerator that had supplanted Alien's original mini-fridge, looking on, laughing. Cheryl sat primly behind the desk in the room. She tried to ignore both guys, focusing instead on the screen of her laptop.

"What happened?" Alien asked, as if it weren't obvious.

"Cheryl got me," Gus said. "I went for one of the apples in the fruit bin of the fridge and found a six-pack."

Cheryl cringed awkwardly. "I'm really sorry," she told Alien. "It wasn't on purpose. I was just going to use one. I tried to put the six-pack where no one else would find it."

Gus slumped. "I *had* to drink it," he said, slurring again. "It's the *rules.*"

Alien toed the empty bottles on the floor. She turned the speaker off. The office looked more like a frat house than any normal place of business. Yet tomorrow morning the four of them were phishing employees of client 6110 —a global law firm with more than a billion dollars in annual revenue.

"Guys, you're *professionals* now," Alien said sternly. After years of working under other people, being an authority figure felt weird to her. But the company's existence was on the line with this—and every—contract.

Alien saw the interns as peers as much as employees. Having a beer while they were working late was fine, if it didn't hinder what they were doing. But a drinking game like this was out of the question.

She had to discipline them, but not stress them out so much that they lost confidence in themselves or TSC.

"Gus—go home," she ordered. "Luke—give him a ride and make sure he's okay. Cheryl—thanks for holding down the fort.

"Get some rest. We were going to go over scripts tonight, but instead we're going to meet earlier tomorrow. Be here at six thirty a.m., or I'm going to put you through our very expensive shredder. Which would be a shame." She paused before continuing. "Because then I'd have to get another one."

Everyone gathered again in the interns' office early the next morning. The bottles were gone, Alien noticed, and the beanbag chair had been pushed back into a corner. Luke brought in a ten-cup cardboard coffee container from a local café.

She watched while "Cheryl in IT" practiced calling Gus, who posed as a 6110 employee. Gus practiced calling Luke. Luke practiced calling Cheryl. Then all three called Alien.

"I hate surprises," she told them. For all the fast-talking she'd had to practice, Alien's model hacker was the mastermind who anticipated in advance where the conversation might go rather than the pure improviser. "Anything they say to you, you should be ready to respond."

First, to warm up her charges, the boss played nice in her responses: "I won? *Really? Oh, thank you!*" Alien enthused. Next, mimicking an inexperienced user—the "grandma," pejoratively—she asked, high-voiced, "*How* do I click on that? Where's the address *bar?*" Finally, Alien threw curveballs: "*Cheryl* in IT? There's no *Cheryl* in IT!" As necessary, they stopped, edited the call script, or discussed how best to respond.

Afterward, Alien sent everyone links to the phishing site and the location on the TSC file server of the final call script and initial cold phish list with each employee's name, position, email address, phone number, and geographic location. Different spreadsheet tabs divided the targeted employees among the interns, with additional columns for the date and time called, whether they reached the person, if he or she followed their instructions, and any other notes. "Look at the column labeled 'ID' for each person," Alien said. "That's the code I'll send you if someone on your list turns hot. Trade only if you get overloaded. And remember to check their region first so you know which location you're calling."

Luke, Gus, and Cheryl flipped their laptops open.

"Oh—and don't forget to block caller ID," Alien said. "They're going to catch on to us eventually. And when they do, we don't want them to call us back."

At five minutes to launch time—ten fifteen a.m.—Alien checked her watch.

"Get ready," she said.

Alien walked back to her own office. She opened the cold phish spreadsheet and an IRC chat window alongside the command line on her laptop. Until you fell for one, it was easy to make fun of phishing schemes, and assume the people behind them were small-time crooks. But what followed was as closely coordinated as a military missile strike.

At the command line, Alien typed:

```
sudo iptables -n --line-numbers -L | less
sudo iptables -I INPUT 40 -p tcp --dport 80 -j ACCEPT
sudo iptables -I INPUT 40 -p tcp --dport 80 -j LOG
sudo iptables -I INPUT 40 -p tcp --dport 25 -j ACCEPT
sudo iptables -I INPUT 40 -p tcp --dport 25 -j LOG
```

"Opening firewall to allow access," she wrote in the IRC window. "Confirmed firewall port 80 open. Confirming external access successful. Opening firewall port 25."

At the command line, Alien typed:

```
./phish-script-1.1.sh -v config.txt
```

"Sending test email," she wrote in the IRC window, "config.txt" being the configuration file containing a pointer to her cold phish recipient list—for test purposes, the email addresses of Alien and her team.

"Test email received," replied Cheryl.

"Received," Luke confirmed.

Alien opened two new terminal windows for her warm and hot phish logs. In the first, she typed:

```
tail -F warm.txt
```

In the second, she typed:

```
tail -F hot.txt
```

"Checking user tracking," she wrote. "Click your links."

They did—and the warm phish log updated accordingly. When each of them filled out and submitted a poll, the hot phish log updated too.

"Confirmed user tracking working properly," Alien wrote. "Loading target list. Launching emails in thirty seconds."

The others waited. In Emacs, Alien updated her cold phish recipient list to include the email addresses of their actual targets, the employees of client 6110. Again, she typed:

```
./phish-script-1.1.sh -v config.txt
```

Hitting the Enter key to put the phishing expedition in motion was the hardest part. In spite of all her experience, it was dreadful every time. There was no way to know just what would happen, except that there was no going back.

Milliseconds later, in some of the most well-appointed law offices across the country, people's computers beeped.

New message!

⊲⊳

Out-of-office replies came first—a good sign. Their messages were getting through. And the information about who was out, for how long, and whom to contact in their absence would let the TSC team customize calls with inside references: "Is Margot back from Hawaii yet?" "Dave gave me your name." "Yeah—Ben mentioned that before he went to Philadelphia."

Still, Alien was antsy as she waited for the first click-throughs. At ten seconds in, she counted two warm phish. Twenty seconds later, she had five. Another fifteen seconds and she had ten.

"Warm phish incoming . . . ," she typed. Alien held her breath, waiting for a submitted poll, like a general holding out for the first word back from the front.

Then their first catch appeared on the hot phish log. One of 6110's billing coordinators, based in Dallas and assigned to Cheryl.

Alien exhaled.

"Cheryl—hot phish," she typed. Alien copied and pasted his ID.

"Hi," she heard a moment later through the thin office walls. "This is Cheryl in IT. Congratulations! You've won the Amazon gift card for participating in our poll! I'm going to direct you to a site to download it . . ."

Two more followed almost immediately—an East Coast marketing associate, assigned to Gus, and a West Coast lawyer, assigned to Luke.

Alien directed each their way.

"Hi," she heard. "This is Gus in IT. Congratulations! . . ." "Hi! This is Luke in IT. Congratulations! . . ."

The round-robin, cross-country phishing chorus continued for almost fifteen minutes.

"Send stats," Alien typed to the members of her call center.

"9 reached, 6 wins," wrote Cheryl.

"6 reached, 3 wins," Gus wrote.

"5 reached, 4 wins," wrote Luke.

So: twenty calls total. And thirteen openings to the law firm's supposedly privileged inner communications.

"We're done," typed Alien. "Great batting average, Luke."

Cheers sounded in the next room. High-fives. Alien heard knocking and opened her office to greet a delivery guy from the sandwich shop around the corner. TSC was treating. It was another way to make the interns feel appreciated—and keep them on task.

As Alien carried the sandwiches in to her employees, "You're the Best Around" started playing in their office.

"Good job today," she said. "Next time, Luke, you're going to run the prep."

Alien was becoming a small business owner with big responsibilities—a lot like her parents, even if information security was a very different enterprise from selling restaurant supplies or preparing tax returns. When Luke graduated in May 2010, she hired him full-time at the same starting salary she'd received at Los Alamos and issued him a company credit card of the kind Elite Defense never provided her. Alien moved the TSC file server offsite, to a secure colocation facility, and brought in new desks for Gus and Cheryl. A part-time office manager came on to keep the books, handle payroll, and arrange health insurance, duties she had previously split with Cheryl.

Each new commitment was a trade-off: greater capability and more to worry about. And Alien was still feeling her way as the boss of young and spirited people for whom this was their first real work experience, and in an unconventional field that deliberately encouraged them to think outside the box. A particular challenge was drafting the company's first human resources policy guidelines.

"No icing in the office," read one of the provisions. "No vacuuming another employee's lap" was another.

And a third: "'You're the Best Around' may be played a maximum of three times per person, per day."

In late July, Alien flew the team with her to Vegas and DEF CON, where their ToneDef contest and a related presentation had both made the program. Earlier in the month, the holding company that owned the Riviera had declared bankruptcy, citing diminished guest visits, yet DEF CON attendees again filled the hotel to capacity—and beyond.

"We're out of rooms," a harried front-desk clerk told Alien when she tried to check in after Luke, Gus, and Cheryl.

"But I reserved *a year ago*," said Alien.

The clerk conferred with her manager. "We can offer you a suite," he said. *It doesn't get better than this.*

To avoid being hacked by other conference-goers, Alien had told everyone to leave their laptops and smartphones at home and got them "burner phones"—cheap, easily disposable flip phones. In addition, she and Luke carried frequency-hopping spread-spectrum walkie-talkies. "Take the rental car and go with Gus to Whole Foods," Alien radioed him upon examining the suite's kitchenette. "Get enough milk, cereal, sandwich stuff, snacks, and drinks for everyone for the weekend. Plus chips and dip." The entire supermarket bill would be less than one group meal at the hotel.

Afterward, all three employees were to roam the conference, handing out newly printed stickers — "TSC" emblazoned in silver letters above a globe on which was a *Charlie's Angels*–style female silhouette, "the ToneDef temptress" — advertising their contest and talk.

"Put these on and pass them out wherever you go," Alien instructed.

She had come a long way since her first DEF CON visit. Who would have guessed, two years after sleeping in a bathtub, she would have her own suite, with her own staff, thinking of ways to expand the range of her own company?

The four of them gathered that night in the suite to coordinate their plans for the rest of the evening. By now, Alien had changed into black high heels, fishnet stockings, and a puffy black-and-white feathered Cruella de Vil dress with an oversized collar and cuffs. Luke and Gus wore jeans and dark dress shirts, Cheryl a mid-thigh little black dress.

"Have fun and keep an eye on one another," said Alien. For the first time, it occurred to her that she had taken three young people from small-town Colorado to Sin City.

"Stay safe. If you go off on your own, please call or text someone to say where you are and where you're going," Alien continued. "And" — the words that followed could have been uttered by her own mother — "if you have *any* problems at any time, call me right away."

———

Four big pentests awaited the week they got back from Vegas. All required tight turnaround times. At Elite, Alien had used Adderall and Ambien to power through one emergency after another. Now the last of her pills was gone. She wanted to get pregnant, so she hadn't renewed the prescriptions. She'd even cut down on drinking tea, lest caffeine affect conception. Her employees had to step up.

Alien supervised the interns closely, writing an Nmap script they could feed lists of Internet addresses to scan by client, checking for thousands of potential holes. With this and other custom scripts, she helped Cheryl penetrate a well-advertised insurer's internal Web server, and Gus avoid the intrusion detection system guarding a Pentagon-funded academic research network. So far, so good.

She looked at the clock. "Don't forget—you have that social engineering gig soon."

"Already on it," Luke said. "We're meeting in fifteen minutes."

The contract was for a "spearphishing" test, or customized phishing attack targeting specific high-value employees—in this case, a Northeast power company's president and vice president. Alien observed as Luke held his prep session, coaching Gus and Cheryl to work separately but simultaneously, trying scenarios similar to what she had practiced in person at Castle Bank headquarters. Then it was go time.

On one side of the interns' office, Gus called the vice president's executive assistant, posing as a member of the IT staff. "I'm seeing a lot of bandwidth usage on your computer," he said. "Is this *business* usage?" Gus asked imperiously.

"It should be," the assistant replied. Her voice sounded shaky, though, Alien overheard. The specter of having been caught doing something wrong —exchanging personal messages, shopping online, idly browsing the Web —scared everyone.

"Hmm." Gus pretended to ponder the situation. "Maybe you have a virus. Let's see. Can you go to this IT page and download a virus scanner?"

As Gus offered directions to a fake IT website they'd set up, Cheryl, on the other side of the room, was tying up the power company's *real* IT help line. Her ploy was pretending to be the executive assistant to the president. "He forgot his password," she said in a panicked voice. "It needs to be reset right away because he's in a meeting and he needs it to present."

Alien watched as Cheryl waited. "*My* favorite color?" Cheryl said into the phone, repeating IT's security question to her. On her laptop, Cheryl flicked to the actual executive assistant's Facebook page, having located it in her preparatory reconnaissance. Social media was a boon to social engineering. First, it was a new, often more informal way to reach people than phone and email. Second, your targets tracked and tagged themselves.

In this case, the executive assistant's profile showed a plump mid-fifties woman in a purple dress, backgrounded by a field of violets.

"Purple," Cheryl answered confidently.

She gave Luke a discreet thumbs-up. "Okay . . . 'Smith3'?" Cheryl asked IT. "With a capital 'S' and a '3' at the end? Got it! Thank you!"

Gus and Cheryl hung up at the same time. Alien shook her head, smiling. A hacker could exploit the power company president's account immediately, stealing files or sending orders under his name. The executive assistant's account was perfect for a long con, intercepting messages and installing malicious software for months or even years to come.

"Great job!" Luke told the interns. "Time to debrief."

Alien moved to Luke's desk when he did. Onscreen was the Medusa password-guessing tool, probing a remote access server for one of Southern California's largest banks.

"ACCOUNT FOUND," it said. "User: test Password: fuckyou."

"Classy," Luke said. They both laughed. Everyone thought hackers were the immature and irresponsible ones, but "fuckyou" and other expletives were incredibly common user passwords, no matter how eminent or prestigious the entity.

"Check the privileges," said Alien.

Luke logged in. "Root," he said incredulously.

The insurer. The military research network. The power company. The bank. Millions of people trusted billions of dollars—and their lives and livelihoods —to these institutions. But when it came to computer security, a trained adversary could pwn almost anyone.

Luke entered a directory full of image files. He typed a quick command to open the first ten.

The monitor filled with loan documents and copies of scanned checks.

<hr/>

Alien, acting as a representative of Antidote, prepared to call her contact in California within the next half hour. Every minute that they knew other hackers could get in and they weren't fixing the problem was a minute the bank could be bleeding both dollars and its clients' vital data. The possible consequences ranged from embarrassment to ruin.

"Take enough screenshots to illustrate what you accomplished," she said. "Black out the account numbers and any PII"—personally identifiable information, specific to a single person. "Do it again and document everything. Fast."

Luke nodded, already moving confidently back through the system. He'd have done the same without her standing next to him, Alien realized. It was a good feeling. A year ago, the guy had been hacking his college professor's desktop. Now he had the skills to save a bank.

Alien thought as she saw Luke work. He'd come so far. But he could still go further.

"What?" Luke asked, seeing her scrutinize his sneakers, jeans, and untucked shirt.

"Do you have a suit?" Alien asked.

——⊰⊱——

Alien introduced Luke to Bill Rogers. "Call him once a week," she told Luke. "I'll handle the other two times." Together, they talked up TSC taking on challenging and generously compensated on-site gigs for Antidote, on par with any Elite Defense engagement.

In late September, a steakhouse chain with franchises in forty states contracted with Antidote for a security assessment of their Miami headquarters. The next day, Antidote subcontracted with TSC.

DEF CON aside, it was Luke's first trip outside Colorado.

Alien did all she could to prepare him. "When you get there, introduce yourself and review the schedule and goals for the week," she told him. "Set clear, conservative, and realistic expectations. And remember: encrypt everything, back it up to the TSC file server at night, and physically remove and store your laptop hard drive in the hotel safe if you leave it behind when you go out to dinner."

Her parting gift was a mini-screwdriver set to keep with him, a useful good luck charm.

Luke left on an afternoon flight. The following morning, Alien pictured her former intern waking up at his hotel, dressing in his new suit (jet black, black button-down shirt, and bright pink tie), and driving a rental car to the restaurant chain's corporate offices.

Pride and happy anticipation swept Alien as she drove to work herself. Luke was a smooth talker. People liked him. And by now his technical moves had been practiced time and time again. She knew he'd do great.

All the same, it was impossible to tell him *everything*. Alien remembered every detail of stepping out of the car with Richard on that first Castle job, and how nothing could have prepared her for the rush of what would follow.

Alien parked. She climbed the stairs to the fifth floor, greeting Gus and Cheryl, who were already vying for Luke's desk. Alien had barely sat down before she received a text.

Luke.

"root dance!" he wrote.

She picked up the phone and called him. "Forty-five minutes," Alien checked the time. "Nice. How'd you do it?"

"Oh, so easy," he said. "The default port scans didn't come up with anything, but the full SYN scans showed open telnet on a weird port. It was the Aloha POS"—the restaurant chain's point-of-sale system. "I looked up the default admin password, and boom—I was in."

⎯⎯◆⎯⎯

Luke uploaded photos and screenshots, and then went to work seeing what else he could do on the network. Gus and Cheryl started working on the report by examining what Luke was sending.

"Check this out!" they called to Alien.

Alien looked. The first photo Luke had taken showed a bland beige-walled basement. Down the hall, though, was the bright-red entrance to a full-scale exact replica of every restaurant in the steakhouse chain, installed in corporate headquarters for training and testing purposes. And the photos continued inside.

Each COWBOY CROSSING sign, set of elk antlers, and other décor was the same as in a real restaurant. So was the kitchen, bathroom, employee break room, and every piece of furniture and silverware. And so was the computer network and point-of-sale system.

Luke had pwned both, his notes showed, from a red-cushioned booth.

"Wow," said Alien quietly. A malevolent hacker emulating Luke from the same seat at any restaurant in the chain could grab the credit card information of every customer.

⎯⎯◆⎯⎯

Antidote sent Luke on other road assignments—one week to one of Washington, D.C.'s most visited museums, the next to a prominent Silicon Valley venture capital fund. "r00t dance!" he texted Alien again, both times within the first hour.

From a public conference room at the museum, he'd plugged into their network, sniffed traffic, and set himself up with administrator credentials. Now, as his screenshots showed and "r00t dance!" proclaimed, he could grab email messages, log every keystroke anyone typed, and access—or destroy—all their files, from payroll records to secret auction notes.

The VC fund was even easier pickings: the usual port scan, combined with a password cracker, gave up confidential records on the financial standing of hundreds of tech companies.

With Luke out of the office, Gus and Cheryl joined forces, pentesting a popular Web hosting service that provided domain name registration and online server space for individual and organizational websites. "Hey—I think I found a directory traversal issue," one of the interns reported their second day on the project. By default, the hosting service made only the Web pages of each site accessible to a browser. But if you figured out where other files were stored on the server, you could access *any* document, no login necessary.

Alien watched as Cheryl bypassed the authentication process for one of the hosted sites, an online pharmaceutical service. Gus scanned their records, finding dozens of familiar names. "Oh my God," he said. "These are all professional athletes."

Alien knelt beside him, studying the list. She wasn't a sports fan, but these people were so famous even she knew who they were. In seconds, TSC could search who had a cold and who had herpes, who was playing on a sprained ankle and who was weaning himself from painkillers. Sports fans would find this intel fascinating, and sports gamblers would find it highly profitable.

"Write it up," said Alien. "No screenshots."

She walked back to her office to call the client. Alien had stopped being surprised by how easy it was to hack everyone. But rather than exult in TSC's success, she found it disturbing. She and her team were cracking open important organizations on a daily basis. Almost every time, what they found was a mess: vulnerable systems and leadership unable to tell where their computers were or who was on them even as they ceded ever more control to technology. And the people who relied on those organizations had no idea. Take the professional athletes. Because the ultimate client was the Web hosting provider, it would get an immediate report of its hole. But the online pharmacy would never know it had been breached. And neither would the pharmacy's clients —the athletes and others.

Each case was like discovering that all the homes in an entire city had been built on rotten foundations, Alien thought. And the larger dilemma presented by the world's dependence on the Internet was that there was no safer place to go.

Alien rubbed her stomach protectively. She and Elliot weren't telling anyone yet, but she was twelve weeks pregnant.

15

Phoning Home

ALIEN SCOWLED, SEARCHING THE racks of the pastel-walled maternity shop in the Parkmont mall for business clothes she could wear to work. She liked to dress professionally, and these would be important in any face-to-face meetings and presentations, as with her lawyer, or at a security conference like SCAN. It was January 2011, and she was well into her second trimester. All they had here were jeans with big black stretchy fabric in place of buttons at the waist, and dresses that looked like pink tents.

Alien gave up on the maternity shop, purchasing nothing but a navy blue baby sling, and then crossed the mall to a regular women's clothing store, where she bought a business-y black skirt three sizes larger than usual. Back in her office, she ordered a nursing pump and Pack 'n Play portable crib online.

What would happen when the baby cried, though? And who was going to pull in work or deal with clients while she was nursing?

She walked next door, where Luke, Gus, and Cheryl sat typing. Alien cleared her throat and waited for all three to look up. "We have to get the business to the point where you can run day-to-day operations without me," she said.

Luke was the first to respond. "Don't worry about it," he assured her. He turned to Gus and Cheryl. "We're ready, right, guys?" They nodded in agreement.

Alien waited to exhale until she had walked out again.

Before the end of January, Alien rented yet another new space in the building, an office area for herself at the far end of the hall with a view to the east of snow-topped mountains. Its crucial feature was a small adjoining room where her baby could sleep and she would be able to nurse or pump milk in relative privacy.

Alien shifted the interns to her old office, so Luke had his own. Then she held an "Ethernet crimping party" during which everyone cut and crimped one thousand feet of cabling into the dozens of new cables necessary for the expanded office network, centered on a new modem, switch, and firewall in the closet of the Playlab, TSC's experimental hacking space.

It was an imperfect, even precarious setup. Each time she entered one of the offices, Alien saw the rough holes in the walls and exposed wiring. Use the microwave and space heater simultaneously and the power flickered out.

And "You're the Best Around" still blasted at any hour.

In the middle of one such serenade, Luke knocked on her new office door. "Gus and Cheryl are graduating in May," he reminded Alien.

"What you're really saying is that you want to hire them full-time, right?"

"Yep!"

Alien let the steam rise from a freshly nuked frozen veggie burrito — today's breakfast, lunch, and, in all likelihood, dinner. Meanwhile, numbers filled her head. She'd just raised Luke's salary by twenty thousand dollars. Add about another forty thousand each for Gus and Cheryl — plus health insurance, company credit cards for them, and other benefits — and she'd need more than one hundred grand in new business per year just to maintain her current income.

In spite of this, Luke's suggestion made sense. Her due date was virtually simultaneous with Parkmont College graduation. If she wanted to keep TSC going while she was off the phone and away from the keyboard, she needed a team.

"You said you could run things," Alien said. "Can you manage everyone, too? Because I won't have the time."

"Sure," Luke said.

"It's a lot of responsibility."

Luke grinned. "I'm on it," he said.

Alien nodded. "Glad to hear it."

Luke returned to his office. Alien sat thinking for a minute until she noticed the burrito still in her hand. Her pregnancy already made her constantly queasy, and now the rice, cheese, and broccoli bits had congealed into a solid mass that was unappetizing under any circumstances. She put it down.

Alien opened her laptop to try and make the numbers work.

⟨⟩

A week later, Alien invited Gus and Cheryl one at a time to her office, where she offered them full-time jobs.

Gus asked for the same position Luke had started with — security consultant. Cheryl, however, said that she wasn't sure if she had enough experience.

"Why not?" Alien asked her. "You've been doing fantastic work. Your report reviews are wonderful. Your scans are perfect. You have an amazing attention to detail."

Cheryl shrugged. "But I'm not as *technical* as Gus is," she said finally.

Alien pushed back. "You do the same work he does," she said. "You read up after hours. Everything else you learn by doing. And he has a lot to learn from you in communicating with clients. I know you can handle this."

It was the truth. Plus, the alternative was a self-perpetuating cycle. Gus would have more experience earlier, which would lead to better opportunities later. And Cheryl would be stuck doing report reviews — at best.

"Well, I am really interested," said Cheryl. "If you think I can do it . . ."

Alien was emphatic. "You've got this. And we're here to support you."

Cheryl raised her chin. "Okay."

⟨⟩

The following week started with two subcontracts for the same client, a Denver hospital. It needed a remote pentest, assessing its network security, and an on-site consultant to check its compliance with federal rules specific to health information privacy.

Alien sat Luke down and went over both subcontracts, line by line, to show him how it was done.

"This is the most important part of the job," she said. "It's not the hacking. It's designing and planning the engagement, and making sure that everybody" — TSC, Antidote, the client — "knows what to expect. Engagements succeed or fail before they ever start."

A social engineering assessment probed human vulnerabilities, for example. If automated spam filters had blocked the phishing emails, there was no way to know if employees would have fallen for them. For that reason, Alien explained, "the statement of work should require whitelisting"—specifically allowing TSC's emails.

"Criminals can spend all day trying to beat spam blockers," she told him. "We don't have time for that, and clients won't want to spend the money to hire us to do it."

Likewise, for the pentest of the hospital, TSC required written permission to hack. They needed to know exactly what systems and Internet addresses they were authorized to probe. And, even after authorization, they had to verify that the hospital actually owned those systems and addresses.

"It's fine to be a little flexible—for instance, testing one hundred and fifty-five Internet addresses instead of one hundred and fifty," Alien said. "But you may *only* conduct the tests included in the statement of work, and you can *never* test other clients or systems. And remember: sometimes clients get their *own* addresses wrong."

What had happened in person with Jim, when Castle Bank gave them an incorrect location for its data backup and disaster recovery center in Chicago, was even more likely to occur when they were dealing with the all-number locaters—172.217.11.174, for example, or 91.198.174.192—that made up an online address. More than once, Alien had caught typos in the information clients provided her that would have had TSC unintentionally attacking someone else.

"If we break into the wrong computer system, whose liability is that?" she warned Luke. "I don't want to find out."

Luke completed the hospital contract reviews with Alien and coordinated with the client. Under his direction, Cheryl took the on-site assignment and Gus the remote one. That day, Gus ran into Alien's office at noon.

"Hey! Hey!" he said excitedly. "I see Cheryl!"

"So?" she asked. The two of them shared an office, didn't they?

"She's in Denver, at the hospital. I'm *watching* her from the DVR system I *hacked*," Gus said.

Alien followed him as fast as she could. On Gus's monitor was a live video feed from the hospital security system.

"All the controls are online," he said. "I had the password in ten minutes.

And look." He pointed to a slim young woman with long red hair, dressed in a gray skirt and matching suit jacket buttoned over a black blouse. She was talking to a middle-aged man in a white coat at a desk behind a pharmacy counter.

The woman turned, as if to face the cameras. *Cheryl.*

"Oh my God—you're right!" said Alien. "Take a screenshot!"

He did, and then they watched together, rewinding back and forth for another minute.

"Tilt and zoom," Alien suggested. "Can you see patients getting their medicine?"

"Yeah . . . I think so." Gus tried it. "*There.*"

They watched as a woman in her thirties, wearing a black nylon jacket, received a little pill bottle.

Gus zoomed out. A long line of other patients waited their turn at the counter.

Their privacy wasn't safe at an online pharmacy. And it wasn't safe in person either.

<hr />

While Gus continued his investigations, Alien called Antidote, which would follow up with the hospital once her team had written up their findings.

"It can probably wait until you see the report," she told Rogers, "but I wanted to give you the heads-up."

"Thanks," said Rogers. Then he lowered his voice. "By the way, did you hear the news?" he asked.

Alien sat up. "What news?" she asked.

"They're selling Antidote."

In the 1980s, computer giants warred over operating systems and office software packages. In the 1990s, it was Web browsers and the onetime fringe business of e-commerce. Then came social platforms, smartphones, and cloud computing. Now the hot new turf was information security. As much as possible, Rogers explained, Antidote's new owners wanted to move everything they did in-house.

"So what's going to happen to subcontractors like us?" said Alien.

"I don't know," he offered glumly. "But all of us here are polishing up our résumés."

Alien felt nauseous, and this time it wasn't the baby. After hanging up, she opened the project management software that had replaced her orange binders.

In the last six months, Tessman Security Consulting had had contracts for close to 120 jobs, with ten more yet to be completed, and five on tap next week. Every single one was from Antidote.

Alien winced. For two and a half years—almost twice her tenure at Elite Defense—Antidote had found the clients, TSC had hacked them, and they had split the fee. It had all been to everyone's satisfaction and profit. But just at the moment when TSC needed more work to stay afloat, there was the distinct prospect of less.

Alien considered her situation. She was six months pregnant. If she dissolved the company and started looking for a job, it would be very hard to find an employer ready to take on a woman about to give birth, let alone at the salary she needed to pay her bills and her mortgage. Besides, she felt an obligation to her employees, who depended on her. And a pride in owning and running her own business.

Alien thought of learning how to ride a motorcycle. And the exhilaration once she had done so.

The key, Piñon had taught her, was not to let fear slow you down, but to lean into the curve and accelerate.

It was time for TSC to make its own name in the security industry.

Get bigger. Go faster. Or crash.

Alien called a meeting with the whole staff right after Cheryl's return.

"We need to market," she said.

The Antidote sale closed in February. By March 1, Rogers had left Antidote. The company still provided TSC some subcontract work, but Alien had to go through a cumbersome new billing system. The first invoices got gummed up, so they weren't paid for a long time, which created a cash flow crisis. And everything could dry up completely at any moment. Even if her staff did most of the actual hacking work without Alien, there was more pressure than ever on her to find work for them to do.

That month, in stolen moments between gigs, Alien built a company web-site accessible to the public. Elliot and the employees designed a professional logo: the initials TSC reflected in a shimmering alpine lake.

Alien, now eight months pregnant and almost thirty-five pounds over her usual weight, stuffed brochures and business cards into promotional folders for Elliot to hand out at SCAN classes.

Alien's due date was the last Wednesday in April. In the week before, she pulled three all-nighters, trying to wrap up different projects before the baby arrived. Her plan was to have a water birth, delivering in a big spa-style tub of warm water at the Parkmont Natural Birth Center, attended only by a doula and certified nurse midwife on staff. On her actual due date, with no contractions yet, Alien arranged a four p.m. checkup with the midwife.

In the hours before the appointment, she started debugging her team's latest phishing site. The contract was with another huge law firm, one of Antidote's VIP clients, and her new handler was tracking it closely. TSC couldn't afford any delays or mistakes.

The poll wasn't working. The client site they had copied had some fancy JavaScript on its Web pages that was interfering with TSC's submission form. But if they cut out the JavaScript, the page didn't look right.

As much as she had tried to prepare her staff for any challenge, Alien was the only one with the technical know-how to fix the code.

"Almost finished," she emailed Luke before rushing to her checkup. At first her midwife was less concerned with the missed due date—nothing uncommon—than with the bags under Alien's eyes.

"You need to take better care of yourself," she told the mother-to-be.

"I know...," said Alien. "I will."

The woman checked her with a portable ultrasound. She frowned and turned to Alien. "You have really low levels of amniotic fluid."

"Oh," said Alien. "I guess I haven't been drinking enough water. Too preoccupied by the computer. But I can drink more now. That'll take care of it, won't it?"

"I'm afraid not. We have to get you to Parkmont Hospital. *Right now.*"

"The hospital?" Alien gulped anxiously. But what about her birth plan? "No, no, no ... I'll drink a bunch of water. Let's check again in an hour."

Her midwife touched Alien's arm consolingly.

"I'm sorry," she said, "but you *need* to go."

Alien slowly paced the halls of the hospital maternity ward in a flimsy gown, shackled to a wheeled IV. The doctor on call had given her until early evening to see if she would naturally go into labor without being medically induced. When a pretty brunette nurse in blue scrubs beckoned her back to her assigned room, Alien knew that she had timed out.

"Do you want an epidural?" the nurse asked.

"No!" Alien answered unhappily, asserting what control she could.

"Okay. We're going to get started."

The woman rolled over monitoring equipment. As she did, Alien couldn't help herself. She checked the screen and identified the operating system.

"Is that *Windows 2000?*" she said.

The nurse paused. "I don't know," she answered slowly.

"It *is*," Alien said. "Wow." Unbidden, the names of major Windows 2000 worms—*Blaster, Code Red, Nimda, Slammer, Sobig, Zotob*—invaded her imagination. And the complete list of security vulnerabilities could fill a phone book.

"It's probably infected," she told the nurse.

The nurse's face indicated her confusion. "Everything is sterile," she reassured Alien.

The doctor—a blond and fit fifty-year-old man—arrived. "Hey," he said in a gentle voice. "We're going to need to induce you now."

After another brief back-and-forth, Alien gave up arguing, allowed them to add Pitocin to her wheeled IV, and resumed walking. Soon, the contractions began in full force. With every one, the body-wrenching pain surged from her abdomen to her back.

Eyes closed, Alien held on to the metal bars along the walls of the hospital corridor. When each contraction subsided, she went back to walking, until the same pain forced her to hold on again. Each time her body seized, she felt like vomiting.

Twenty-eight hours later, the baby was still not ready to emerge. Alien collapsed into the hospital bed, shaking with a 103-degree fever. She heard the doctor say, "We've got to get this baby out."

The monitor beeped. Panting and soaked in sweat, Alien surrendered herself to medical science, computer technology, and fate.

⎯⬥⎯

At midnight Thursday, Alien turned to the sight of her daughter—Adrienne—stirring beside her. Elliot slouched in a corner chair, gently snoring, but Alien had yet to sleep herself.

The baby woke. She stared at Alien with clear gray eyes. Alien held out her hand and Adrienne took it. Her tiny fist curled around Alien's index finger. Adrienne squeezed.

We did it.

Alien rose gingerly, picked up the baby, and placed her on her chest. Adrienne latched easily. She suckled. Alien felt warm milk flow naturally from her body, no hacks necessary.

"I love you," she whispered to her daughter.

Half a minute went by. Alien hesitated, but then stretched her arms to reach her laptop on the tray in front of her, scooting aside an untouched cup of peaches.

Using a VPN—virtual private network—to secure the patchy Wi-Fi available in the maternity ward, Alien logged in to the TSC server.

"We're all set for Friday," their client on the phishing engagement had emailed her. "I just need to see a copy of the email."

"No problem," Alien wrote back. "I will have a copy of the test email to you in your inbox first thing in the morning, so we can kick things off at eleven a.m. as planned."

Adrienne murmured contentedly as Alien pulled up the phishing site code and continued debugging.

Their first all-nighter together had begun.

⎯⬥⎯

The sun rose before Alien finally fixed the phishing site from the hospital and emailed the client.

It felt as if she had given birth twice.

"What happened? How do we do better?" she asked herself and her employees about her emergency debugging. They had to get past the point of relying on her programming skills to save them in a pinch.

Alien returned to the office five days later, with Adrienne. She bought TSC's second fifteen-hundred-dollar professional software license for Nessus, an automated vulnerability scanner. Together with Metasploit, an all-purpose penetration testing tool, this supplemented many of her custom computer scripts.

Now the others could work with or without her, both here and on-site.

While they did, Alien pored over the books. She tallied close to fifteen thousand dollars a month in rent, salaries, and other expenses. And no new work had come yet from the promotional folders or the website.

Adrienne cried.

Alien looked out the window, imagining the wilderness just beyond the mountains, and lifted her daughter to her breast.

Alien felt like she spent the entire summer with her fingers crossed, hoping TSC would drum up enough business to make payroll. She wasn't going to short her employees, or make them front their own expenses, as she'd had to do at Elite Defense. But the thirty-day gap between submitting a new invoice and getting paid by Antidote was more anxiety-inducing than her climb up the abandoned elevator shaft at MIT.

"We *have* to turn the report in right away," she told Luke, Gus, and Cheryl each time they completed a project.

At first, they didn't understand. "The client doesn't care if it's another week."

"The client doesn't care about your paycheck."

In June, six weeks after the birth, Adrienne started day care. Alien developed a drop-off and pickup routine, and playdates at the park and public library. She joined a monthly book group with other mothers. One connection led to another, and soon two Parkmont police officers had asked Alien and her team to consult on recovering deleted cell phone texts and photos for a cyberstalking investigation.

With TSC's tools and talents, meeting the technical challenge would be easy enough. Yet hosting the cops in her office—surrounded by her books and (hidden) breast pump, business papers and (air-freshened) burrito funk—Alien felt exposed. And the more local work she had the opportunity to take on, the more often the issue would come up.

In July, Alien rented and furnished the fifth and last office available on the fifth floor, in the middle of the hall, as a conference room to receive current and potential clients. The same month, she advertised for a new intern and hired Milo, a self-taught computer programmer in his mid-twenties, with neat black-framed glasses and sandy-colored hair. His initiation was running ToneDef 2, TSC's second annual hacking challenge at DEF CON.

Whether the conference room or contest led to anything else, Alien was back to the broadest form of social engineering: *Look successful to be successful.*

<hr />

For a while, Alien held back her own salary and lived off her credit cards, like many small-business owners, considering it another investment she would someday pay down. Although he didn't know it, Luke was taking home more than she was. Alien couldn't share this information with him, not because it would embarrass her, but because she needed everyone to have faith in the future of the company.

One day in mid-September, she spent the morning editing project reports. Alien checked her email afterward and saw a new message to the general TSC address.

The sender was an IT network manager at one of the largest companies in the Rockies — Treeline Bank. He had taken a SCAN class taught by Elliot at which he had picked up a TSC folder.

"Enclosed is a request for proposal for Treeline Bank's annual security testing," Alien read.

Alien took a deep breath. It all had to start somewhere, and this could be it. The first real chance to do business on their own, independent of Antidote. If they got the job, and Treeline liked them, a big bank was the ideal reference for other clients. But she'd need to convince them that TSC was the right hire.

<hr />

In her proposal, Alien provided a quote for a remote pentest, an on-site pentest, and a social engineering assessment. She landed the contract. The entire TSC team conducted the work in October and November. They were successful enough that the bank signed an agreement for a year of quarterly assessments. The first-quarter phishing test, in late February 2012, went off perfectly. The second phishing test started on a clear seventy-degree morning in mid-June.

Sitting forward in her chair with her fingers never leaving the keyboard or her eyes the screen, Alien jumped back and forth between the command line and her simultaneous online chat with Luke, Gus, and Cheryl in their offices:

```
<alien> opening firewall port 80
<alien> confirmed firewall port 80 open
<alien> confirming external access successful
<alien> opening firewall port 25
<alien> sending test email
<alien> please confirm and click when you receive
<cheryl> received
<gus> received
<alien> two clicks recorded
<alien> two form submissions recorded, username MrMan
    and thisisatest
<cheryl> confirmed
<gus> confirmed
<alien> target list loaded
<alien> launching emails in 30 seconds
```

Alien checked her watch, her heartbeat increasing steadily as the second hand ticked forward. Fifteen seconds. Ten. Five. *Now.*

As the countdown ended, Alien hit Return to start her phishing script. "Emails launched," she typed. She watched a separate terminal window that showed the mail server logs. It scrolled automatically as hundreds of emails were sent.

And then, suddenly, it stopped.

Alien hit Enter. Nothing. She opened a new terminal and SSH'd into the server again. No luck.

Chat, command line, warm and hot phish logs, Web browser—everything onscreen that used the Internet had frozen.

Alien felt a sudden jolt of alarm throughout her body. The worst thing was that she had no idea of the status of the phishing attempt, so there was no clear way to fix it.

Had the emails been sent? If so, only some of them, or all? If some, which ones? How many undeliverable and how many out-of-office messages had they gotten? Were employees reading now? Were they clicking? How long until the first person filled out and submitted a poll? How long until a dozen did?

She rushed out of the office and into the hall. Luke joined her a few seconds later, followed closely by Gus and Cheryl. Everyone clutched their printed call scripts.

"What's going on?" they asked.

Luke threw open the door of the Playlab. Milo had been set to work inside, trying to organize stray chargers, cables, circuit boards, memory boards, processing chips, CD drives, power strips, and keyboards into sealed plastic tubs. At some point, however, the cleanup efforts had taken him into the network closet, where he was standing now.

In Milo's left hand was a mini-Maglite. In his right was a thick black cord.

"What?" he said drily.

"You broke the Internet!" Luke yelled.

⟨◇⟩

Replugging and restarting didn't work. They tried again—and again. Nothing changed.

Treeline was a fifty-thousand-dollar contract. The test this time covered almost five hundred employees. Equally important, two smaller banks, a local law firm, and a community health clinic had all hired TSC on the strength of their work for Treeline.

The life of her company flashed before Alien's eyes.

"Grab your stuff and get in the car! Everybody in the car!" she shouted.

Everyone but Milo swooped up phones and laptops. They stampeded down all five flights of stairs, nearly flattening a blue-suited attorney carrying a cup of coffee.

At the parking lot, Alien hopped in the driver's seat of the dark green Subaru Outback with which she'd finally replaced her Volvo. Luke joined her in front. Gus and Cheryl shared the rear, shoveling aside Duplos and a yellow plush giraffe. A black car seat encrusted with Cheerios held in place by dried apple juice forced them close to one side.

Alien peeled out. Less than five minutes later, she screeched to a halt at the end of her street. Alien jumped out of the car, ran up the flagstone walk, and threw open her front door.

"Go! Go! Go!" she yelled, along with the Wi-Fi password.

⟫═══⟪

The hackers spread out—Alien to the master bedroom, Luke to the square oak kitchen table, Cheryl to the red velour living room couch, and Gus to Adrienne's bedroom, strewn with stuffed animals, board books, boxes of fresh diapers and containers of baby wipes, and a crib on whose railing was mounted a musical mobile.

Alien's hands shook as she logged in. "Remember to block caller ID!" she shouted. "We can do this!"

We have to.

Alien loaded the phishing spreadsheet and logs from the server and started handing out assignments.

"Hi," she heard a moment later. "This is Luke in IT . . ." "Hi. This is Cheryl in IT . . ." "Hi. This is Gus in IT . . ."

⟫═══⟪

Half an hour later—less than forty minutes after the botched launch—they reached their thirty-call target. "Done!" Alien typed, her entire body still trembling.

In the few minutes TSC had burned in the emergency relocation to Alien's house, hundreds of Treeline employees had "self-alerted," warning others throughout the company that the online poll was a scam.

But not everyone. Gus pwned a commercial loan officer. He'd done this under circumstances as difficult as they were absurd: sitting on the floor, his shoulders and head up against the slats of Adrienne's crib. And in the dark, since in his rush he hadn't been able to find the light switch. "woot!" he sent over IRC.

The win was enough to keep Treeline committed to further testing. But rather than congratulate themselves, Alien and her team thought about how they could have pwned the bank harder — and that they'd only barely escaped disaster.

⟢

The TSC Internet outage was a far louder and more urgent wakeup call than the buggy phishing site. "What happened?" Alien again asked everyone. "How do we do better?"

It was clear that they needed procedural changes for improved communications and workflow, as well as a more robust infrastructure, with a backup power supply and multiple network connections. Either way, the company had outgrown its jerry-built arrangement of offices. A new space was required to ensure the effectiveness of the security services TSC was selling. And to set a stage where it could continue to expand in the future.

The following week, Alien drove to a new five-story glass-and-steel building one block east of the Parkmont mall. A made-up blonde with a stylish bob — her Realtor — was waiting for her. The woman carried a black leather attaché case with which she beckoned Alien inside.

"It's *very* modern," the Realtor said. "They don't use keys, they have *cards*." She demonstrated by swiping her own card by an RFID reader, which beeped to allow access.

Alien affected a calm and appraising expression. Inside, however, her heart swelled with each new security feature. A bank, the embodiment of safety and stability, anchored the street level. Taking the elevator required a special fob. When they reached the L-shaped space available to rent — ten rooms along two interior hallways and occupying 2,500 square feet — a small lobby and solid wooden door separated it from any other offices.

Alien entered first, expecting traffic noises, cross-chatter from elsewhere in the building, or the whir and rumble of various vents and pipes, as in her current offices. Instead, the loudest sound was her own heels swishing on fresh pale gray carpeting almost identical to the floor covering in her father's accounting firm.

Light streamed in from tall glass windows. An airy break room with round tables offered a central space for people to gather. There was central HVAC with programmable thermostats and a full kitchen with a built-in microwave and pod coffeemaker.

As the Realtor chatted about "great signage" and "ample parking," Alien was already picturing who and what would go where.

Luke would get a corner office and she'd get a middle one, so she could keep an eye on everything. Gus, Cheryl, and Milo could all have their own work areas, with more room for future interns, a salesperson, a full-time office manager, a bookkeeper, and a safe. They'd build out a conference room (that phrase alone—*build out*—felt delicious to contemplate), along with a new, improved Playlab and a dedicated forensics lab. But what to do with the open space by the front door, just big enough for a single desk?

"And here's your receptionist area," the Realtor said, reaching it.

Alien nodded. Her *receptionist*. How about *that?*

This was a long way from the Fireberry spare bedroom. Her primary identity wasn't hacker, or pentester, or even "senior security consultant" anymore. It was business owner and manager. And her *business* needed someone to welcome visitors and answer the phones.

⟫⟪⟫

Alien scrimped and saved to staff up. With the receptionist and other new hires, TSC grew to nine employees. Four were older than Alien. Unlike her former interns, now all full-time, they had conventional job experience and expectations. Having to help them cover as many as thirty open projects a week pushed Alien to her limits. Then came the slow season, when she never knew how she was going to pay the bills beyond a two-week window. In early 2013, Alien went to the bank and took out TSC's first line of credit. And she negotiated TSC's last major subcontract with Antidote, for client 0666.

At first the deal seemed a dream come true: 0666 was a vast retail chain that needed remote and on-site penetration tests, mobile and Web app assessments, and a security review of its credit card processing systems. Each was an interesting assignment worth eighty to ninety thousand dollars. Taken together, it was enough work to occupy and fund the company for months.

That was the upside. The downside was that Alien soon discovered Antidote had handed off the gig only because the client was so difficult. The company's technology was severely out of date, and it was strapped for the cash it needed to deal with this and several other priorities. Its management didn't have the resources to improve its security more than the absolute minimum necessary to comply with state and federal regulations. On top of that, 0666 was very disorganized, which resulted in its imposing odd conditions on TSC. The client required that all testing take place after hours—which meant any consultants on the job had to work seven p.m. to four a.m.

In April 2013, Alien escaped the office just long enough to host Adrienne's second birthday party. A battery-powered blower filled the air with soap bubbles as a dozen happy children and their parents gathered in her grassy backyard. Alien herself felt terrible, however. Her head hurt. Her limbs ached. Her clothes irritated her skin. She was nauseous and completely drained.

Could *stress* do this? Her team was begging her to refuse any further work with 0666. Yet monthly payroll and overhead were more than fifty thousand dollars, no matter how many or how few their paying clients. The overwhelming pressure to bring in new business, preferably long-term contracts, never stopped. She kept thinking that if she just continued growing the company, eventually she'd be able to step back.

With her skills, Alien could rob a bank and run away to Vietnam, or anywhere else with good weather and loose extradition laws. And if she was ever short on cash, she could always go phishing. All she needed was an Internet connection and a phone.

But Alien never even imagined going rogue. She was thirty-two years old, and building lasting relationships. Her friends and neighbors were here. Her lawyer. Her banker. Her local clients. And, of course, her family and her employees. After four and a half years, Parkmont wasn't just her base of operations anymore but her home.

Alien watched her daughter, dressed in a pink jumper and purple hair bow, tear through the wrapping paper of her presents.

"Say 'thank you,'" Alien told her.

"Cake!" Adrienne responded.

"Cake! Cake! Cake!" the kids all clapped and screamed together. But Alien heard and saw them only in a haze, and took what seemed like hours to find and light the necessary candles and then carry out the birthday cake, though she'd had everything set up since morning.

Weeks later, still feeling sick, Alien finally visited her doctor.

"I'm exhausted," she said. "Maybe I'm going through early menopause?"

The doctor examined her carefully and ran a few quick tests.

"It's not menopause," she said. "You're pregnant again."

It was clear to Alien how naïve she had been during her first pregnancy when she thought a larger staff would mean less work. Now, with triple the team and a second kid on the way, she needed a full-time director of operations. Life had thrown her into another curve, and it was time to hit the accelerator again.

Alien hired a tech-savvy Denverite in her mid-forties, Susannah, who was seeking a change of scene after twenty years in government, where she had overseen a staff of thirty. Susannah, not Alien, would lead the team, assigning technical work and managing projects. As her welcome to the role, Alien gave Susannah a small statue of a bulldog draped in the British flag, modeled after the equivalent prop in the James Bond movie *Skyfall*.

"You're the new M," said Alien, referring to Bond's boss, fictional head of MI6, dishing out assignments to her agents.

Alien knew the new hierarchy was working when she stopped a young man at the office door one day that summer.

"Can I *help* you?" Alien interrogated him.

The stranger stammered nervously, surprised. "I'm the new intern," he said.

Susannah hastened over to intervene. "He was just hired," she explained. "It's his first day."

"Ah," said Alien, shaking hands. "I'm Elizabeth. Welcome."

As she walked to her office, Alien passed Gus, Cheryl, and two new pentesters gathered around the break room table discussing their latest work with client 0666.

"Who's on-site now?" asked Alien.

"Milo," Gus answered. "He cracked their wireless network from a café inside one of their stores, and then wormed his way into the company's central systems."

"He got root on the badge-printing system," said Cheryl. "He could add his name and photograph to the badge system and give himself access to any building. Any room. You name it."

One of the new pentesters piped up, "We found this internal database that had the entire shopping history of every single customer."

"*Every* customer?" asked Alien. She shopped at 0666. Everybody did.

Gus hemmed. Cheryl tittered.

"What?" said Alien.

"We found you!" Cheryl said. "The earliest entry was from *nineteen ninety-three*" — ancient history to the twenty-four-year-old.

"Congratulations." Alien opened the fridge and grabbed a water bottle. She pictured the entire break room papered with her life story as told through 0666 receipts, from her first bra to Adrienne's crib. The feeling was akin to crossing the Fifth East ledge naked.

That was fifteen years ago, though. It was in the dark. And François's towel theft aside, being naked had been her choice.

The Internet was much, much worse, exposing everyone in far profounder ways that were beyond anyone's control.

—◆—

In mid-September, Treeline Bank called TSC on behalf of one of its customers, a construction company based in Salt Lake City. A day earlier, the company's payroll manager had clicked on a phishing email link that infected his Web browser with a "man-in-the-middle" attack, allowing hackers to see everything he typed and even replace his familiar Treeline online banking page with an exact replica asking for additional credentials. Only a second layer of security, requiring special executive approval for large wire transfers, had stopped the firm from losing almost sixty thousand dollars to an offshore account.

Could TSC investigate and find out what happened and how to fix it?

Susannah sent Luke on-site to image any affected computers and interview staff. When he returned, Milo took over, using the equipment in the forensics lab to inspect everything carefully. The payroll manager had clicked on *nineteen* links in as many different phishing emails, he discovered.

Alien volunteered to help finish the job. Business operations aside, having to come up with original material every year for ToneDef, TSC's DEF CON contest, gave her an extra reason to keep up with new hacking developments.

"I'll do the malware analysis," she said.

—◆—

To understand how the malware worked, Alien set it up in a "sandbox," or cordoned-off virtual machine environment, on a computer in the Playlab. This gave her the digital equivalent of a high-level biosafety lab, where the software could be safely stored, inspected, and dissected. Alien started by viewing the page source for the emailed link that led to the man-in-the-middle attack. It was neatly written by sophisticated programmers.

These bad guys are good.

Of late, the best black hats had emulated successful Silicon Valley entrepreneurs, licensing the use of their work through cloud-based commercial software suites called "exploit kits." To begin a mass attack, you didn't have to know how to write a computer program — or even have your own computer. You just logged in from anywhere, chose the kind of hacks you wanted, and paid by the day, month, or year. Some black hat services accepted payment by deducting a percentage of the take.

Alien infected the virtual machine, and then came back forty-eight hours later to check what the digital thieves had been doing.

The software began by configuring itself to run at startup. Then it phoned home once every twenty minutes, seeking updates or further instructions from one of a series of modern command-and-control servers around the world.

"What do you want me to do?" the program asked, in essence.

And the criminals at the other end of the connection could order whatever they wanted.

"It's impressive," she told Susannah afterward. "And more than a little frightening." Not just in itself but for what it portended. This wasn't a solo hit-and-run operator. It was the work of a group of professional hackers, just like TSC.

As she had gone from novice to student, student to practitioner, practitioner to teacher, and managed to manager, all as a white hat hacker, black hat hackers across the globe had followed a parallel path, organizing their operations, establishing reputations, and finding clients. And bringing in money to their communities.

Alien had never realized it, and she had never wished for it, but one could even say she had needed the black hats to keep growing and getting new opportunities herself.

"How many employees do you think *they* have?" Alien asked.

"I don't know," Susannah said. "But their sales team is definitely bigger than ours."

Alien laughed. From Susannah's desk, she picked up the little bulldog statue she had given her. "I wonder if they have an M ...," Alien said. "Maybe somewhere, on the other side of the world, there's an evil Susannah."

Susannah raised an eyebrow wryly. "Well, then there would have to be an evil Elizabeth, too."

⫸⫷

Tuesday mornings, Alien took off work to spend extra time with Adrienne. Ten a.m., the day before Christmas, the two of them moved through the aisles at the supermarket with Adrienne in the kiddie seat of the shopping cart. Alien was eight months pregnant, dressed in stretchy jeans and a loose black sweater, while Adrienne, now two and a half years old, wore her favorite princess pajamas and sky-blue faux-fur booties.

Leaving the produce section, they passed a stand with the *Denver Post*, *USA Today*, and the *Parkmont Messenger*. Each paper featured a photo or illustration of a computer screen on its front page. And every other headline seemed to be about information security.

In May, former NSA contractor Edward Snowden had fled the country with hundreds of thousands of files documenting secret government surveillance programs around the world. Then, this past week, 70 million Americans learned they'd had their credit cards and personal information compromised by shopping at Target—all because an employee of a heating and cooling subcontractor in Pennsylvania had clicked on a phishing email link, letting his or her computer be captured and used to reach the rest of the company network, then Target's network, and then its point-of-sale machines nationwide.

Overnight, ordinary people realized they were being tracked and targeted. New revelations came daily—not necessarily because hacking had increased, but because the media were finally on the lookout for it.

Alien turned in to the snack aisle. A moment later, she felt her cell phone vibrate in her pocket. It was her main contact at Treeline Bank, one of their senior vice presidents.

"Our cash management representatives really need some cybersecurity training," he said. "They're the ones who have the relationships with our corporate clients. And they're the ones who get a call if there's a suspicious wire transfer. Can you come in and give a presentation?"

Spend an hour showing you exactly how TSC can protect your biggest clients?

"Absolutely," said Alien. "We can make videos of the malware in action from one of your recent customer cases. That'll drive the point home."

Her phone beeped—incoming call—before she was even off the line. Susannah.

"We just got a new client," she said when Alien picked up. "Never seen a request like this before, but I told them we could handle it."

"Okay," said Alien. She looked down at Adrienne, trying to raise herself out of her seat to snag a box of graham crackers from the nearby shelf. "I'll be in this afternoon," Alien closed out the call. "Let's figure out a battle plan."

She lifted up Adrienne and rested the toddler against her left shoulder. Alien was in a good mood, and excited about both new projects.

"Crackers?" Adrienne pleaded.

"No," Alien said. "*Hackers.*"

Adrienne looked at her quizzically.

Alien smiled. "*And* crackers," she said, grasping the box her daughter wanted with her free right hand and placing it in the cart before returning Adrienne to her seat. "When we get home," she added.

Adrienne clapped enthusiastically as Alien leaned over to kiss her on the head.

Fast Forward

I N THE YEARS THAT followed, TSC expanded to employ more than two dozen people. Today, her staff, not Alien, perform most of the company's pentests, forensics investigations, and incident response work, under the direction of the chief operating officer, Susannah. Alien, meanwhile, leads TSC and focuses on community and training events.

It's a growth field. In 2014, not long after the birth of her son, Isaac, the company moved again, to larger offices in downtown Parkmont.

One year later, Alien bought the building.

⊐━━⊏

I slid an orange laminated card across Alien's kitchen table. When she recognized what it was, she smiled.

Months had passed since she'd agreed to share her story with me. In the interim, I'd crisscrossed the country, with and without her, interviewing other members of the diverse hacker and information security communities —American and international, activist and academic, government and corporate, legal and illegal. Now I had my own souvenirs from Las Vegas nightclubs and Los Alamos research labs, the bar scene by NSA headquarters and the tunnels, tombs, ledges, and domes of MIT. My favorite item, however, had been a loaner.

Soon after we got back from traveling to DEF CON together, Alien had let me borrow her old MIT hacking card. That was what I had just returned to her. One side listed eleven different "Methods of Entry" to be used, in order, in trying to access any physical location. The other side contained a code of conduct to follow in pursuing these methods. The card itself was bent from late-night use opening locked doors almost twenty years earlier.

It was a guide, a belief system, and a tool—all in one.

Along with the many twists and turns, the successes and dead ends, the risks and rewards, important continuities ran through Alien's path from freshman hacker into unknown or forbidden physical spaces at MIT to Info-Sec expert and entrepreneur. These went beyond her intelligence, ingenuity, and energy to her attraction to situations, problems, and challenges that most of the rest of us would rather avoid or ignore.

"Where's cybersecurity going next?" I asked.

"Have you heard of the Internet of Things?" she said.

I nodded. The term included networked security cameras, spy drones, and missile launchers, but also "smart" watches, pacemakers, baby monitors, and slow cookers.

By 2020, Alien told me, "there are going to be an estimated thirty billion connected devices with really no security management, ready to do a hacker's bidding." Imagine ransomware in self-driving cars, she elaborated. Bot armies of "enslaved" fitness trackers, covertly "mining" cryptocurrency. Remote-control voting machines.

"That's off the top of my head," Alien said. "And it's just the beginning."

I got a sinking feeling in the pit of my stomach. After researching and writing this book, I now locked my phone and logged off my computer when I wasn't using them. I set up hard drive and email encryption, and a VPN, or virtual private network, for my phone, laptop, and other devices, so I could access public wireless networks more securely. I used multi-factor authentication and a program that generated and managed strong unique passwords for all my online accounts. I updated system software regularly, to keep security patches up to date. And I deleted suspicious email attachments and double-checked Web links to defend myself against phishing attacks.

Anyone could do this quickly and easily, following instructions online. Everyone should.

But Alien's quick summary of technology's growth and dynamism made it clear that there was no such thing as absolute security in this world, or any definitive and final fixes. Black hats would keep striking where and when they could, in ways that were impossible even for her to predict. That made white hats like Alien all the more essential. They were the best defense we had.

＝＝＊＝＝

Her phone rang. It had done so repeatedly during our conversation. Now I more fully understood why she still did so much work after midnight. This was the only time when calls wouldn't interrupt her.

I closed my notebook and stood up to go. I could just let myself out while she spoke with whoever was on the line, but Alien raised an index finger to signal that I should hold on.

"Uh-huh, uh-huh . . . ," she said into the phone. "Sure . . . We can do that . . . Yes . . . Of course . . . No problem . . . I'll call you back in fifteen minutes." Alien hung up and looked at me.

"Sorry," she said. "It never stops."

Alien picked up the worn MIT hacking card and looked it over fondly as she walked me to the door. "You can teach hacking processes, but people either have the personality or they don't," she told me.

"You mean it's impossible to *become* a hacker?" I asked.

"The only thing you can become," Alien said, "is yourself."

While one of her recurring fantasies was to live a normal, boring life, for her that would be the hardest hack of all.